GREEK

CITY-STATES

KATHLEEN FREEMAN received MA and D. Litt degrees from University College, Cardiff, Wales, and was for many years lecturer in Greek there.

She published a dozen studies in Greek history and literature, some thirty novels and detective stories, several children's books, and many other volumes.

GREEK
CITY-STATES

by

KATHLEEN FREEMAN

The Norton Library

W · W · NORTON & COMPANY · INC

NEW YORK

FIRST PUBLISHED IN THE NORTON LIBRARY 1963

ISBN 0 00193 8

PRINTED IN THE UNITED STATES OF AMERICA

7 8 9 0

Geographic factors count for much in history; but personality is an even greater force.

M. CARY, *The Geographic Background of Greek and Roman History.*

CONTENTS

MAPS AND PLANS

PREFACE

INTEREST in Greek thought, Greek art, the Greek way of life, continues to grow; but when most people speak of Greece, they mean Athens or perhaps Sparta. It is not generally realized that the Greek world consisted of a number of small units called city-states (*polis* is the Greek word, whence is derived "politics"), which were entirely independent of one another, with different constitutions, laws, ways of life and means of defence, and even different ways of speaking the same language and worshipping the same deities.

Athens and Sparta were always recognized by the Greeks themselves in historic times as the first of these city-states in importance, and most of our information is about them; but there were hundreds of other city-states, great and small, which when Greek civilization was at its zenith occupied sites from the western Mediterranean to the coast of the Levant, from the Black Sea to North Africa. Most of these produced a civilization which, though still Greek, had an individual flavour due to their very different circumstances. If the Greek world is really to be understood we must know not only about Athens and Sparta, but about the islands of the Aegean Sea, the Greek cities of Sicily and Italy and Asia Minor, and the other cities of mainland Greece. To the inhabitants of these states their way of life was of passionate interest, as they showed by their readiness to defend it against foreigners and against each other.

To build up a comprehensive picture from these many units would be a formidable task, even in so far as it is possible with the material available. I have therefore taken for my purpose nine city-states which illustrate the immense and fascinating diversity existing within the Greek world. The reasons for choosing these nine out of hundreds is their diversity of origin, environment, size, way of life, destiny. Massalia, the most westerly, on the edge of barbarian Gaul, Byzantium at the entrance to the Black Sea, Corinth, third greatest city of the mainland, Seriphos, tiny island in the Aegean, have a continuous history which has brought them, however much changed, to the present day; Acragas on the south coast of Sicily survives only as an awe-inspiring group of abandoned temples; Miletus and Cyrene are a mass of ruins interesting mainly to archaeologists; the very sites of Abdera and Thourioi are hard to find. Yet in their day all were flourishing; all played their parts in the development of Greek civilization; many of them produced great men comparable in genius and influence, though not in numbers, to the Athenian galaxy, and actually contributing much to Athenian thought and art.

In ordinary histories of Greece we see these places only in glimpses, as they happen to impinge on the history of Athens and Sparta. I have attempted not only to tell their continuous story, but also to reconstruct their way of life, to recapture their peculiar flavour; to rebuild the streets and market-places of old Corinth and Cyrene and the rest, and set their citizens walking and talking, until we see and hear them as vividly as, by the labours of scholars, we see and hear Socrates talking in the gymnasia or the Spartan boys enduring without a murmur their competitive floggings on the altar of Artemis. I have also attempted in a concluding chapter to suggest the lesson for the modern world which is implicit in the rise and fall of these communities.

NOTES

1. A circumflex is used to denote a long vowel. In the text this has generally been confined to the first appearance of unfamiliar or difficult words. In the Index it is used throughout.

2. The line drawings at the head of each chapter are exact copies of the principal coin type of the city-state concerned.

3. The first and last chapters are reprinted with minor alterations from an article in *World Affairs* (July, 1948), to the Editors of which my thanks are due.

K.F.

GREEK CITY-STATES

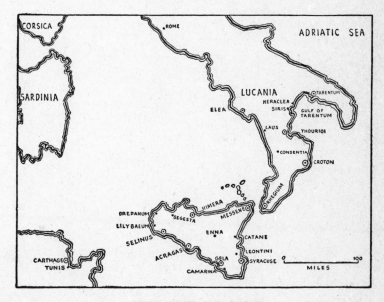

SOUTH ITALY AND SICILY

1. THE RISE AND FALL OF THE GREEK CITY-STATE

THE OUTLINE of the history of ancient Greece reads like a tragedy in three acts.

The first act is full of promise. A series of migrations of Hellenic peoples populates the peninsula of Greece, overwhelming the inhabitants by force or by peaceful pressure; the last and most violent of these migrations, the Dorian invasion, drives earlier Greek invaders further south and even overseas. A period of assimilation follows; and out of chaos there emerge the principal city-states of the ancient Greece we know: the new Athens, centre of government for Attica; Sparta, Corinth, Megara, Thebes and the rest; the Aegean island-states and the great commercial city-states on the coast of Asia Minor. These communities flourish; overseas trade expands; new sources of wealth are eagerly sought; and a new colonization movement, lasting over two centuries, begins. The shores of the Black Sea, the coasts of Sicily and southern Italy, are occupied; and trading-posts are planted further west and on the coast of North Africa. The Mediterranean, the Aegean and the Black Sea have become largely Hellenic, though the Phoenicians and their colony Carthage remain to challenge Greek trade supremacy.

This Hellenic world, far from being a solid *bloc* like a nation, consisted, like the solid-seeming substances analysed by Democritus into atoms and void, of countless units separated in space and varying in size from large communities like Athens and Syracuse to mere trading-posts like Sestos and Abydos. Nearly all these communities were completely independent: each was free to ally itself or go to war with a neighbouring city-state; each judged its own policy at every step by the standard of immediate self-interest. The colonies, even, in spite of a sentimental regard for the mother-city, were not bound to pay any heed to her wishes in peace or in war; and racial ties within the Hellenic people, such as those forming the Dorian and Ionian groups, did not prevent these groups from being split by the wedge of self-interest, as the Peloponnesian War was to show.

It is a curious fact that in spite of the Delphic injunction "Nothing too much," and the reputation of the Hellenes for devotion to Reason and the Mean, they themselves tended to extremes in the experiment of living. In fifth-century Athens an extreme form of equalitarianism among free adult males still arouses astonishment: all officials, except the War Board of ten generals, to be chosen by lot from those eligible. In Sparta there was an extreme cult of physical fitness and militarism which can still provide a bad example. Acragas went to extremes in religion, as the magnificent ruins on her crowded hill-top still demonstrate. In the same way the Hellenic race displays to the historian the most intense passion for separatism that the world has ever seen. The hundreds of city-states had nothing in common except their descent from a common stock and their basic language, both of which meant a small common heritage of beliefs and ideas. Yet they contributed in less than a millennium more to the human treasury of civilization than all the rest of the world put together throughout all its known history.

Why did their civilization perish? It is generally believed that it perished because they were unable to sink their differences and combine. The second act of the tragedy, while showing superb intellectual achievement, also shows constant wars between city-states which weakened both victor and vanquished. There was not only the great struggle lasting for twenty-seven years between Athens at the head of her empire and Sparta at the head of her confederacy: there were many smaller struggles from time to time, in which neighbour destroyed neighbour and weakened Hellas in the face of the barbarian. For instance, the flourishing city-state of Sybaris on the south coast of Italy was wiped out in the late sixth century B.C. by her neighbour Croton, only sixty miles away, so that the very site remained uninhabited for over half a century after: this though the Greeks formed a mere fringe on the coast, with a hinterland of natives whose attitude was often hostile and always uncertain. On the island of Sicily the Greek settlers were never in full control: the interior was occupied by native Sicels and Sicans, and the western tip by the bitterly hostile Carthaginians, whose base lay across the Mediterranean at a distance of only one hundred and fifty miles. Yet the Greek city-states were never able to achieve unity. Syracuse, for instance, which by its size and strength was obviously destined for the rôle of leader, turned on its own colony, the little town of Camarina fifty miles away on the south coast, and destroyed it in 552 B.C.; recolonized it in 495 B.C., and destroyed it again ten years later, at a time when the Hellenic world was facing its great struggle against the barbarian, Persia in the east, Carthage in the west. These are only two examples among many.

But, it is often believed, the Greeks of the mainland at any rate, though apt to quarrel in times of peace, were able to unite in times of external danger. This is quite untrue: it is an opinion based on the famous stand of the defenders of Greece against the Persian invasions of 490 and 480 B.C. Few realize even now how very far the city-states were from achieving unity. In the former of these invasions the Persian army came by sea across the Aegean to Attica, and landed at Marathon; they had no fear about what was happening in their rear, because the whole of northern Greece, Thessaly, Thrace and Macedonia had already given tokens of submission to the Persian envoys, as also had the island of Aegina, actually within sight of the Peiraeus. The victory of Marathon was almost entirely Athenian: the Spartans, having no great love for the Athenians, came too late; they themselves, only sixteen years earlier, had sent an army into Attica in an attempt to interfere in Athenian internal affairs. In the second great invasion, that under Xerxes in 480 B.C., the Spartans did send an army further north; but when this was wiped out at Thermopylae they were very ready to abandon Athens to her fate, and Athens was actually evacuated and occupied by the enemy. The sea victory of Salamis reversed this; but Athenians owed their salvation to their own exertions, not to any concern on the part of the more southerly city-states for their preservation. In later days the Greeks themselves liked to look back on this period as a time of Hellenic unity; but it was nothing of the kind. It was a brief spell when certain of the city-states consented unwillingly to fight side by side in the pressing cause of self-preservation.

The moment the immediate peril was relaxed they returned to the expression of their mutual enmity: the Peloponnesian cities to the building up of a confederacy hostile to Athens, the Athenians to their policy of the domination of the Aegean. All the city-states, in whatever they did, were governed by immediate self-interest: those that joined Sparta—Corinth, for instance—did so because they hoped that Sparta would use her military power to check Athenian expansion, which menaced their prosperity; those that joined Athens, in the hope of enjoying profitable trade relations and the protection of her fleet. When they found that Athens intended to use them in order to build up her own power, the larger states, such as Samos, attempted to break free, and were brought back into the Athenian power-orbit by force. Others, like Chios and Lesbos, revolted during the terrible Peloponnesian War, which broke out in 431 B.C. and lasting twenty-seven years drained both sides of their strength; they became, in the following century, an easy prey for the military adventurer, King Philip of Macedon, a man who, though his race and language were Greek, was nevertheless completely un-Hellenic in outlook, and who, with his son Alexander, did in fact destroy for ever the civilization of the city-states.

It was during this second act of the tragedy that all the best of what Greece has given us, with the exception of the epic, was produced. This period saw the rise of science and philosophy in Miletus, Sicily and southern Italy, and its perfection in Plato and Aristotle; the lyric poetry of Pindar; the Athenian drama; the prose historical work of Herodotus and Thucydides; the work of Solon and other legislators; Athenian oratory; the birth of scientific medicine under Alcmaeon of Croton, Empedocles of Acragas, and Hippocrates of Cos; mathematics, astronomy, biology, the art of education, painting, music, sculpture, architecture and much more. Truly, as Heracleitus said, "War is the father of all and the king of all". The constant struggle for power and wealth between the city-states themselves was mirrored in their internal strife, in which oligarch and democrat plotted and murdered (judicially or by straightforward massacre), and where the opposition party was usually willing to sell its state to the enemy in return for political power. Philip of Macedon brought the use of the bribe and the internal band of supporters (or fifth column, as we call them) to a fine art, preferring them to the sword; but long before his day they were a familiar weapon everywhere. When the struggle between Athens and Sparta was at its height plot succeeded plot in Athens to dislodge the democratic government: exiles were scheming outside; the anti-democratic, pro-Spartan party within. When the Spartans were victorious they were able at once to put the government into the hands of a committee of thirty Athenian oligarchs, who were not only the willing tools of the conquerors but who also indulged during the eight months of their power their passion for wealth and their political and private hatreds. Athens was surely paying for her many political and military crimes: her subjection of the Greek islands, her cruelty to Melos, her attempt to subdue Syracuse. And while Greek destroyed Greek, the Persian power intrigued in the east, and the Carthaginians attacked the Sicilian

Greeks in the west, capturing the wealthy city of Acragas after an eight months' siege and destroying her neighbours on that coast—Gela, and the unfortunate Camarina, already twice destroyed by fellow-Greeks. This was in 406–405 B.C. The surrender of Athens to Sparta was in April 404.

The third act of the tragedy, the break-up of the city-state system, bringing with it the end of the distinctive thought and work of ancient Hellas, begins from then onward. Throughout the first half of the fourth century the menace grows. Yet the mainland Greeks do not unite. Fresh combinations are formed: Thebes invades the Peloponnese and attacks Sparta; Athens goes to Sparta's aid for a time, but the uneasy alliance cannot last, since neither side has good will towards the other. Philip of Macedon comes to his throne in 359 B.C. and at once begins his activities, aimed at the domination of the Hellenic world. His Athenian opponent, Demosthenes, completely clear-sighted and completely courageous, has to see his efforts to rouse his fellow-countrymen to a sense of the danger thwarted by time-serving rivals like Aeschines and sentimental doctrinaires like Isocrates, the former hoping for political power, the latter preaching the out-of-date cause of union against Persia. There was at this time a spate of rhetoric about "concord" and "unity", but to all such talk the common citizen opposed a scepticism that baffled even the plainest speaking, and a lethargy that was impervious to all warnings. To those of us who suffered from a similar sense of impending disaster during the years between the First and Second World Wars, there is no more poignant reading in all history than the speeches of Demosthenes, in which that great man strove with all the force of piercing insight and consummate oratory to awaken his fellow-citizens to the danger. Again and again he warned, and his warnings came true; but still the response was "too little and too late". And yet, only a quarter of a century ago, an historian of Greece could write of Demosthenes: "To the last, indeed, he failed to see things in proper perspective", and of Philip as the "lover and promoter of Hellenic culture". Truly, as Mr.

Churchill once said in another connection, this "falls into that long, dismal catalogue of the fruitlessness of experience and the confirmed unteachability of mankind".

Sixteen calamitous years saw the crushing defeat of Athens at Chaeronea; the death of Philip two years later, in 336 B.C., and the brief revival of hope; the campaigns of Alexander, in which the opposition of the Greek city-states was hardly sufficient even to delay the main enterprise, the subjugation of the east; the death of Alexander in 322, and the second brief resurgence, easily quelled; the flight of Demosthenes and his suicide to avoid capture. With these events the political life of the independent city-state ends for ever, as Greek philosophy dies with Aristotle in exile at Chalcis. Macedon was not Greece: the rule of the Macedonian generals in Asia Minor and in Egypt begins a new uneasy period of history, when the Hellenic world awaits absorption into the unifying realm of Rome.

What is the moral of this tragic story? Why did the vivid and distinctive Hellenic civilization not survive, or survive only as an influence in those of other peoples? The customary explanation is "lack of unity"; but this is to mistake the symptom for the cause. Perhaps a closer view of some of the most representative city-states other than Athens and Sparta will suggest an answer less superficial and more instructive to the modern world.

2. THOURIOI

(*Thurii*)

ON THE coast of southern Italy, just before the coastline changes its direction from south-west to south-east, there was in ancient times a place where the high mountain range stood back a little, and in front of these mountains a series of semi-circular terraces formed a kind of giant's amphitheatre looking out to sea on the Gulf of Tarentum. At this spot two rivers flowed close together into the sea; their alluvial deposit had built up a small fertile plain, and the route taken by the larger of them down from the mountains pointed to a short cut to the sea on the other side, the Etruscan Sea. Here, in the latter half of the eighth century B.C., a band of settlers from Achaea in the north of the Peloponnese built a town between the two rivers, which they named, as colonists tend to do, after a river and a spring in their homeland: the larger river they called Crathis, "the Mixer", and the smaller Sybaris, "the Gusher". The newly-built town took its name from the Sybaris. Both these rivers are there today: the Crathis is still called the Crati, and the Sybaris, which now flows into the Crati, is called Coscile.

On the brief but notorious history of Sybaris a great deal of nonsense was written in ancient times. Sybaris was extremely prosperous, and it attracted the envy and hatred of its poorer neighbours. Strabo the geographer, grossly exaggerating, says that in its heyday it governed four neighbouring tribes, twenty-five cities and could put 300,000 men in the field. The stories of Sybarite luxury vied with one another in prodigiousness; and when disaster finally befell the city in 510 B.C., some two centuries after its foundation, this seemed to historians one more example of the work of Nemesis. A quarrel broke out between Sybaris and the neighbouring Greek city-state of Croton, where the philosopher Pythagoras was living and teaching. The people of Croton, though at first afraid of their powerful neighbour, took the advice of Pythagoras and chose war. The result was that Sybaris was captured, the inhabitants either slain or driven away to the hills, and—so the story goes —the river Crathis was diverted by the Crotoniates over the site of the town, so that not a trace remained. Some modern writers maintain that this would have been beyond the powers of the Crotoniates as an engineering feat; but Herodotus, who later lived at Thourioi, believed it: he wrote of the dry bed of the old river, and of a temple of Athene that had later been built there.

For a time the site remained completely deserted. The scattered survivors lived at other Greek cities on the west Italian coast, and from time to time attempted to return to the old site. Once, nearly sixty years after the disaster, the site was occupied by some Greeks from Thessaly. But all these attempts were foiled by their jealous neighbours, who refused to allow the town to rise again; and the settlers were never strong enough to resist them. At last the persistence of the exiled Sybarites—by now the children or grandchildren of those who had survived the disaster—was rewarded. The possibilities of the place attracted the eye of Pericles, then at the height of his power as virtual ruler of Athens. He saw how useful it would be to have an Athenian outpost there on the coastal route to Sicily, at a spot where in bad weather the passage of overcrowded boats through the strait could be avoided by sending the men across land and the ships round to meet them. He therefore took pity on the Sybarite remnant (it is said that these had sent delegates to Sparta and to Athens, but the Spartans paid no attention), and decided to take the initiative in refounding Sybaris.

And so we come to the founding of Thourioi, as the new city-state came to be called. All was done with due form and ceremony. This colony was to be no haphazard affair like the settlements of the old adventurers; it was to be as well begun as modern Periclean science and political skill could make it. It was not to be a purely Athenian venture: a proclamation was sent round the cities of the Peloponnese, offering a place to anyone who wished to join. Many accepted. Among these was a Spartan named Cleandridas, banished from Sparta on suspicion of having accepted a bribe from Pericles not to invade Attica the previous year. This man's son was to prove a bane to Athens thirty years later: he was Gylippus, the man mainly responsible for the disaster which overtook the Athenian army and navy blockading Syracuse.

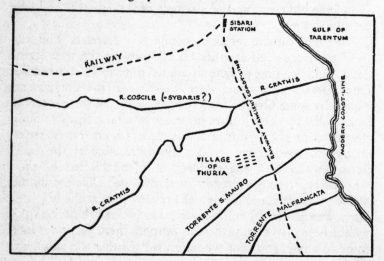

Meanwhile the Delphic oracle was consulted, according to custom. The Pythian priestess rose to the occasion with a special riddle: "You must found your city where you shall drink water by measure, and eat barley-cake without measure." Other professional seers were called in: Athens had no lack of these. Altogether ten seers made the voyage to Thourioi, perhaps one for each of the ten ships that sailed; they took such a prominent part in the expedition that one or other of them was often said to have been its leader, or even to have founded Thourioi. They were certainly prolific in prophecies about the future of the colony; and they evidently founded a school of seers there. Twenty years later they were being held up to ridicule on the Athenian comic stage as a type of lazy humbug.

The expedition sailed. The number of colonists sent by Pericles is not recorded; but besides the Athenians many others to whom the proclamation appealed or who had reasons for wanting to leave home joined *en route*. When they reached the coast of Italy and had sailed round to the mouths of the rivers Crathis and Sybaris, they were no doubt met by the original Sybarites and others wishing to share in the new venture. The first thing to look for was the spot indicated by the Delphic oracle; and they soon found something that would do. They came to a spring from which the water flowed through a bronze pipe, which the natives called *medimnos*. The *medimnos* in Athens was a dry measure; they therefore decided that this answered the riddle: "The place where you shall drink water by measure, and eat barley-cake without measure." This spring was called Thouria, "the Rusher", and was shortly afterwards to give its name to the new city. But at first the settlement was given the name of the old city Sybaris: the first coins struck there bore the head of Athena and the inscription SYBARI.

Ancient writers are agreed that the new city was not laid out on exactly the same spot as old Sybaris. Perhaps the latter was actually annihilated and obliterated by the diversion of the river; at any rate, the site of Sybaris has not yet been determined. The site of Thourioi, however, is known; and Italian archaeologists claim to have discovered even the spring "the Rusher" which led to the choice of site. The lie of the land has altered considerably since those days; the two rivers have now joined, and flow together into the sea, and their alluvial deposit has altered the coastline, adding considerably to the plain. A railway now runs across the plain, and it is thought that its course approximately marks the ancient coastline, so that ships in those days could come much closer than they would now be able to do. There was never a good harbour; but this was of less importance in times when ships could be drawn up on the shore.

The two rivers were reputed to have remarkable properties. The Crathis had the reputation of being able to bleach the hair of those who bathed in it; Aristotle jotted this down in his notebook of "Strange Things Heard". Euripides in his play *The Trojan Women* makes the Chorus sing of "the fairest of rivers, Crathis, which imparts a golden sheen to the hair". Strabo says that those who bathe in the Crathis go blonde or even white-haired, and that its water has healing properties. Theophrastus thought that sheep and cattle, if they drank it, turned from black to red to white; and Pliny thought that it produced whiteness and softness of flesh as well as straight hair. The opposite properties were attributed to the river Sybaris, which, Pliny believed, turned cattle and sheep black, and made men darker, harder and curly-haired. In one of the Idylls of Theocritus, a goat-herd who has won the prize in a singing competition promises his goats a wash in "the mere of Sybaris" as a treat, in celebration of his victory. Others, however, said that it made men and horses who drank it timorous, and that men kept their cattle away from it. Ovid says that both streams could make the hair "like gold or silver-gold".

The river Crathis had also a connection with ancient legend. Here, it was said, the Trojan women captured by the Greeks after the fall of Troy managed to set fire to the ships of their masters; their leader, a woman named Setaea, was hung up in chains on a cliff near the mouth of the Crathis and left to die.

A learned poet of Alexandrian times depicted the prophetess Cassandra as saying of Setaea: "Poor woman! For thee awaits an unhappy fate upon the rocks, where most pitifully outstretched with brazen fetters on thy limbs thou shalt die, because thou didst burn the fleet of thy masters; bewailing near Crathis thy body cast out and hung up for gory vultures to devour. And that cliff, looking on the sea, shall be called by thy name in memory of thy fate." The cliff was called Setaeon.

In the neighbourhood was a third stream called Lousias, "the Washer". This was said to have the clearest, most transparent water, and to produce black fish in considerable quantities. It was haunted by the Muses, and there was a cave of the Nymphs near by.

The town was therefore well served with water. No pains were spared to see that it was well laid out. With the expedition there sailed a famous town-planning expert, Hippodamus of Miletus, who had already made his name by replanning the Peiraeus as a residential and commercial district for Pericles. He was the inventor of a new system, called by Aristotle "the modern or Hippodamian method", that of wide straight streets crossing each other at right-angles in place of the old-fashioned narrow crooked streets. He now had a golden opportunity, and he made the most of it. He planned the new city with four main streets running longitudinally, called Heracles Street, Aphrodite Street, Olympus Street and Dionysus Street; and three crossing these, called Hero Street, Thouria Street, and Thourina Street. The houses were then built in the intervening spaces, and the effect was excellent. What public buildings or temples were erected, or how they were arranged, is not known; the only adornment we hear of is a statue of Diomedes, one of the heroes of the siege of Troy.

The town-planning expert was also an amateur political theorist: Aristotle says that he was the first man not actively engaged in politics to attempt to frame an ideal constitution, so that he probably left his mark on the city-state's new laws as

well as on her streets. His provisions for the ideal state are
recorded by Aristotle in the *Politics*. Hippodamus thought that
the best number for a city-state was ten thousand male citizens,
divided into three classes: artisans, farmers, soldiers. The land
also was to be divided into three: sacred, public (for the maintenance of the army) and private. So, too, the legal code was to
have three categories: assault, damage and homicide. There
was to be a court of appeal composed of elderly men chosen
by election. The verdict of the ordinary jury-courts was not
to be given by voting for absolute acquittal or condemnation:
each juryman was to have a tablet on which he recorded his
decision on each separate charge. It is clear that these ideas were
suggested by a critical observation of the Athenian legal system
rather than by any practical considerations; but whether he
was able to introduce any of them at Thourioi is not known.
Hippodamus was a man of strong personality, an eccentric
whose oddities of dress used to amuse the Athenians. He wore
his hair long like a Spartan, and his clothes were of the cheapest,
"even in summer", Aristotle says; but he also wore very valuable jewellery, and he may be one of the set of "sophists,
medical quacks, all rings, hair and laziness" mentioned along
with the "prophets of Thourioi" by Aristophanes. Whether
Hippodamus picked up these ways in Thourioi or helped to
introduce them there one cannot tell. He himself came from
Miletus, a city which had enjoyed a peculiar affinity with
Sybaris: the citizens of Miletus had lamented the destruction
of Sybaris with the deepest sorrow.

The constitution of Thourioi, however, was not left to
amateurs: it was as carefully thought out as the street plan.
The legal code was eclectic, a selection of the best laws of
several famous legislators of the past. What seems to have been
aimed at to begin with was a moderate oligarchy, something
like that of Solon's at Athens, with a property-assessment as
a qualification for citizen rights and a small number of govern-
ing offices in the hands of the upper class. The land was divided
out fairly, perhaps equally at first; but this did not last. Thourioi

was destined to show a rapid evolution from oligarchy to democracy, and to become a byword for civil strife.

The first trouble arose over the original Sybarites. The newcomers entirely failed to assimilate them, and ended by turning them out. We do not know the Sybarite case; we only know that the new colonists complained that the Sybarites behaved as if they owned the place: they assigned the best offices to themselves, expected their wives to take precedence on ceremonial occasions, tried to keep the land nearest the city and give the more distant pieces to the newcomers—in short, behaved with all their traditional arrogance, coupled with the contempt of an established caste for a heterogeneous crowd of *parvenus*. Their behaviour was foolish, since they were in a minority. Friction grew and became so serious that soon fighting occurred. Some of the Sybarites were killed, others fled; and so once again they found themselves looking on from the outside. This time the remnants collected on the Traeis, a nearby stream, and here the fourth and last Sybaris came into being. The refuge lasted a little while, until it was finally wiped out by the Bruttians, an Italian tribe.

The next trouble for Thourioi came from outside; the new colony was already full to overflowing, and it was desired to found another along the coast to the north, at a convenient distance. The site chosen was some forty miles away, on the navigable river Siris. There was already a settlement here called Siris; and the attempt to found a new one from Thourioi brought the latter into collision with the powerful Spartan colony of Tarentum. There was some fighting; the two peoples ravaged each other's fields. The Thourians had the advantage of being led by the exiled Spartan Cleandridas, and held their own; but the result of many small skirmishes was negligible, and soon the two city-states came to terms. The Thourians were given the right to send immigrants to the spot, but the colony was adjudged to belong to Tarentum, and was given the Dorian name of Heracleia. It was three miles inland, away from the older town Siris, which served as its dockyard.

Next the Thourians turned their attention to Croton, the ancient enemy of Sybaris. There was no wish on either side to continue the feud; and a pact of friendship was entered into. This left the Thourians free to attend to their own affairs: their internal arrangements and their commercial prosperity.

Now that the Sybarites had been expelled, the citizens were divided into ten tribes, on a racial basis. Three tribes were composed of men who came from the Peloponnese: the Arcadian tribe, the Achaean, and the Elean; three of men of the same race from outside the Peloponnese: the Boeotian, the Amphictyonic and the Doric; and four from other races: the Ionic, the Athenian, the Euboean, and the Islanders. The Athenians, evidently, were only a small part of the whole, although they had played the leading part in organizing the expedition. But they claimed the colony as theirs; and a dispute arose as to who could claim the title of Founder. It was decided to refer the matter to the Delphic oracle; the priestess replied that Apollo must be regarded as the Founder. This excellent solution was accepted, and the people "returned to their previously existing harmony", as one historian put it.

The territory was extensive and good; the newcomers had only to begin where the Sybarites had left off. The alluvial land gave grain in sufficiency, the terraced land above gave good and plentiful wine. Thourian wine became famous, though it was never quite so much prized as the sweet Lagarian wine of the highlands, which also produced wool and silver. The colony also dominated the land route across the hills to the western coast of Italy, sending that way its own wares and other goods which came for further distribution, just as Sybaris had done of old.

It is a pity that more is not known of the men who came to visit or reside in Thourioi. Perhaps the most famous resident was Herodotus, who came here to spend his latter days and to complete his History, so that he was sometimes even called "Herodotus of Thourioi". The date of his arrival is not known, but tradition says that he died there. Another famous visitor was Empedocles of Acragas. From Athens came two colonists, a young man and his brother aged fifteen, both of whom were destined to be remembered: Polemarchus and Lysias, sons of Cephalus, the Sicilian shield-manufacturer from the Peiraeus, friends of Socrates; Polemarchus destined to unjust execution at the hands of a terrorist government, the Thirty Tyrants of Athens, Lysias destined to win as an orator a fame second only to that of Demosthenes. From Syracuse came Teisias, the expert on oratorical composition and author of a handbook on rhetoric; it is said that he gave lessons to the young Lysias. There were openings for teachers of all sorts, and among them were a certain number of charlatans: Euthydemus and Dionysodorus, the irritating brothers whom Plato satirized in a dialogue, migrated to Thourioi from their native island Chios, but were subsequently expelled and went to Athens, where there was a wider field for the practice of their profession as teachers of sophistic argument.

The Peloponnesian War, between Athens at the head of her Empire and Sparta at the head of her League, broke out in 431 B.C. Thourioi at first remained neutral; but when the war moved to the west, she became an important link on the sea-route to Sicily. In 415 B.C. a great Athenian expedition set out to attack Syracuse. One of the Athenian commanders was Alcibiades; but he was under a cloud of suspicion, and soon the Athenian State vessel *Salaminia* set out after him, with orders not to arrest him but to summon him home to stand his trial for sacrilege. Alcibiades was at Catane on the east coast of Sicily when he received this command. He and others implicated with him had no choice but to board his own private ship and leave Sicily under the escort of the *Salaminia*. The vessels, coasting along in the usual way, came to Thourioi. Here Alcibiades went ashore with his friends, and when the time came to set out again they could not be found. The crew of the *Salaminia* were sent to search for them in the town; but they found good friends to hide them, and finally the *Salaminia* had to leave without them. As soon as she had sailed, Alcibiades reappeared, and himself left Thourioi for Argos in the Peloponnese. It was at Argos, apparently, that he heard the news of his condemnation, and from there he went straight to Sparta; but it was from Thourioi that he departed as an exile, determined to wreak vengeance on his native city which he adored and which had rejected him. There is a story that when he heard that the Athenians had condemned him to death in his absence he said: "All the same, I'll show them I'm alive!"

Thourioi at this time was torn with internal dissension, between those who favoured the Athenian cause and those who opposed it. For a time the balance was held evenly, and the result was neutrality. Then, by Alcibiades' advice, the Spartans sent Gylippus to help Syracuse against the besieging Athenians. On his way from Sparta to Syracuse he crossed over from Greece to Italy and, staying for a while at Tarentum, wooed the Thourians from there. He sent an embassy and renewed the citizenship which his father Cleandridas had enjoyed at Thourioi; but the Thourians observed how few ships he had, and despised him. They did not know that the main body of his fleet was to follow; and thinking him of no account, they rejected his overtures. Soon Gylippus sailed, to bring relief to Syracuse and disaster to the Athenians.

Gylippus' fate was strangely like that of his father: after the defeat of the Athenians at Aegospotami in 405 B.C. the Spartan commander Lysander entrusted him with the escort of the spoils to Sparta. These included 1,500 talents ($9,000,000) of silver in bags; in each bag was a scroll with the amount contained written on it. Gylippus, not knowing this, opened the bags and took 300 talents ($1,800,000); but when the Spartan officials inspected the cargo, the scrolls revealed the deficit. Gylippus fled and was condemned to death; but whether he found refuge in Thourioi as his father had done is not known.

Tempers in Thourioi now began to run high. Shortly after Gylippus' visit there was a civil war, in which the anti-Athenian party was turned out. The Athenians were not slow to take advantage. Their general Demosthenes [1] was bringing over a new fleet, asked for by the besiegers of Syracuse. He sailed along the south Italian coast, picking up men and ships where possible; and when he came to Thourioi he decided to hold a review before proceeding.

The Thourians still did not want to join the Athenians; they wished to remain neutral. But their internal warfare had left them too weak to resist the pressure of Demosthenes with his imposing array of ships and men; and they were obliged to make a comprehensive alliance and to furnish a thousand men: 700 infantry and 300 javelineers. The commanders then reviewed the whole of the land army, and led it across along the river Sybaris. They had ordered their fleet to meet them farther along the coast, at Croton; but the people of Croton, always suspicious of anything coming from that direction, refused them a passage; so Demosthenes and his army were forced to embark again and to leave the shores of Italy for ever. Thus a contingent from Thourioi fought in the final Athenian disaster at Syracuse, and very few, if any, came home again.

At once, when the news came through that the Athenians were utterly defeated at Syracuse, there was a reversal of policy in Thourioi. They had sent their forces unwillingly, under pressure; and now these were wiped out. Down with the Athenians and all who sympathized with them! The exiles returned, and the pro-Athenian party was now driven out instead. Among those who had to leave were Lysias and Polemarchus; this was in 412 B.C. The brothers returned to Athens and took up the family business of shield-manufacturing again. Thus we have the odd spectacle of two men whose father was a Syracusan, uprooted from their adopted city Thourioi and returning to their father's adopted city Athens, because Athens had failed to destroy Syracuse. This shows how completely Athenian Lysias and Polemarchus had become, and remained even throughout their residence in Thourioi.

[1] Not to be confused with the orator Demosthenes, who was born thirty years later, in 385 B.C.

From now onwards we find Thourioi violently on the side of Sparta. The war is now transferred to the Aegean; and in the Peloponnesian fleet are Thourian triremes. This part of Thourian history is linked up with the career of a remarkable man named Dorieus, originally from the island of Rhodes. He was the youngest son of a famous athlete, Diagoras of Rhodes, for whose victory at Olympia in the boxing-match Pindar wrote the magnificent Seventh Olympian Ode in 464 B.C. Diagoras trained his sons and his daughters' sons to similar feats; and Dorieus, his youngest son, was victorious three times in the Pancration, a very difficult event in which boxing and wrestling were combined; he was also victorious eight times at the Isthmus, nine times at Nemea, and at the Pythian Games in javelin-throwing. Diagoras' daughter Callipateira dressed herself in men's clothes in order to be able to take her son Peisirhodus to Olympia, where women were not admitted as spectators of the contests; she saw her son win the boxing-match for boys. Other members of the family were equally successful.

But Rhodes, a Dorian island, was annexed by Athens. The family of Diagoras was exiled, and Dorieus left Rhodes with his nephew Peisirhodus for Thourioi. Dorieus, as one would expect, was a passionate admirer of Sparta; and when the Thourians, soon after their revulsion of feeling against Athens, sent ten ships to join the Spartan fleet, Dorieus was given command of them.

At least four of these ships were captured by the Athenians in the Aegean in 411 B.C., but the crews escaped. Another five, perhaps all that remained, which had been left at Miletus, sailed with others from Syracuse and elsewhere to help the island of Chios in its defence against the Athenians; and though this relief squadron numbered only twelve, they successfully held the Athenian contingent of thirty-two ships, until night put an end to the battle. Then comes the most vivid picture of all. The Peloponnesian fleet at Miletus, kept there inactive by the inefficient Spartan admiral Astyochus, threatened mutiny.

They were paid seldom and inadequately, and they said that they would either fight their way out or desert. They all blamed the admiral; some even accused him of treason. These discussions led to an uproar: the Thourian and Syracusan sailors, being mostly free men, not slaves, clamoured most boldly of all for their pay.

The admiral Astyochus, not used to such insubordination, gave an angry answer, and when the Thourian captain Dorieus joined with his men in their demands the Spartan admiral raised his staff against him. When the men saw this gesture, they made a furious rush at Astyochus ("as sailors will," remarks Thucydides, who tells the story) and the admiral was saved from death by stoning only by taking refuge on an altar. Shortly afterwards he was recalled and replaced.

Dorieus, however, remained faithful to Sparta and continued to fight on her side. Shortly after the episode at Miletus, we find him trying vainly to get his ships through the Dardanelles to join the Spartan fleet there. But finally, four years later, in 406 B.C., he was captured with two Thourian triremes—probably all he had left—by an Athenian squadron and sent to Athens. He was still under the original condemnation which had led to his flight from Rhodes to Thourioi, and he had by now a long record of anti-Athenian service. But when he was led before the Athenian Assembly in a slave's dress and in chains, the people of Athens were ashamed to see such a fine figure of a man, a famous athlete, thus humiliated; and they let him go without even exacting a fine.

Meanwhile Thourioi, for all its vicissitudes, was prospering. The constitution had gradually changed from the original oligarchy to democracy: the property-assessment was lowered, the number of offices increased. The upper class had tried at first to seize the whole land; but the people, having had practice in warfare, were able to thwart them, and the land was divided equally. Laws such as the one limiting the generalship to a five years' term were relaxed by popular consent, and this opened up the way to further changes. The original code of laws said to have been accepted by the Thourians contained some very democratic provisions, including free education for all; and it also contained a provision to prevent tampering with the laws, namely that the person wishing to propose an amendment of an existing law must speak with his head in a noose; if he or she failed to convince, the noose was tightened instantly and the complainant was strangled. Nevertheless, the Thourians seem to have managed the change of constitution from oligarchy to democracy without great difficulty.

Life at Thourioi, apart from the fighting, was pleasant enough. The Spartan institutions of the common mess for men and the gymnastic exercises were introduced to some extent; and Spartan dress, especially long hair, was favoured. But in other ways the Thourians resembled the Ionian Greeks, or even the Persians; their environment had made them luxury-loving like the Sybarites. But the admixture of races, the fighting, and the constant coming and going kept them from sinking into indolence. The plenty in which they lived, however, was notorious. A comic poet of Athens, one Metagenes, a contemporary of Aristophanes, wrote a burlesque called *The Thouriopersians*, which, although it was never produced on the stage, enjoyed some vogue among readers and was often quoted. Most of the play is lost. The longest surviving passage gives one of those lists of food of which the Athenian comic writers were so fond: in it the river Crathis is depicted as flowing with barley-cakes which have kneaded themselves, while the river Sybaris rolls along a wave of cheese-cakes, meat and stewed skate. The streamlets run with baked cuttle-fish, bream and crayfish, or else with sausage and mincemeat. Sardines are here, anchovies there; slices of haddock, automatically steamed, float from above into one's mouth, and scones swim round one in a circle.

The wine, as already mentioned, was good, and the olive oil the best in the world. Vessels to contain oil and wine were manufactured, and, as at Athens, a special style of pottery of a pleasing rotundity was evolved that was much favoured by connoisseurs. Thourians at home enjoyed life thoroughly, eating, drinking, dancing—though their dancing was not in the best Hellenic style: "What's this?" exclaims a character in *The Thouriopersians*. "Are they horses galloping? They dance like a lot of savages!" But they were not lacking in the spirit of adventure. There were Thourians in the army of Greek mercenaries that marched upcountry with Prince Cyrus against Babylon in 401 B.C. Xenophon, who brought the leaderless Greek army through many perils back from Mesopotamia to the Black Sea, tells how when they reached the coast at last a conference was held to discuss the best way of getting home. Thereupon a man from Thourioi named Leon made a speech which won general favour, and which, brief as it is, exemplifies the Thourian character:

"Comrades, so far as I'm concerned, I'm sick of packing up, marching, running, carrying my kit, standing in formation, keeping guard, fighting. What I want is to be through with all this work. As we have now reached the sea, I should like to sail the rest of the way home and arrive like Odysseus, lying down stretched out at my ease."

The next we hear of Thourioi is during the reign of the tyrant Dionysius the Elder at Syracuse. It was in the year 385 B.C., when Dionysius was in the throes of his persecution-mania: furious because his poems were not appreciated at the national festival at Olympia, insane with spite against everyone. He had Plato sold as a slave, so it is said, after inviting him to his court; and he drove many of his friends into exile. Among the latter were two brothers named Philistus [1] and Leptines, men of great courage and outstanding services to their country during war. Visited by the tyrant's capricious displeasure, they fled to Thourioi, where they met with a great welcome; but Dionysius recovered his senses, and soon afterwards at his request they returned. They were not only reinstated to their

[1] Later wrote a history of Sicily. See page 74.

former favour, but Leptines was consoled with the hand of the tyrant's sister.

But now, in the middle of the fourth century B.C., the clouds begin to gather. It is the period before the outbreak of the First Samnite War in 343 B.C., when the Romans began their fifty-odd years' campaign for the subjugation of southern Italy. Mixed bands of runaway slaves and others are gathering in Lucania, the province surrounding Thourioi, terrorizing the natives and proceeding to the siege of the rich towns of the coast. The Bruttians, Thourioi's other neighbours, who occupied the extreme toe of Italy, had now organized themselves. They dominated the Crathis valley, which was the route over the hills, with their capital Consentia. The Lucanians became so threatening that the Thourians had to call up 14,000 infantry and 1,000 cavalry against them; but they were severely defeated on the west coast, and so lost their control of the profitable land route. Syracuse was hostile; and Tarentum, jealous of Thourian prosperity, would give no help.

However, in 344 B.C. Thourioi was visited by some guests, who made themselves useful. Dionysius the Younger, son of the preceding tyrant, had just been driven out of Syracuse by Timoleon, sent from Corinth for this purpose. The Corinthians sent Timoleon a reinforcement of 2,000 infantry and 200 cavalry, who got as far as Thourioi and found themselves unable to cross to Sicily because the sea was controlled by the Carthaginians with a large fleet. The Corinthian troops were therefore obliged to wait; and unlike most soldiers billeted on a foreign town, they spent their time in the way most serviceable to their hosts: they took over the city of Thourioi as if it were their native land, and guarded it "blamelessly and faithfully", the historian says, while the Thourians went off on a campaign against the Bruttians. These good Corinthian soldiers later managed to slip across the Straits of Messina without interference from the Carthaginians, and moreover, the weather worked what looked like a miracle in their favour. It had been blowing a gale, when the wind suddenly dropped and they crossed with the utmost ease on ferry-boats and fishing-smacks; it was so calm that the horses were able to swim behind on ropes.

Ten years later the Thourians are in even greater trouble. King Alexander of Epirus had been called in by the city-state of Tarentum to be their general in their campaign against the Lucanians. But he found himself unable to agree with the Tarentines. A Congress of the Greek city-states of Italy, usually held at the Tarentine settlement Heracleia, was now due. In his annoyance, King Alexander tried to remove the meeting-place from Heracleia to a site in Thourian territory, between the rivers Siris and Sybaris. This brought the Tarentines against the Thourians. War seemed imminent; and in their fright the Thourians took a momentous step: they called in the Romans to help them against all their enemies, Tarentines, Lucanians and Bruttians. The Romans agreed.

From now onwards the fortunes of Thourioi declined. In 282 B.C. a Roman garrison moved into the city, having been temporarily driven out of Tarentum, and on this occasion Thourioi was plundered. We hear nothing more of it until nearly the end of the century, during the Punic Wars, when Thourioi unwillingly joined the Carthaginians under Hannibal against Rome. Thourioi was then presented with an addition to her population which cannot have been welcome: Hannibal sent there the inhabitants of two Italian towns, who can hardly have mixed well with the Greek citizens. But Hannibal had never liked or trusted the Thourians; and so, during his retreat in 204 B.C., he caused the city to be sacked, and 3,000 inhabitants to be removed to Croton.

Thourioi was now completely exhausted, as well as underpopulated. After Hannibal's withdrawal and the defeat of Carthage, in about 194 B.C. the Romans sent a colony of 3,000 settlers and 300 cavalry to the city, but without granting full citizen status. They also changed the name to the very appropriate one of Copia or Copiae (Plenty). This was the name now stamped on its copper coinage; and its official title appears to have been Copia Thourioi. It appears to have received citizen rights from the Romans in 90 B.C. but fifty years later its status had again been reduced for a reason unknown. The old Greek name, Thourioi, tends to persist, and to oust the Roman name Copiae; but its history as a Greek city-state is over.

Yet during the most troublous times some, at any rate, of the Greek inhabitants must have found consolation in religion. At Thourioi, as elsewhere, a number of gold plaques have been found of the kind which were sometimes buried with those who held Orphic beliefs. These gold plaques were for the guidance of the soul when it reached the next world. They bore extracts from an Orphic poem describing what the soul might expect to experience there. If a man or woman had fulfilled his or her religious duties throughout the whole cycle of existence, there was hope of everlasting life, a godlike existence free from care, when the soul had stood before the throne of the dread goddess Persephone and the other judges and had passed the test of purity. "I come pure from the pure, O Queen of the Underworld and ye other deities!" says the soul. The judges answer: "You are no longer a mortal, but divine. You have fallen as a kid into milk. Welcome, welcome! Pass to the right, to the sacred meadows and the groves of Persephone!"

In 40 B.C. Sextus Pompeius, son of the great Pompey, besieged Thourioi in the interests of Mark Antony, who was at variance with Octavian, the future Emperor Augustus. But the Thourians were strong enough to repulse the attacker, to the annoyance of Antony and the delight of Octavian, who remarked: "What a blow for Pompeius, miserable villain, miserably beaten off as usual—this time from Thourioi!"

This episode really ends the known story of Thourioi. By the second century A.D. the site was deserted. Four hundred years later a harbour of Thourioi is mentioned by an historian describing the Gothic conquest of this region; but no important settlement was ever again built on the alluvial land. The nearest settlement after the Gothic conquest was no longer on the coast but three miles away, on the edge of the coastal range of hills. The plain had always been malarial, and also there were the descents of pirates to be feared.

And so the Crathis and the Sybaris flowed on unhindered, piling up the mud, joining their waters. Today there is nothing but a heap of stones, called by the inhabitants Le Muraglie, beside the road from Terranova to Corrigliano, to mark the site of Thourioi. The district has occupied the attention of archaeologists, who have disputed the supposed site of Thourioi, have failed to find Sybaris, and while accepting the river Crati as the ancient Crathis, have denied that the Coscile is the Sybaris, and have given this honour to a much smaller stream called Torrente San Mauro, farther south. But Thourioi has its surprises still. The German archaeologist Kahrstedt based his argument concerning the site of Thourioi on the presence of certain mounds near the coast, which he and others thought to be an ancient cemetery. These were excavated in April 1932; and they proved to be sand-dunes.

3. ACRAGAS

(Agrigentum, Girgenti, Agrigento)
"Fairest of mortal cities."—PINDAR.

THERE IS no doubt that Acragas on the south coast of Sicily was one of the most beautiful of all the beautiful cities of the Greeks. Pindar, who worshipped colour and splendour, calls Acragas "glorious"—the tribute that elsewhere he bestows on Athens—and "lofty city lavish above all in gifts to the gods". Acragas was, to him, "the sacred settlement by the river", and the very "eye of Sicily".

When Pindar visited Acragas—probably in 476 B.C. for the performance of two of his greatest Victory Odes—the city had not yet reached the zenith of its glory; most of its many temples were still unbuilt. But the progress made since its foundation was amazing.

The Greeks had begun arriving in Sicily and founding city-states from the eighth century B.C. onwards. Naturally at first they settled on the east coast. Syracuse, the greatest of all the Sicilian colonies, was founded in 734 B.C., where that coast afforded a splendid harbour. Nearly fifty years later a band of settlers from Rhodes and Crete founded Gela on the south coast. Gela flourished so exceedingly that it soon had to seek an outlet for its surplus population. A leader from the mother-island Rhodes was sent for; and the "swarm" from Gela set out along the coast to a site further west, where there was a high hill about two and a half miles from the sea, suitable enough except that it lacked a good harbour. This was Acragas, last of the Dorian colonies of Sicily, as Syracuse was the first, and destined to have a history no less remarkable.

The crag on which the city was established has an area of less than four square miles; yet on to it were to be crowded such a cluster of temples as were to be seen nowhere else in the whole Greek world. This crag was steep on the east, but more gently sloping on the west, and was itself divided by a deep valley, now called Valle della Croce; the whole eminence is encircled by two small rivers which join to the south of the town: one called Acragas, which gave its name to the city, the other called Hypsas. Both streams may still be seen, though they have been renamed the San Biagio and the Drago.

The settlers took a considerable risk when they chose a site so far to the west. The extreme western end of Sicily was a stronghold of the Phoenicians, the greatest trade-rivals of the Greeks in the Mediterranean; and Carthage, Phoenicia's greatest offshoot, was only one hundred and fifty miles distant across the sea to the south-west, on the African coast. There was, it is true, another Greek city-state, Selinus, between Acragus and the Phoenician tip; but Selinus, founded a hundred years earlier, had long reconciled herself to her dangerous neighbours, and was eventually to become more of a menace than a friend when a mortal struggle arose between Carthage and the Greeks for possession of the island. Besides this danger, there were the native inhabitants of Sicily: before the Greek settlers at Acragas could take over the site they had to dislodge the Sicans who were in occupation and had been for many centuries. These Sicans were unable to prevent the seizure of their home, in spite of an ingenious system of far-branching tunnels which they and their ancestors had hewn in the rock for defence purposes. So, like the other natives ousted by the Greeks, they retired inland to watch events and take sides against the invaders whenever this was profitable.

The Greeks at Acragas, left in possession, began at once to fortify their hill with walls, especially on the western side where it was more vulnerable. They provided the walls with three gates, one leading to the sea, one leading back to their mother-city Gela, and the third leading westward to a small coastal settlement called Heracleia. They also laid out on the highest point of the crag a temple dedicated to the Zeus of their ancestral place of origin, Rhodes, and entitled him Atabyrios after a Rhodian mountain. There are no written records of this busy time; but tradition says that a dozen years after their arrival one of the leading citizens named Phalaris, having been given high office, managed to seize dictatorial power. Appointed finance minister, he was put in charge of the arrangements for building the Temple of Zeus. When the work had been started, he pretended to the people that building material was being stolen, and persuaded them to let him not only fortify the height but arm the workmen, some of whom were prisoners of war, while others were foreigners hired for the purpose. Then, using these men as a personal body-guard, he descended on his fellow-citizens during a religious ceremony, and overpowered them with much slaughter. It is said that he succeeded in disarming the citizens by organizing a sports festival outside the walls; then, shutting the gates against them, he instituted a house-to-house search for weapons and confiscated all that he found.

During the sixteen years of his reign Phalaris showed the greatest energy, waging war on the hostile natives, and using every means, cunning as well as force, to establish the new settlement on a firm basis. But in this enterprise he also displayed a ferocious cruelty that made his memory execrated for centuries afterwards, until it later became fashionable to excuse him on the grounds of pressure of circumstance. Perhaps the story that he roasted his victims alive is an invention by a sensation-loving anecdotist; [1] but Pindar heard it, and he was there only two generations later, when memories of Phalaris' reign were still vivid in the minds of descendants. At any rate, after sixteen years the people of Acragas could stand the tyrant no longer, and during a furious rebellion he was assassinated. The leaders of the rebellion took his place, at least in influence, though they did not at first assume despotic power; but after a while the need for strong leadership was again felt, as the menace of Carthage loomed near; and the supreme power was given to Thêrôn, a descendant of the man who had led the movement against Phalaris.

Theron too reigned for sixteen years, from 488 B.C. until his death in 472. His reign was a period of the greatest splendour and progress, unmarred by cruelty. His reputation stood high, not only in Sicily but throughout all Greece; in fact, he was said to have excelled all Sicilian rulers in nobility, wealth and benevolence towards his people. Even before he received the monarchy he and his house were noted for their hospitality, their culture, their kindliness, and the good use they were making of their vast riches. Above all, they were known for their successes in the Great Games.

A few years before Theron's accession, his younger brother Xenocrates won a victory in the chariot-race at the Pythian Games at Delphi; and at the same festival another Acragantine, named Midas, carried off the prize for flute-playing. This Midas had as his pupil an Athenian named Lamprocles, who became the teacher of Sophocles; so that Athenian tragedy, at any rate on the musical side, owed something to Acragas. Both these successful competitors commissioned Pindar to write Victory Odes; and Pindar, still at the beginning of his career,

---

[1] Or it may represent a tradition of human sacrifice to the chief deity. The Bull was so constructed that the cries of the victims sounded like its bellowings. The first victim was said to have been its inventor Perillus (cf. the tradition regarding Dr. Guillotin), and the last, Phalaris himself.

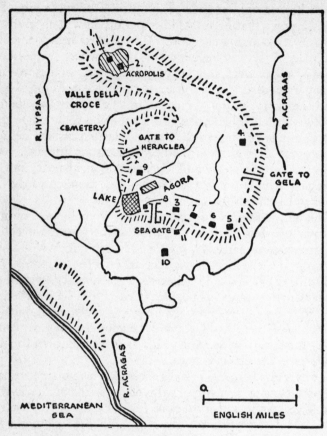

1. *Temple of Zeus Atabyrios.*
2. *Temple of Athena.*
3. *Temple of Olympian Zeus.*
4. *So-called Temple of Demeter and Persephone.*
5. *So-called Temple of Hera Lacinia.*
6. *So-called Temple of Concordia.*
7. *So-called Temple of Heracles.*
8. *So-called Temple of the Dioscuri.*
9. *So-called Temple of Hephaestus.*
10. *Temple of Asclepius.*

lavished the best of his unique art on these two works. For Midas the flute-player he invoked the city-state of Acragas herself to welcome the victor home:

"*I pray thee, lover of radiance, fairest of mortal cities,*
Seat of Persephone, who dost dwell on the banks of the river,
Sheep-nurturing Acragas, on a fair-built hill, O Queen!
Graciously, with the good will of gods and men,
Receive this garland from Delphi, awarded to illustrious Midas,
And welcome the victor himself, who has conquered all Hellas
  with his art!"

For Xenocrates, the king's brother, Pindar wrote a longer Ode, in which he praised not so much the owner of the victorious team, but his son Thrasyboulus, who had driven the chariot, and with whom Pindar seems to have struck up a lasting friendship. Of this young man he writes most charmingly, praising him for his filial devotion, his moderation, his love of the arts, and, above all, for his sweetness of temper. Comparing him with Nestor's son Antilochus in the *Iliad*, who sacrificed his life to save his father's, Pindar writes:

"*But that is the past.*
Today, there is Thrasyboulus,
Who comes nearest to the standard of filial duty,
While approaching his father's brother (Theron) in brilliance.
Wisely he uses his wealth,
Not plucking the pleasures of a wicked or violent youth,
But culling the flowers of Art in the secret haunts of the Muses,
And with a spirit thou lovest, O earth-shaking Poseidon,
Pursues the chariot-races first invented by thee.
Sweet too is his temper,
And as a boon companion
He rivals in sweetness the honeycomb, labour of bees."

It is not surprising that in later years, when Theron himself was victorious at Olympia, greatest of all the Games, he too commissioned this poet to celebrate him in song. He did well:

his reputation lives and breathes still in these wonderful crea-
tions, for as Pindar himself proudly claimed:

*"It is from poems of praise, framed by skilled craftsmen, that we
know men's names.
Excellence lives long in glorious Odes,
But to few is given the making of them."*

Two great external events marked the reign of Theron. One
was the defeat of Carthage, by Theron in alliance with Gelôn,
king of Syracuse. The other was the avoidance of what looked
like inevitable war with Syracuse itself. The defeat of the
Carthaginians in Sicily was almost as celebrated as the defeat
of the Persians by the mainland Greeks at Marathon and
Salamis; and in fact the two hostile movements were made in
collaboration. While Persia was planning the invasion of Greece
Proper, the Carthaginians were by arrangement with them
planning to throw the Greeks out of Sicily. The story of their
defeat, less well-known than that of the Persians, is just as ex-
citing, and was just as vital to the salvation of western civilization from oriental tyranny.

The Carthaginian attempt was a most serious menace, above
all to the city-state of Acragas, which was directly opposite
the enemy base, and was farthest to the west except for the
untrustworthy city of Selinus. The Carthaginians chose as their
general a very able man named Hamilcar, and gave him command of an enormous force: an army of at least 300,000, with
200 warships and over 3,000 supply vessels. This expedition,
however, was wrecked by a storm, in which the cavalry and
war-chariots were lost, so that Hamilcar on arriving at the
Carthaginian base in west Sicily, Panormus, at first reported
that he could do nothing: he feared that the war was over—
the sea had rescued the Sicilian Greeks. Nevertheless, having
rested his forces, he decided to proceed, not against Acragas
itself but against Himera, a city on the north coast, which a
century earlier had placed itself under the protection of Ac-

ragas because of the Carthaginian menace. He invested Himera with his ships and his land forces, and settling down there, sent home his cargo vessels for fresh supplies.

Theron was already in Himera with a large defence force. When he saw the magnitude of Hamilcar's preparations, he was greatly alarmed, and sent an urgent message to Gelon, the ruler of Syracuse, who had married his daughter Dêmaretê and was his ally. This man, one of the ablest and most energetic of the Sicilian Greek nobles, had had a spectacular career. He belonged originally to Gela, the mother-city of Acragas: but this state was too small for his ambitions, and seizing an opportunity offered by internal dissension at Syracuse, he made himself its ruler and bent all his efforts on its aggrandizement, transferring the population of other cities to his new realm. He was so powerful that the mainland Greeks sent envoys to him asking for help against the Persians; he offered substantial aid provided that he were given the chief command. When this condition was rejected, he dismissed the envoys with the contemptuous words: "The Greeks have lost the springtime out of their year." He was the only ruler in Sicily who wielded greater power than Theron. Theron, shrewdly recognising this, formed an alliance with him and gave him his daughter Demarete as his wife.

Gelon was prepared. He responded at once to Theron's appeal and marched to the relief of Himera. His first efforts, after pitching a fortified camp outside the city, were directed towards restoring confidence to the inhabitants. He sent out his horsemen to capture stragglers and had them brought into the town. These not only provided information: the sight of them heartened the defenders. Gelon's next action was to order the removal of the barricades which Theron had had built across the gateways; thus the defenders were encouraged to feel contempt for the enemy. Then Gelon was rewarded with a piece of good luck.

Gelon's plan was to try to set fire to the Carthaginian fleet; and while he was considering how to attack their naval camp, a letter fell into his hands which revealed the ideal opportunity. The government of Selinus, now completely under Carthaginian influence, wrote to Hamilcar saying that they would send the required contingent of cavalry on the day on which Hamilcar would be holding a great sacrifice to Poseidon. This gave Gelon his chance. He sent a contingent of his own cavalry to the Carthaginian camp with orders to pose as the expected band from Selinus. As they were Greeks, the Carthaginians would not see through the deception and would admit them. These were then to kill Hamilcar and set fire to his fleet, while Gelon would await their signal and attack simultaneously.

The ruse worked. Gelon's men were admitted. They immediately rushed to the shore and fired the ships, while Gelon led all his forces against the camp.

At first the Carthaginians inside the camp fought bravely; but at the height of the struggle flames began to rise from the ships, encouraging the Greeks and terrifying the enemy. The slaughter of Carthaginians was huge: Gelon had given orders that no prisoners were to be taken, and it is said that about 150,000 were killed. The rest fled inland to a deserted place, and at first defended themselves, but were soon overcome by thirst and obliged to surrender. Their lives were spared. As for the general Hamilcar, he was never seen again, dead or alive. The Greek soldiers claimed to have killed him at the altar; the Carthaginian tradition was that when he saw defeat at hand, he threw himself into the altar fire and himself became the burnt offering.

For this great victory, which the Greeks liked to believe had taken place on the same day as the battle of Thermopylae (August 480 B.C.), Gelon was given most of the credit, and rightly so; it had been won by his brilliant generalship and his daring. He was regarded with wonder, as the man who had killed the greatest number of the enemy and taken the most prisoners.

After the rout, Gelon showed great mercy, principally through the influence of his wife, Theron's daughter Demarete, who was active in promoting peace and in obtaining lenient terms for the defeated. The Carthaginians in gratitude voted her a golden crown. The Syracusans struck a magnificent commemorative silver coin worth ten Attic drachmas (about $10), carrying on one side a woman's profile surrounded by four dolphins, and on the other a four-horse chariot over which a winged Victory is flying with a garland. The coin was called after her, the Demareteion. The profile is thought to be that of the patron goddess of Syracuse, Arethusa, a regular feature of Syracusan coinage; but the artist may also have given it a resemblance to the queen, whose kindness of heart reminds one that she was a cousin of Pindar's sweet-tempered friend Thrasyboulus.

Theron's part in this great victory, which freed Sicily from the Carthaginian menace for seventy-five years, almost till the end of the fifth century B.C., was somewhat overshadowed by that of his brilliant son-in-law Gelon. Yet no city-state of Sicily was more directly affected by its results than Acragas. The prisoners were divided among the Greek cities in proportion to the numbers of men from each city who had fought; by this reckoning, Acragas was allotted the largest number. Like the other states, the Acragantines shackled their prisoners and turned them on to public works. Moreover, they received still further additions of slave-workers as those of the Carthaginians who had escaped alive and had fled to the interior gradually came drifting in, driven by hunger and thirst. Most of these too came to Acragas. The city was packed with prisoners: there were so many that no one knew what to do with them. Some of the wealthiest citizens had as many as five hundred as private servants. Most of those who were used for public works were employed in hewing stones for a vast new building programme, that of the great temples of the gods which were now to adorn the height. Others were set to labour at constructing huge underground pipes for drawing away water from the city. These pipes were so large that they were one of the wonders of the place, though often despised because of their prosaic purpose, in contrast to the magnificent temples. The superintendent of this drainage scheme was called Phaeax, and the drains were called after him, "Phaeaces".

But the most enterprising undertaking of all was the construction of a magnificent ornamental lake, fifty feet deep and nearly a mile in circumference. This too was excavated by the prisoners of war. It was fed by river- and spring-waters, and it became a breeding-pond for fish, yielding a vast number of every sort for food. Moreover, large numbers of swans settled on it, so that it came to present a most delightful spectacle. In later days, after the fall of Acragas, this lake became silted up through neglect, until by the beginning of the Christian era it was almost filled up. In modern times its outlines can still be traced, the bottom being used as an orange-grove.

The whole of the surrounding district controlled by Acragas was good fertile land. This they now, by means of the prisoners' labour, planted with vines and every sort of tree, from which later they drew a large revenue. The number of prisoners throughout all Sicily was so great that, as one of their historians records, it was as if all Libya had been captured by the island.

Gelon did not live long to enjoy the honour in which he was held not only by his own subjects but by all Sicilian Greeks. He died of dropsy in 478 B.C., two years after the battle at Himera, and was commemorated at Syracuse by a magnificent tomb. He was succeeded by his brother Hieron, who was destined to raise Syracuse to new heights of prosperity and power; but before Hieron was established trouble arose, in which Acragas was involved, and which nearly caused war between the two city-states, now the most influential in Sicily.

Gelon before his death had entrusted the care of his wife Demarete and their small son not to Hieron but to another brother, Polyzêlus, evidently intending the latter to succeed him; but Polyzelus was unable to make good his claim, and for a time the two remaining brothers lived uneasily at Syracuse, full of mutual mistrust. After a while Hieron decided to get Polyzelus out of the way, and planned to send him in command of a battalion on an overseas expedition, hoping that he would be killed. Polyzelus, seeing through the plot, fled to Theron at Acragas.

Preparations for war against Hieron were made at Acragas with a view to setting Polyzelus and Demarete on the throne of Syracuse. But neither of the rulers really wanted war. One story is that Hieron took the initiative in making friends: he had received a message from Himera asking for help against their oppressive governor, who was Theron's son Thrasydaeus, and offering to hand Himera over to Hieron. Hieron, wishing to earn Theron's gratitude, it is said, revealed the plot to him, in return for which service Theron, having punished his son's opponents at Himera, withdrew his opposition to Hieron's rule at Syracuse and reconciled him to Polyzelus. Other historians prefer the more sensational story that the two armies were actually confronting each other when a reconciliation was effected by the poet Simonides. At any rate, peace was made, and the pact was sealed with further intermarriages. Theron's daughter Demarete was now the wife of Polyzelus. Theron himself took as his wife one of Polyzelus' daughters. Hieron married a daughter of Theron's brother Xenocrates. Thus the two dynasties were more firmly linked together than ever; but the two city-states, though completely reconciled, remained also completely independent, in the Hellenic way.

There followed for Acragas a period of unexampled prosperity. After Gelon's death, Theron's name, as that of the joint victor of Himera, stood highest in Sicily, and his court became famous, in a city already noted for its hospitality. Again Theron and his family, now that the Carthaginian danger was past, were able to send their racing chariots to the Great Games in Greece. In 477 B.C. Theron's brother Xenocrates won a victory at the biennial festival on the Isthmus; and some years later, Xenocrates having died, Pindar wrote a commemorative Ode at the request of Xenocrates' son Thrasyboulus, whose charming character he had celebrated in song

twenty years before. It is pleasant to know that Pindar's affection for this family had not diminished. He calls Thrasyboulus
"my trusty friend", and his father Xenocrates "light of the
people of Acragas". "In the past," he says, men were less com-
mercially-minded:

"*In the past, poets wrote poems to beauty,*
   Not for money and as a trade.
   But now, 'money, money is the man.'
   However, it is an easy journey to bring praise to the homes of the
      great.
   Your father Xenocrates excelled all men in sweetness of temper:
   He was gracious towards his fellow-countrymen,
   And he pursued the breeding of horses in the Panhellenic way.
   He welcomed every festival of the gods,
   He was world-famous for unremitting hospitality.
   Thrasyboulus can afford to ignore envy in singing his father's
      praises."

A year later, Theron's chariot carried off the greatest prize
of all: victory at Olympia.

Pindar was commissioned to write the celebratory Ode. The
theme suited him well: a great king, lavish of hospitality,
formerly beset by troubles which are now safely past, ruler
over a prosperous city-state, where love of the gods and regard
for one's fellowmen are supreme. The magnificent opening
is, in the original tongue, like the sound of the music it invokes;
and even in paraphrase its beauty and force and passion for
nobility ring out challengingly:

"*Lords of the lyre, my songs,*
   What god, what hero, what man shall we celebrate?
   Zeus first, patron of Pisa.
   Heracles next, who founded the Olympic award.
   Theron third, whose victory in the four-horse race
   Deserves a triumph-song:
   Theron, kind to strangers,
   Bulwark of Acragas,

Flower of noble sires,
Pillar of the State."

The poet prays for the safety of Acragas, "eye of Sicily":

"Men and women alike must suffer sorrow.
 No man knows whether his end will be peaceful, in undiminished
  prosperity.
 But when success crowns our efforts, the mind is released from
  cares.
 Wealth, when adorned with virtue, brings varied opportunity.
 If a man who has it knows the future . . ."

There follows a description of the after-world, as envisaged
by the mystical religions: a judgment which sends the wicked
souls back into the world to pay the penalty for their sins,
while the good are given a life free from toil and suffering.
Significantly the poet adds:

"I have many swift arrows in my quiver,
 Bearing a meaning for those who understand.
 For the masses, their meaning needs interpreters . . .
 Come now, my soul, bend thy bow upon the mark!
 At whom shall we aim,
 Shooting arrows of fame from a kindly heart?
 Acragas is my target.
 I shall declare in all sincerity, and swear upon oath,
 This city has not within a century produced a man more benef-
  icent to his friends,
 More lavish of hand,
 Than Theron!"

In another song, written to be sung at the newly-built
Temple of Castor and Pollux, Pindar writes:

"Water is first among liquids,
 Gold is most valued among treasures.
 So today Theron has reached the limit of achievement,

And has touched the Pillars of Heracles in his voyage.
Beyond that, let no man go,
Be he wise or foolish!"

The poet's intuition was in one regard correct: Theron had touched the height of his achievement. Four years later he died. He was succeeded by his son Thrasydaeus, who had already proved himself tyrannical at Himera. The son's reign was brief and inglorious. Soon after his accession he reopened the quarrel with Hieron of Syracuse, was defeated in a battle, and disowned by the people of Acragas, who settled down to self-government for sixty prosperous years.

Throughout the next three decades, while Athens and Sparta were in the early stages of their struggle for supremacy in Greece, Acragas was undisturbed by any shadow of impending disaster. The city and its surrounding territory were overflowing with riches. By this time, the trees which had been planted with the help of the Carthaginian prisoners of war had grown to a prodigious fertility. The vines were of surpassing size and beauty, and the olives with which the greater part of the land had been stocked gave a huge harvest which was sold, ironically enough, to Carthage. The coast of Libya, with the exception of the district round Cyrene, was not yet planted; and so the landowners and farmers of Acragas were able to dispose of their crops at a huge profit, accumulating enormous wealth. Vast revenues also accrued to the State from the public and sacred lands; this wealth was spent mostly on building temples to the gods, the remaining ruins of which testify to the money and labour at the disposal of the Government and the magnificence of their ideas.

The small area on the top of the eastern crag already carried at least four temples, the earliest, that of Zeus Atabyrios, at the highest point. Close beside it was a Temple of Athene, built in Theron's reign. On the south cliff there was a Temple of Heracles. Most important of all, on the east cliff was a Temple of Demeter and Persephone, the revered goddesses of the mystery-religion to which Acragas was devoted. There now rose other temples, to deities who can no longer be named with certainty, until the south slope was crowned with a row of huge Doric edifices built of the local porous stone, which is (to quote a modern visitor) "of a warm red-brown colour, full of fossil shells and easily corroded when exposed to the air". The best-preserved of these, the so-called Temple of Concord, lacks nothing but its roof, having been preserved by being converted into a cathedral in the sixth century A.D. by a Bishop of Girgenti. The so-called Temple of Hera close beside it is almost as impressive. These two are among the finest Doric temples that survive.

In front of certain of the temples stood a huge altar for burnt offerings, as long as the façade of the temple itself. But the biggest temple of all, dedicated to Olympian Zeus, and begun in about 450 B.C., was still being built when the second war with Carthage broke out in 406 B.C.; it was never quite finished. It was 361 feet long, apart from its steps, and 173½ feet wide. Its huge columns, originally thirty-eight in number, have a height of 60 feet and a diameter at the base of 14 feet. Between these columns, half-way up the wall, stood gigantic figures of Atlas 25 feet high, which helped to support the roof; some of them can still be seen. The temple was adorned, says a writer of the first century after Christ, with sculptures of outstanding size and beauty, the subjects of which were the battles of the Giants and the capture of Troy; it also had several porches of correspondingly colossal size.

This passion of the Acragantines for building mighty temples was unique in Greece; it expresses the outlook of the whole community. They were, amid all their material splendours, devoted to religion. They worshipped all the gods of Olympus: Zeus, Athene, Hera, Castor and Pollux, Hephaestus; and some of the demigods: Heracles and Asclepius. Even after their downfall they did not cease to build. One cult, wherever it appeared, aroused a special fervour: that of Demeter and Persephone, which had one foot in the underworld. Acragas was the home of a particularly intense worship of these two goddesses, who are associated with the Mysteries, with Orpheus and Dionysus, who offered something more than the conventional, cheerful ritual sufficient to propitiate Zeus and his consort and their capricious but immortal children. This cult of the Mother and the Maiden was particularly favoured in Sicily: according to Sicilian legend, Persephone was picking narcissi in a meadow at Enna on the road from Catane to Acragas when she was carried off to the underworld by Pluto; a temple to Demeter was built on the spot to commemorate the Mother's loss. The principal tenet of the cult, that which most attracted its devotees, was a belief in reincarnation, in a cycle of existences in which the purity or sinfulness of the soul met with rewards and punishments, the reward for purity being a final apotheosis, a translation to a blissful life in the company of the gods. All these beliefs, with their message of hope, received a tremendous accession of vitality through the work of Pythagoras, who migrated from Samos in the Aegean to Croton in southern Italy in the sixth century B.C. and founded a religious school in which disciples were taught an ascetic way of life based on Orphic doctrine and, if they were capable of assimilating it, advanced mathematics and metaphysics. The influence of Pythagoras on both scientific philosophy and religion was immeasurable. One of his disciples was a native of Acragas named Empedocles.

This great man, who was active in the middle of the fifth century B.C., at the height of his native city's prosperity, became in later times a magnet for miraculous stories. The truth about him is simpler and nobler than the sensational anecdotes now associated with his name, such as his jumping into Etna; when examined, these stories all turn out to be inventions, arrived at by exaggerating passages in his own writings. He wrote two great poems, one an account of the origin of the universe and an explanation of its phenomena, the other a religious poem setting forth the Orphic doctrine concerning man's destiny: his fall from grace, his cycle of existence, his final apotheosis if all the precepts of Orphism were observed. These precepts were, above all, abstinence from animal slaughter and the eating of meat. From these poems we learn that Empedocles was no miracle-mongering seer, but a man inspired by a passion to understand nature, to control its destructive manifestations and to help his fellow-men. His interests ranged over all natural phenomena; but he had a special interest in biology and medicine. He travelled, and attained to great fame, especially as a healer. His religious poem is addressed to the people of Acragas, in an eulogistic preamble:

"Friends, you who dwell in the great town on the city's heights looking down on the yellow river Acragas,
You who are occupied with good works,
Who are harbours of refuge, kindly to strangers,
Without part in wickedness,
Greeting!
I move among you as a god, no longer a mortal,
Held in honour by all, as they think I deserve,
Crowned with garlands.
When I visit prosperous cities,
I am honoured by all, men and women.
They follow me in thousands, to ask my advice,
Some wanting oracles,
Others a prescription for their various ailments and chronic pains . . .

Friends, I know that Truth is present in the story that I shall tell.
But it is very difficult for mankind.
They do not want to feel the pressure of conviction on their minds."

To his favourite disciple Pausanias he wrote the glowing creed of these early investigators:

"You shall learn all the drugs that exist for our protection against illness and old age.

You shall check the force of the tireless winds
Whose blasts lay waste the crops,
And again you shall bring them back.
You shall create drought after rain,
Rain after drought in their season.
You shall restore a dead man to life."

These were not vain boastings. They were the passionate faith of one who believed in the power of knowledge, and who wished to use that power solely for the benefit of mankind.

Much could be written of Empedocles and his theories; but we are here concerned rather with the city-state that produced him. From his poems we get the same impression of the Acragantines as that which emerges from the poems of Pindar: they were, above all things, kindly, considerate towards each other and towards "foreigners", that is, Greeks from other city-states. How they treated their prisoners of war is not directly recorded; but since these were present in such large numbers, and yet we hear of no repressive measures such as the Spartans were forced to use against their Helots for fear of an uprising, we may assume that the masters at Acragas were not too harsh. This view is supported by the fact that throughout the fifth century B.C. Acragas was at peace with Carthage and was enjoying a busy trade with her. The attitude of the Acragantines to Empedocles, a man of original outlook and way of life, is notable if one compares it with the treatment that Athens accorded to Socrates and Anaxagoras, to mention the most famous of all examples. To take a lesser-known case: Heracleitus of Ephesus wrote scathingly of his fellow-citizens:

"The Ephesians would do well to hang themselves, every grown man, and bequeath their city-state to adolescents, since they have expelled Hermodôrus, the most valuable man among them, saying, 'Let us not have even one valuable man; but if we do, let him go elsewhere and live among others!'"

"May wealth never fail you, men of Ephesus, so that you may be convicted of your wickedness!"

Contrast the scorn felt towards the Ephesians by their greatest man with Empedocles' dedication of his poem to the men of Acragas!

There are tales of Acragantine love of luxury; but there are no tales of their arrogance, as of the prosperous citizens of Sybaris. Luxury at Acragas did not breed licence; it did, however, lead to a neglect of military training and physical hardness for which they were later to pay dearly.

In the middle of the fifth century B.C. the Acragantines experienced a brief scare from which they would have done well to take warning. A native chieftain named Ducetius had succeeded in reviving the hostility of the inland tribe, the Sicels, against the Greeks. For a time he proved himself a considerable danger. His headquarters threatened Syracuse rather than Acragas; but in 451 B.C. he marched across country against the wealthy and less well defended city-state, which sent to Syracuse, as usual, for aid. At first Ducetius defeated the combined forces of the Greeks; but finally the Syracusans defeated and captured him. He was sent across the sea to live at Corinth, the mother-city of Syracuse, with whom Syracuse retained close relations. Ducetius was allowed to return to Sicily in 446 B.C., much to the annoyance of the Acragantines; but the trouble died down, and no more was heard of him. The Acragantines returned to their life of busy trade and to the enjoyment of their prosperity.

Life at Acragas in the fifth century B.C. must have been pleasant. The citizens were fond of social activity. For recreation, they had their great artificial lake, by now full of every kind of fish for public banquets, and the nesting-place not only of swans but of many other birds, which gave great pleasure to the spectators. They were particularly fond of birds; numbers were kept as pets in their houses, especially by girls and children. The breeding and training of race-horses was one of their chief preoccupations; all took the keenest interest in the results of the Games, and when towards the end of the century an Acragantine named Exaenetus won a victory with his team at Olympia, the whole city turned out to escort him home, drawing him along in his chariot. The procession included three hundred pairs of white horses, all belonging to Acragantines. Famous horses when they died were buried in separate graves marked by monuments, usually pyramidal; these, with the magnificent tombs erected to illustrious citizens, and the memorials to pet animals, even birds, were a wonder to tourists centuries later, when Acragas had become an unimportant town in the Roman province of Sicily.

The chief public occasions were the festivals to the gods whose temples crowned the height; these were joyous gatherings, true holidays, with processions and singing. Perhaps because of the number of them the Acragantines seem to have felt no need for a theatre; the centre of Sicilian drama was Syracuse.

The citizens lived luxuriously from childhood. They wore the softest possible clothing, and golden ornaments; even their toilet equipment—the oil-flask and scraper indispensable to the bath—was of silver and gold. One of the surviving signs of their prosperity is their coinage, remarkable for its variety and beauty, and for the size of the largest pieces. When first they began striking coins, in the last quarter of the sixth century B.C., they used as types an eagle and a river-crab, with the name of the city beside the type. These were two-drachma silver pieces. But in the fifth century B.C. they began, like most Sicilian city-states, to issue four-drachma pieces, on which the original types of eagle and river-crab were retained. In the second half of the century, as their wealth increased, they began to vary the types: the eagle was sometimes shown tearing a hare, and the river-crab was accompanied by fish, bivalves and molluscs (no doubt from the lake). Then two eagles were shown instead of one, and Scylla was shown with the crab. Sometimes a four-horse chariot was used for the reverse, as at

Syracuse and elsewhere. Then towards the end of the century some splendid ten-drachma pieces were struck, with the two eagles holding a hare in their claws on the obverse, and on the reverse a charioteer steering his team round the turning-point of the racecourse. Perhaps these handsome coins served to commemorate the already-mentioned victory of Exaenetus at Olympia in 412 B.C.

The richest citizen of Acragas at this time was a man named Gellias. He became proverbial for the virtue on which all Acragantines prided themselves: hospitality. Gellias had a large mansion with many rooms. He used to keep servants posted at his gates, whose duty it was to invite strangers to come in and stay. A story was current in Sicily that once a contingent of five hundred cavalry from Gela were driven by a storm to take shelter in Acragas: Gellias not only entertained them all at his house, but also gave each man a cloak and a tunic from his store as a parting gift. A visitor from Greece who had seen Gellias's wine cellar described it thus: it had 300 large winejars hollowed out of the rock, each holding 900 gallons; there was also a "reservoir" holding 9,000 gallons, from which the jars were filled, thus making a total of 279,000 gallons of wine.

Gellias himself was of a remarkable character; though insignificant in appearance, he was sharp of wit. Once he was sent as a delegate to a small neighbouring city-state. When he entered the assembly, the crowd burst out laughing. He retorted: "Don't be surprised! Acragas sends her handsomest men to the important states; she keeps her insignificant-looking men for states of corresponding kind."

Gellias was not the only example of wealthy munificence. Among many others, Empedocles himself was said to have given away some of his wealth to provide dowries for the daughters of poor citizens. The Acragantines liked a fine wedding. When Antisthenes, surnamed "the Rhodian", celebrated the marriage of his daughter, he entertained the citizens to a feast in the streets where they lived. The bride's procession consisted of 800 pairs of horses, as well as the state cavalry and many contingents invited from neighbouring cities. At his own expense Antisthenes had all the altars in the temples and in the streets throughout the city built up with faggots, and gave orders to the workers' overseers everywhere to light these when they saw a beacon-light lit on the height. This was done. When the bride was being escorted to her new home at night, after the wedding-feast, in a torch-light procession, the whole city blazed with light, and the whole population thronged the streets to do her father honour. The population was now about 20,000 Acragantines; if the foreign population which settled there are included, the number must have been not less than 200,000.

The war between Athens and Sparta which broke out in 431 B.C. affected Sicily only indirectly for the first sixteen years of its varying fortunes. Then, in 415 B.C., the Athenians carried the war westward by sending a great expedition against Syracuse, which they wished to destroy, among other reasons because it was the daughter-city and close friend of their second greatest enemy, Corinth.

Acragas, like the other Greek city-states of Sicily, had now to decide on her policy. In the first winter of the siege the Syracusans, heartened by a temporary success, sent delegates throughout the island to ask for help in dislodging the Athenian invaders. Sicanus, one of their generals, was sent to Acragas with a squadron of fifteen ships, in the hope of winning the city over to the Syracusan side, as there was now a pro-Syracusan minority and opinions were sharply divided. The question was whether Acragas should remain neutral or join the Syracusans; there was never any question of her helping the Athenians. But by the time that Sicanus arrived the internal strife at Acragas had been composed: the pro-Syracusan party had been expelled, so that he was unable to obtain any help. From then onward the Acragantines remained neutral, even when it became clear that the siege was a failure. As the chances of victory receded, city after city joined the Syracusan side. The Acragantines refused even transit-rights to the rein-

forcements sent to Syracuse by allies, who could not therefore
use the south coastal road. On one occasion this enabled the
Athenians to arrange with the natives to ambush a body of
reinforcements obliged to traverse the interior, so that 800 men
were killed. Thus, like all neutrals, Acragas helped one side
by not helping the other.

As the struggle drew to its close, almost all Sicily joined
Syracuse against Athens: Gela, the mother-city of Acragas;
even Selinus to the west of Acragas; and many other states who
until now had looked on. Acragas, refusing to remember old
debts, persisted in her neutrality to the end.

The Athenian host in Sicily was destroyed. Yet the war,
transferred to the Aegean, continued for another nine years,
when it ended with the destruction of the Athenian fleet at
Aegospotami in the Dardanelles and the surrender in the following year, 404 B.C., of Athens herself. By the time that this
happened Acragas, for all her caution, lay in ruins.

How had this disaster come about?

The Carthaginians, watching the suicidal struggle that was
draining the life-blood of the Greeks, now planned a new attempt to conquer Sicily. In 409 B.C. they sent over an army
under a general named Hannibal,[1] son of Gisgo, who captured
Himera in the north and Selinus in the south, thus bringing the
Carthaginian borders up to the territory of Acragas. For the
next three years the Carthaginians prepared for the major assault. First they offered the command to Hannibal. When he
pleaded to be excused on the ground of age, they refused to
allow him to retire, and gave him as his second-in-command a
younger man named Himilco, son of Hanno. A conference
was held, and measures were decided upon. At home, the fittest
of their own men, as well as Libyans, Numidians and Moors,
were enrolled, and envoys were sent to Spain and the Balearic
Isles with much money to raise troops. Even Italians from
Campania were engaged as mercenaries, but these were sent

---

[1] Several Carthaginian generals of this name are known to history. The
famous Hannibal, the opponent of Rome, lived from 247 to 183 B.C.

to Africa, because the Carthaginians could not trust them to remain loyal in Sicily. A final review revealed an army of 120,000 according to one historian; another gives the number of men as 300,000.

The Greek city-states, hearing of the magnitude of the preparations and realizing that they were faced with a life-and-death struggle, were in great alarm. The Syracusans sent to the Greeks of southern Italy, and even to the Spartans, as well as to any other Sicilian state prepared to fight for freedom. The Acragantines were aware that the brunt of the attack would fall on themselves; they therefore decided to bring all their corn and other produce, and all movable property, inside the city walls. This done, they could do nothing but wait. They were entirely unprepared for war, and entirely unused to the conditions it was soon to create. It is recorded that soon after the siege began the authorities had to issue a decree that men on night duty on the walls should not have with them more than a mattress, one blanket, one coverlet and two pillows. "If this was the hardness of their couches," comments the historian sourly, "one can surmise the luxuriousness of the rest of their way of living!" This story reads like a joke invented against the Acragantines rather than history; but it is an exaggeration based on fact.

By the spring of 416 B.C. the Carthaginians were ready. An advance squadron of forty ships was intercepted by the Syracusan fleet and defeated off western Sicily. In order to prevent further such mishaps, Hannibal set sail with the remaining forces and, having landed in western Sicily, at once proceeded against Acragas. Here he established two camps, one on some neighbouring hills where he planted the troops from Libya and Spain, 40,000 in number; the other not far from the city. This second camp he fortified with a deep ditch and a rampart. Then they sent envoys asking the Acragantines to join them, or at least to maintain a friendly neutrality while they attacked the rest of Greek Sicily. The Acragantines, to their credit, rejected this proposal. Siege operations were begun against them.

Inside the city, all men of military age were armed and the walls were manned in relays. The defenders were much heartened by the presence in their midst of a Spartan named Dexippus, who had recently arrived from Gela with 1,500 mercenaries. The reputation of the Spartans for military efficiency was now at its highest because of their successes against the Athenians, and in particular because it was the Spartan Gylippus who had directed operations at Syracuse when that city had repelled the invader. The Acragantine government, therefore, hearing that Dexippus was at Gela and free, had eagerly invited him to come to their aid with as many mercenaries as he could hire. Meanwhile they themselves had secured the services of the Italian troops, about 800, who had served with Hannibal three years earlier; and these were posted on the Hill of Athene which conveniently overlooks the city.

On the first day of the siege Hannibal and Himilco made a tour of inspection round the walls, and having discovered a place which looked vulnerable, they brought up two large "towers", as they were called: movable wooden structures which overtopped the wall and from which picked troops could attack. In a sharp fight many of the defenders were killed; but the attack was beaten off and the Carthaginian generals sounded the retreat. At nightfall the Acragantines sallied out and burnt the "towers".

The next move of the Carthaginians was nearly fatal to themselves. Some of Hannibal's officers, anxious to attack at other points, gave their men orders to break up the monuments in the cemetery outside and pile up the stones against the city wall. This was quickly done. There were so many monuments that the task was easy; but among these was the enormous tomb of King Theron, which, having been struck by lightning, was so much broken up already (or so the Carthaginians said) that the soldiers did not recognize it. They had already begun the destruction when some of their own religious advisers, seeing what was happening and dreading the consequences, intervened. But it was too late. At once, we are told, a plague attacked the camp and many died, while large numbers of others suffered severely. Men posted on guard reported that at night the ghosts of the dead appeared. The superstitious terror of the Carthaginian troops reached its height when the elder general Hannibal fell a victim to the prevailing sickness and died.

The surviving general Himilco first stopped the destruction of the tombs, and then (according to the Greeks) performed a ceremony of contrition. The national custom of Carthage (they alleged) required the sacrifice of a boy to Cronos and the drowning of a vast number of animals in the sea in honour of Poseidon. Himilco carried out these rites; but he did not relax his military activities. He dammed up one of the rivers, the Hypsas, which runs close under the walls; he brought up all his siege-engines and carried out daily assaults.

The Syracusans, watching the course of the siege and afraid that Acragas, like Selinus and Himera, would be wiped out, were anxious to send help. As soon as they could collect enough ships, they despatched an army under a general named Daphnaeus to Acragas by coast road, while thirty of their warships accompanied them by sea. Their total forces were 30,000 foot and at least 5,000 horse. Himilco sent out a force of Italian and Spanish troops, at least 40,000 according to the Greeks; these crossed the river Himera and there met the Syracusan army.

A long battle was fought. The Syracusans were victorious, killing over 6,000 and pursuing the rest back towards Acragas. When the defeated troops came into sight, the Acragantines begged their own officers to lead them out; but the commanders checked their enthusiasm, some said through a prudent regard for the safety of the city, others said because they were bribed. The Syracusans also, afraid of a reverse, did not pursue too far. Thus an opportunity was lost. The troops fighting for the Carthaginians made a safe retreat to their camp near Acragas, while Daphnaeus and the Syracusans took over the camp the enemy had deserted.

The Acragantine soldiers, headed by Dexippus, marched out to join their new allies. A furious conclave was held, in which the generals of Acragas were accused of gross negligence in allowing thousands of the enemy to escape. In the midst of the uproar, the men's leader, one Menes of Camarina, came forward and attacked the conduct of the commanders so bitterly that the men refused to hear any defence and, taking to stone-throwing, killed four out of the five accused; the fifth was let off because of his youth. Even Dexippus the Spartan was not excused. He had come to them with a high reputation for military competence, and had been given great authority. Yet he too had failed, and many said that this was due to treachery.

After the meeting, Daphnaeus and the Syracusans thought of storming the Carthaginian camp, but gave up the idea on seeing its strength. Instead they patrolled the roads with their cavalry, catching foragers and intercepting supplies so effectively that they soon had the Carthaginians in difficulties. The Carthaginians were not strong enough to risk a battle; yet their men were suffering so badly from hunger that things looked dangerous. In particular, the Italian and Spanish mercenaries were losing patience. They crowded round Himilco's tent demanding their rations and threatening to change sides if they were not given food. Himilco persuaded them to wait for a few days; and as a pledge of his confidence in the outcome he gave the mercenaries the drinking-cups of the Carthaginian soldiers. He had information that the Syracusan supplies were coming by sea, and he believed that he could yet save the day. He sent to his own base for forty warships, and launched an attack on the Greek supply-vessels.

The Syracusans, thinking that the sailing-season was over—it was now autumn—had no thought of being intercepted. Himilco's warships caught them off their guard, sank eight of the escorting warships, and drove the rest ashore. The whole of the cargo-vessels were captured. With one stroke Himilco had so transformed his prospects that he not only completely quelled all mutiny in his own camp, but also was able to persuade—by means of a large bribe—the Italians fighting for Acragas to change sides again, in disgust at Greek incompetence.

The Acragantines were now in the direst peril.

In the early days of the siege, thinking that relief would soon come, they had used their corn and other supplies without stint; and now, when Carthaginian hopes were revived, Acragas found itself without food to maintain the many thousands in the city. Those who had come to help began to desert them. Dexippus the Spartan is accused of having accepted a huge Carthaginian bribe: he told the leaders of the Italian mercenaries that supplies had run out and that the war would have to be fought elsewhere. The Italian commanders therefore pretended that their commissions had expired, and withdrew their troops to the Straits of Messina. After their departure, the Acragantine leaders held a conference, followed by an inspection of the corn reserves. These were found to be very small. And so the desperate decision was taken to evacuate Acragas.

At nightfall the order went round that all were to get ready to leave.

When this became known, every house was filled with lamentation, as the great population of men, women and children prepared for departure. Fear of the enemy vied in their minds with the bitter necessity of leaving their precious possessions behind for a barbaric enemy to plunder. Still, though fate was robbing them of their treasures, they considered themselves lucky if they could save their lives. It was not merely the wealth of this great city that they were abandoning, but many living souls as well. There were the sick whose relatives thought only of their own safety and deserted them; there were those too old to travel. Many of those who could have gone committed suicide, preferring to die in their own homes rather than leave their beloved native city.

However, the great procession started, escorted by the armed forces. The Carthaginians did not interfere, having decided to let them go. The Acragantines took the coastal route eastward to Gela, whence their ancestors had set out nearly two centuries earlier. The roads and all the countryside towards Gela were crowded with women, girls and children; the women, who were exchanging a life of luxury for a strenuous journey involving great hardships, nevertheless bore up well. The refugees all reached Gela safely. Later they were sent to Leontini, north of Syracuse, which city the Syracusans gave them as their new home; and two years after that they were again transferred, this time to Syracuse itself, where they helped to swell the population of Dionysius the Elder's new city, and soon lost their national identity as Acragantines.

Meanwhile, at daybreak, Himilco led his troops into the abandoned city of Acragas.

The Carthaginian soldiers killed almost everyone they found, even those who had taken refuge in the temples. Then they sacked the houses and the temples, making diligent search, and amassed a huge booty, as was to be expected from a city of 200,000 inhabitants, perhaps the richest of all the Greek city-states of that time, especially as its citizens had always been connoisseurs of the fine arts and crafts of every kind. There were large numbers of exquisitely-wrought pictures and statues, as well as many other treasures; the best of these were sent to Carthage, the rest were sold as spoils of war. Among the looted objects which Himilco despatched to Carthage was a bronze bull said to be the one in which Phalaris had roasted his victims. Two and a half centuries later, when Scipio captured Carthage, he found the famous Bull there along with the other surviving spoils, and returned it to Acragas, where it was seen by the Sicilian historian Diodorus in the first century A.D.

Among those who died in the capture of Acragas was Gellias. He had decided to stay behind and take refuge with some others in the Temple of Athene on the highest point of the crag; but when he saw the sacrilegious looting by the Carthaginians, he set fire to the temple and perished in the flames, as an atonement to the gods for so much wickedness.

When the disaster became known, such terror fell on the rest of the Sicilian Greeks that many of them removed to Syracuse, fearing that they would be unable to defend their own cities; and others sent their wives, children and property across the Straits to Italy. Those Acragantines who had escaped sent representatives to Syracuse accusing their generals of having caused the destruction of Acragas through treachery. The Syracusan people also were blamed for having appointed commanders who had brought all Sicily into danger. This movement found support among the Syracusans themselves. A party of opposition to the Syracusan government sprang up, and found a leader in Dionysius. Backed by Philistus, who later chronicled the events of his life, he so fomented public dissatisfaction at the handling of the siege of Acragas that he was able to establish himself in power. Neither the Carthaginians, with whom he waged war for fourteen years, nor his many enemies could dislodge him. He ruled as absolute monarch in Syracuse for thirty-eight years, and is known to history as Dionysius the Elder, to distinguish him from his son Dionysius who succeeded him.

The year of the fall of Acragas, 406 B.C., was also that in which Sophocles died in Athens and Euripides in Macedonia. Plato was then twenty-one years old and had just met Socrates, who had another seven years to live.

Himilco did not complete the destruction of Acragas at once, because he wished to use the houses as winter quarters for his troops; but in the spring he broke up everything that could be destroyed, including many valuable sculptures and other works of art, with senseless barbarism. Then, with his whole army, he moved out, leaving Acragas to desolation. He marched against Gela, and then Camarina, both of which he captured; but after that his progress was arrested by the Syracusans under their new leader Dionysius. In the same year, 405 B.C., the Spartans destroyed the Athenian fleet at Aegospotami; and in the spring of the following year Athens surrendered to Sparta. The Greek world, divided against itself, was fatally weakened at a time when the barbarian was threatening its outposts in the west. The city of Acragas never recovered from this blow, and Sicily and the whole of Greece suffered accordingly.

.   .   .   .   .

Nearly seventy years passed before the deserted city was repeopled: uneasy years, in which Sicily was torn with conflicts, first between Greeks and Carthaginians, then between Greeks and Greeks in a struggle for power. At last Corinth sent a man to free Syracuse of its second tyrant Dionysius the Younger: this was the great Timoleon, who pacified the island by expelling not only Dionysius but also many other tyrants from other city-states in Sicily, and by inflicting a decisive defeat on the Carthaginians at the river Crimissus in the spring of 339 B.C. Timoleon's career, however, belongs rather to the history of Corinth and of Syracuse. He re-established democracies in almost all the cities; and he did his best to encourage immigrants, whose labour was much needed in a land that through the devastation of war and through neglect had almost reverted to the wildness of nature.

Timoleon, among many other constructive actions, recolonized the deserted sites of Acragas and Gela. The new population of Acragas came from Elea, a Greek city on the Italian coast over a hundred miles south of Naples. Elea's population came from Phocaea in Asia Minor, the city-state from which the colonists of Massalia also came; they had tried first to found a colony in Corsica, but having been expelled, had settled on the west coast of Italy in 543 B.C., not quite forty years after the founding of Acragas. The Acragantines were Dorians. The people of Elea were Ionians, and had become famous during the fifth century as the home of a new school of philosophy headed by Parmenides and Zeno. It is not known why Timoleon invited men from Elea to take over the ruined city of

Acragas; perhaps it was because Elea was one of the centres of the worship of Demeter and possessed a fine temple dedicated to that goddess. It may have been thought that settlers from Elea would be best suited to revive the old religion at Acragas and to restore the temples.

The history of the new settlement curiously repeats that of the old. There was progress and prosperity, though nothing equal to the past. There were hostilities with Agathocles, the Syracusan soldier-adventurer who succeeded for a time in dominating all Sicily and who carried the war against Carthage into their own country. While he was in North Africa, the new Acragantines tried to rouse the Sicilian Greeks against him, but without avail; his return quelled the movement, but cost him the loss of his African campaign. After the death of Agathocles in 289 B.C. the government of Acragas was seized by a dictator named Phintias, who for a time exercised considerable power, and brought several other cities, including Gela, under the rule of Acragas. He was probably in alliance with Carthage. The usual stories are told of his tyrannical and oppressive reign and attempts to subvert it; but he remained in power until his death. Historians account for this by saying that he mellowed as he grew older and governed more mildly.

But worse troubles were in store for the new colony.

Acragas was now virtually a part of the Carthaginian Empire. In 264 B.C. the First Punic War, between Rome and Carthage, broke out. The Carthaginians, recognizing the importance of Acragas and its suitability as a base, collected all their troops and equipment there. The Roman generals decided to concentrate on an attempt to reduce the city. They encamped a mile away; and so Acragas was subjected to another prolonged siege, this time with a large Carthaginian army within the walls.

At last, after months of skirmishing, both sides were driven by supply difficulties to decide the issue by battle. The Carthaginians were completely routed, though their general (another Hannibal, son of Gisgo) escaped. Next day, the victorious

Romans fell upon the city and, encountering no opposition, sacked it, taking many prisoners and much booty. The sufferings of the Greek population during all this must have been severe; 25,000 were taken away and sold into slavery.

Six years later, the city was recaptured by the Carthaginian general Carthalo, and again sacked. At the end of the First Punic War in 241 B.C., all Sicily was ceded to Rome. In 218 B.C. the Second Punic War broke out; and at the instigation of the great Hannibal (son of Hamilcar Barca) the Carthaginians decided to make another effort to capture Sicily.

When the Carthaginian general Himilco landed troops in the west and south, the Acragantines went over to his side without resistance. They had no choice. The Romans would not defend Acragas; they were busy trying to reduce Syracuse, which had revolted. Syracuse was captured by the Roman general Marcellus, with great glory and great gain, in 212 B.C., in the siege in which Archimedes the engineer was killed. It is said that the booty brought by Marcellus to Rome after this victory started the Roman passion for Greek works of art and the unrestrained looting of all such works, sacred and profane, for the adornment of the Roman temples.

The Romans were now free to deal with the rest of Sicily. There remained considerable unconquered forces round Acragas (or Agrigentum as the Romans called it). Here were assembled, with their troops, the defeated Syracusan general Epicydes, the Carthaginian Hanno, and a Libyan Phoenician named Muttines, a pupil of Hannibal's. Muttines at first displayed great energy in opposing the Romans; but his efforts were thwarted by the other two commanders, who were jealous of his successes, and who refused to heed his advice not to sally forth from their base at Acragas during his absence. During a vital battle, his Numidian cavalry stood quietly on the wing, declining to fight, after having informed the Romans that this was their intention. Marcellus made short work of the rest, and the defeated remnants fled once more to Acragas.

The task of finally subduing Acragas fell to the succeeding

Roman consul Laevinus, Marcellus having finished his term of office and returned to Rome. Laevinus dealt first with the affairs of Syracuse; then he turned to the reduction of the last Carthaginian stronghold. Fortune helped him. Hanno, long jealous of Muttines, now removed him altogether from his command and gave it to his own son, thus estranging the whole of the Numidian cavalry. Muttines also, unable to tolerate this last insult, at once established communication with the Romans and arranged to betray Acragas: the Numidians were to overpower or kill the guards at the Sea Gate and admit a band of Romans sent for the purpose.

All happened according to the plan. The Roman soldiers were admitted. Hanno, hearing the noise of fighting and thinking that it was one of the not-infrequent disturbances created by the Numidians, came out to suppress it. He was confronted with crowds of men and with shouting that was Roman—a sound not unknown to him, as the historian grimly remarks. He fled before coming within javelin-range, and leaving by a back gateway with Epicydes the Syracusan and a few men, he managed to reach the coast. Here they found a small ship; and thus they left Sicily, so long contested, for the last time to Rome.

The rest of the crowd of Carthaginians and Greeks in Acragas attempted no further resistance. They rushed blindly in flight, but the gates were all closed, and they were slaughtered in large numbers.

The consul Laevinus took over Acragas. He executed the rulers by scourging and decapitation. The other inhabitants were all sold into slavery. The livestock was sent to Rome, and the other booty was sold.

The news of this victory caused the war in Sicily to go suddenly in favour of the Romans. Twenty towns were betrayed to them, six were taken by force, and about forty surrendered. The consul, having assigned appropriate rewards and punishments to their rulers, compelled the other inhabitants to lay down their arms and turn to agriculture. About 4,000 men who had given themselves up to a life of plundering were transported to Italy and used to repopulate the south.

Thus ended the war in Sicily, in 210 B.C. The island, under Roman control, was now to become the "granary of Rome". Shortly afterwards, the consul M. Valerius was able to report to the Senate that "Sicily, for nearly sixty years ravaged by war on land and sea, is now settled as a province. No Carthaginian remains in Sicily—not a single man who is not Sicilian. All those who had fled through fear have been brought back to their towns and fields, to plough and sow. The deserted countryside, now once more under cultivation, will eventually yield crops not only for its own farmers but for the Roman people in peace and in war—a very reliable supplement to our own harvest".

The life of Acragas as a city-state was ended. We get one brief glimpse of its constitution between the two Punic wars: an inscription which names as Chief Magistrate an official called the Sacrificial Priest and President of the Council, showing that the tradition of ancient Acragas which gave religion the paramount place survived, at least nominally. Other officials are named as a Speaker, a Recorder and Treasurers. The Council or Assembly had 110 members. The population was divided into Tribes, as at Athens and elsewhere. All this vanished after the conquest of 210 B.C. Acragas henceforth was merely Agrigentum, a town in the Roman province of Sicily.

Nevertheless, its beauties remained to astonish the visitor. Polybius, an Arcadian Greek writing in the middle of the following century, can still say:

"Acragas is superior to most cities, among other things in strength, beauty and adornment. It is built only two and a half miles from the sea, so that it enjoys all marine products; and its boundary both by nature and artifice gives it a special security. Its wall is built on a high rock, very steep, partly by nature and partly by construction. Two rivers encircle it. The heights dominate the east; the outer side is protected by an inaccessible ravine, while on the inner side there is only one road from the city. On the acropolis is built a temple of Athene and one of Zeus Atabyrios; and the city is magnificently adorned with temples and porticoes. The Temple of Olympian Zeus, though never finished, is unsurpassed in size and design by any in Greece."

.   .   .   .   .

As if in compensation for the loss of its liberty and its population, Acragas under Roman rule recovered many of its lost works of art, not from Rome itself, but from Carthage. Scipio Africanus, victor over Hannibal in 202 B.C., returned the treasures stolen by Carthage to all the Sicilian cities. Acragas received back the Bull of Phalaris, among many other things. Scipio asked the Acragantines which they preferred: to be the slaves of a home-grown dictator or to be the subjects of Rome and enjoy her clemency. Their reply, though not recorded, can be guessed; but they might have pointed out that they, or rather their predecessors at Acragas, had themselves got rid of their domestic tyrant.

Scipio also gave Acragas new laws, which ensured a fair representation on the Council of both classes of the population —the old, those who survived the conquest, and the new, those sent from other Sicilian towns by order of the Roman Senate in 207 B.C.

Thereafter Sicily, including Acragas, had nothing to fear from outside attack. Carthage, even before its destruction in 146 B.C., had long ceased to be a menace. But in the following century a new kind of depredation arose: that of the unscrupulous Roman official sent out to administer the provinces of the Republic.

One of the most notorious of these, Verres, was praetor of Sicily from 73 to 70 B.C. He had plundered before, as an official on the staff of the governor of Cilicia in Asia Minor. When he was sent as governor to Sicily, the richest of all the Roman provinces, he could not keep his hands off her treasures, great and small. It was said that in his three years of office he caused more misery and desolation in the now prosperous island than it had suffered since the First Punic War.

After Verres had left, the people of Sicily retaliated. They brought a case against him before the Roman lawcourts for extortion, and briefed Cicero to conduct the prosecution. Verres' own advocates attempted to postpone the action, but were foiled by Cicero's eloquence. The actual trial was never finished. After the first speech for the prosecution, Verres fled from Rome and was condemned in absence.

His condemnation rang throughout the Roman world. There is no doubt that Cicero in pleading the cause of the Sicilians was completely sincere. He spent fifty days in Sicily, and returned with a crowd of witnesses and a mass of evidence, collected from all parts of the island, including Acragas. Cicero knew Sicily well, having himself held the office of quaestor only five years before; when he left, he promised the islanders to help them if ever they needed it. His speeches against Verres are packed with detailed information, so damning that Verres' own advocate advised his client to flee.

The speeches concern every city in Sicily: Syracuse, Lilybaeum, Panormus, Thermae, Messina, Catane, Gela, are mentioned again and again with Acragas. Incalculable sums are said to have been extorted by Verres from the farmers and businessmen. Listing the robberies, Cicero promises the court that they shall hear corroboration from many witnesses, among whom will be the "fine men, keen farmers" of Acragas. Here, the orator says, Verres broke the laws established by Scipio for the composition of the Acragantine Council; during Verres' administration a councillor of the "old" class died, but his seat was sold to the highest bidder, a member of the "new" class. The people of Acragas sent a deputation to him to point out the law; but he remained unmoved.

One of Verres' tricks was to collect the farmers' contribution of corn into one place and, having inspected it, to refuse to "pass" it. He then exacted money from the farmers in place

of the corn, and sent to Rome a tithe of corn obtained elsewhere by illegal means. This he did at Acragas and other
places. He appropriated tapestries, statues, even jewellery: he
once received from one of his agents a letter bearing a seal
which he admired. When he asked where the letter came from,
he was told "Acragas." He wrote at once to the agent demanding the seal ring which had been used—an incredible story,
Cicero calls it, how this Roman dignitary removed a ring by
letter from a fellow-citizen's hand.

The great Scipio, Cicero points out, restored to Acragas
many of the treasures plundered by Carthage: besides the famous Bull of Phalaris, an extremely beautiful statue of Apollo
signed on the thigh in small silver letters MYRON (the sculptor
of the Discobolus). This statue was secretly purloined from
the Temple of Asclepius at Acragas, thereby causing the
greatest agitation in the community; the statue was to them a
memento of Scipio's generosity, a symbol of their religion, an
ornament to the city, a trophy of victory over their ancient
foe, and a proof of their alliance with Rome. Verres did not
dare openly to remove whatever he fancied to Acragas; probably, says Cicero, because there was a large and respected
group of Roman citizens living there on excellent terms with
the Greek inhabitants and carrying on business.

After this secret theft, the magistrates of the city ordered
the temples to be watched at night, so that Verres' next attempt was frustrated. Cicero tells the story as follows:

"There is at Acragas a Temple of Hercules not far from the
market-place, an object of great reverence to the townspeople.
Inside it is a bronze statue of Hercules himself, one of the finest
I have ever seen—though I don't pretend to be as expert in
these things as the number I have seen might suggest. This
statue is so deeply adored that the mouth and chin are worn
smooth with the kisses of the worshippers.

While Verres was at Acragas, suddenly one night there was
a rush of armed slaves upon this temple. The temple guards
raised the alarm, and on offering resistance were roughly

handled and beaten off. The bolts were torn off, the doors were broken open; and the assailants began trying to dislodge the statue and lever it off its pedestal with crowbars. Meanwhile the whole city was in an uproar at the cry that their country's deities were being reft away, not by enemy invaders but by a band of armed gaol-birds from the Governor's residence. Everybody in Acragas, even the oldest and most infirm, rushed to arms and gathered at the temple.

All this time a gang of men were still trying to dislodge the statue; but it would not budge. They began to try using ropes, when the people of Acragas came to the rescue, and pelting them with stones, drove them away. The robbers got nothing for their trouble except a few small statuettes.

Sicilians are always ready with a joke, no matter how serious the occasion. This time they said that this hog's [1] trick ought to be counted among the Labours of Hercules . . ."

This was one of Verres' biggest efforts; but nothing was too small to excite his greed. Among the crowd of witnesses was a Greek from Acragas named Nymphodôrus who complained of the theft of a censer. It was a Greek orator from Acragas, Sôsippus by name, a man most highly distinguished for learning and integrity, who was chosen to address the consul Cn. Pompey before a large audience on the injustices suffered by the Sicilian farmers. He spoke at length and with great earnestness; and what excited the greatest indignation in his hearers was his declaration that whereas the Roman Senate had treated the farmers with generosity, Verres had robbed and ruined them, doing so as if he were acting within his legal rights.

After the condemnation of Verres, Sicily settled down again to her destiny as the granary of Rome. The fertile island soon began to recover, though the south coast was less prosperous than the north. The geographer Strabo, writing in the reign of Augustus (29 B.C. to A.D. 14), gives several prosaic descriptions of this stretch of coast, which, he says, is deserted except

[1] The name Verres means "Hog".

for traces of the ancient Greek colonies such as Camarina. However, Acragas and its harbour, and Lilybaeum in the extreme south-west, still survive. These cities, being opposite Carthage, suffered long and repeated wars through which they perished. The north side of the island, though not populous, is still fairly well inhabited. Strabo speaks also of the inland region, and mentions incidentally that the meres round Acragas taste salt like the sea, but differ from the sea in that divers cannot submerge in them, but float on the surface like wood.

But the final picture of a great city in decay is best given by a poet who had an eye for vanished glory and an unsurpassed gift of expression. Vergil must have sailed along the south coast of Sicily from east to west and seen for himself the distant view he describes in the *Aeneid*. He was so carried away by his sense of the majestic past that he forgot his hero Aeneas, who is supposed to be sailing westward after the fall of Troy, and put into his mouth a description of the Greek cities which did not come into being here until many centuries later:

> "*Thence past Pachynus' cliffs and jutting rocks*
> *We round the point, and lo! before our eyes*
> *Stands Camarina, that the Fates forbade*
> *E'er to disturb; and then the plains of Gela,*
> *Gela, named from its river's furious stream.*
>
> Then lofty Acragas displays afar
> Her mighty walls, *where long ago were reared*
> *High-mettled horses.*
> *   Then with favouring breeze,*
> *Palmy Selinus, leaving thee, I thread*
> *The channels dangerous with sunken reefs*
> *Of Lilybaeum, till I come at last*
> *To port at Drepanum on that joyless shore . . .*"

4. CORINTH

"Not for every man the trip to Corinth."
—GREEK PROVERB.

THE GREAT city-state of Corinth, third in importance to Athens and Sparta, owed its rise to its position, which controlled the land-route through the Isthmus from northern Greece to the Peloponnese, and the route across the Isthmus from the Gulf of Corinth to the Aegean Sea. Its preoccupation was always with commerce and the crafts—Corinth was the only city-state in Greece where the craftsman was held in higher esteem than the soldier—and though under its monarch Periander the art of entertainment was brought to a high level, the artists were immigrants invited by Periander from other Greek states. Corinth produced no great native writer.

The old city lay some three and a half miles from the sea. The ruins of its market-place and buildings of different ages can still be seen. Before the modern excavators did their work, the only outstanding relic of the city was a fragment of the Temple of Apollo, seven monolithic columns in the Doric style, one of the oldest surviving remains of this kind, dating from the reign of Periander in the sixth century B.C. Above the city, to the south, rises the steep hill of Acrocorinth, one of the keys of the Peloponnese, and therefore much coveted and fought over. From its summit is one of the most remarkable views in Greece, comprising the snowy mountains of Arcadia and the peaks of Parnassus, Helicon and other heights north of the Gulf. In clear weather the Acropolis of Athens itself, with the Parthenon, can be seen. Corinth was to find in Athens her greatest trade-rival, and to strive, though vainly, for her destruction. In the end an even greater power rose to subjugate Greece and lay Corinth in ruins for a century: Rome.

The origins of Corinth, like those of most of the mainland Greek city-states, went too far back into the past to be remembered, and were therefore matter for numerous legends, not all of them consistent with one another. The Corinthians liked to believe that their city's name was derived from a son of Zeus called Corinthus; but this claim was laughed at by the other Greeks. Another Corinthian legend told of three dynasties of early kings. The first, they said, was placed on the throne by Helios the Sun-god. When the last ruler of the first dynasty died without an heir, the Corinthians of those days sent to the distant eastern shore of the Black Sea (then still unexplored and so a land of mystery) for the true heir, who was the princess-magician Medea. She married Jason, the first explorer of those regions, and he ruled Corinth through her. But, the story continued, Medea and Jason quarrelled over their children: when she gave birth, she used to hide the baby in the Temple of Hera, believing that this would make it immortal; but she failed, and when Jason discovered what she had been doing, he left her. Medea then handed over her rule to Sisyphus, who began the second dynasty.

This Corinthian story is quite different from the Athenian version which Euripides used in his *Medea*. There Medea is a "barbarian", a foreign woman brought by Jason to Corinth. She kills the king's daughter Glaucê whom Jason wishes to marry, and then murders her children to avenge herself on Jason. The Corinthian story makes Medea comparatively innocent, though there was one version even at Corinth which said that the townspeople stoned Medea's two sons to death because they had carried the poisoned robe sent by Medea to the princess. The tomb of Medea's children was shown to visitors as late as the second century A.D.; on it was a sculptured figure of Terror; and in the days when the town was still Greek, a yearly sacrifice which had been decreed by an oracle was held to propitiate the victims. The variations of the Medea-legend were many; naturally the Corinthians adopted those most favourable to her, since they regarded her as one of their early rulers. But whether any historical fact is embedded in the legend cannot now be ascertained.

The legendary founder of the second dynasty, Sisyphus, may be a historical character. Among the rest of the Greeks he was a byword for cunning; he seems to typify the Corinthian character as seen by those who had dealings with them. In the *Odyssey*, Sisyphus is depicted in Hades, condemned to roll a large stone to the top of a hill; when he has nearly reached it, the stone bounds down to the bottom again. This legend prevailed, except at Corinth. To the Corinthians Sisyphus was a great king, godlike in his resourcefulness.

Sisyphus had a grandson, Bellerophon, whose legend was dearest of all to those born at Corinth. His adventures were made possible by his capture of the winged horse Pegasus. Bellerophon was sleeping in the Temple of Athene when the goddess appeared to him in a dream, and offered him a bridle and bit with which to subdue the immortal steed while he was drinking at a spring on Acrocorinth. Hence the Corinthians were credited with the invention of the bridle, "golden tamer of a horse's spirit". In historic times there was a temple dedicated to Athene of the Bridle, with a statue made of wood with marble face and hands.

All these events were supposed to have occurred before the siege of Troy in about the twelfth century B.C. Corinth was not strong enough to send its own army with the Greeks to the Trojan War; but a contingent was despatched under the lead of King Agamemnon of Mycênae. A descendant of

Bellerophon who was fighting on the Trojan side happened to encounter the Greek hero Diomedes, and after a long conversation, discovered that they were relatives and must not fight; thereupon he gave his suit of gold armour to Diomedes in exchange for a suit of bronze. Such an unprofitable exchange seemed to the Greeks not chivalrous but merely foolish. "Zeus," says Homer drily, "took away his wits."

After the fall of Troy came the Dorian invasion, which changed the face of mainland Greece, and drove many of the earlier inhabitants overseas, so that the eastern Aegean was fringed with Greek city-states. The changes that took place are unrecorded except for archaeological remains. Corinth, when it emerges into the light of history, is a completely Dorian city, if it was not so before. Its kings have been superseded by the rule of a powerful clan of nobles called the Bacchiadae. Apparently this family ousted from power another clan called the Heracleidae and drove many of them into exile with their supporters; in this way the colonies of Corcyra (Corfu) and Epidamnus (Durazzo) on the Adriatic were founded. Others went oversea to Sicily to found the greatest of all the Corinthian colonies, Syracuse.

The family of the Bacchiadae ruled at Corinth for about one hundred and forty years, from 750 to 610 B.C. During this period Corinth was laying the foundations of her naval power. The Corinthians led the Greeks in the building and equipping of triremes; fought the earliest known naval battle in 640 B.C., with their colony Corcyra; and established themselves as masters of the Isthmus. They cleared the neighbouring seas of pirates and offered a market for the exchange of goods, thus acquiring from the tolls a revenue which made them rich and powerful. Then the Bacchiadae in their turn were ousted, this time by a noble named Cypselus, who set himself at the head of a discontented faction and made himself absolute ruler, or, as the Greeks called such unconstitutional monarchs, "tyrant" of Corinth.

Very little is known of Cypselus' rule. Some writers describe

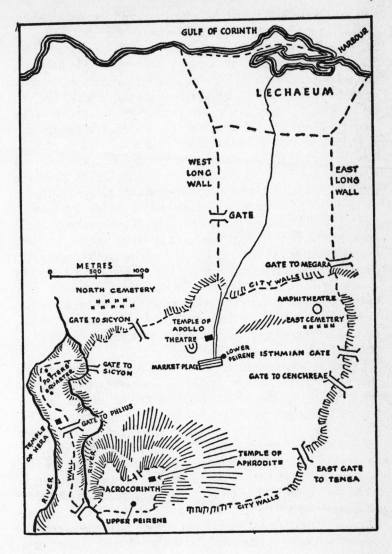

him as a tyrant in the modern sense, cruel and repressive, and it appears that the nobles were driven out of Corinth during his reign. Others say that he was a mild ruler, who was loved by his people, who went about among them without a bodyguard, and who disliked war. He certainly took no part in the wars of his time, and tried instead to extend the influence of Corinth by planting colonies in the west, under the leadership of his sons. He stood in good relations with the religious community at Delphi; he built a treasury there, and sent valuable gifts. In this treasury were also placed, by arrangement, the splendid gifts sent by the kings of Lydia; visitors to Delphi could see there the six golden mixing-bowls given by King Gyges, the six silver jars sent by King Croesus, and a golden lion sent by Croesus to adorn the Temple of Apollo. This had been placed on a foundation of gold blocks; but when the temple was burnt down in 548 B.C. the lion fell off its blocks and partly melted. Its remains were then set up in the Corinthian Treasury, as the Lydians, not being Greeks, had no treasury of their own, and were in friendly relations with Corinth. Cypselus' most magnificent gift was to the Temple of Zeus at Olympia, to which he presented a gold statue to the deity as well as personal relics.

Cypselus was succeeded by his son Periander, under whose rule Corinth reached the height of her prosperity. There is the same uncertainty about the character of his rule as over that of his father. Some say that he governed mildly at first, and later with harshness and cruelty. Others accuse him of every possible crime: incest, the murder of his wife, the systematic elimination of outstanding men. He was credited by Aristotle with the invention of most of the safeguards of dictatorship: the "lopping off of the tallest heads" is attributed to him, though some say that he learnt it from his fellow-dictator Thrasyboulus of Miletus. Other measures were: the destruction of the proud, the prohibition of club life and common meals, as well as education and everything else that might engender pride and confidence, such as study-circles and debating-societies. He liked the people to be kept busy and poor. He liked them to stand about his palace gates, so that their activities should be visible and their spirits cowed. He disliked intimacy between friend and friend, or between the masses and their betters, noble or rich. He kept spies continually busy in their midst. Moreover, unlike his father he engaged in warfare. He was at variance with Corcyra, Corinth's island-colony, which was a refuge for exiled nobles, and subdued it. He engaged in a war in aid of Miletus, with which he was on the friendliest terms. He founded several new colonies in the northern Aegean as tradeposts, the most important being Potidaea. His relations with Egypt and Lydia were cordial; and his influence at Athens was great. He was several times called upon to arbitrate in the quarrels of other city-states.

Strict though his rule may have been, Periander was too shrewd to neglect the importance of recreation in keeping the people contented. The Olympic Games had been instituted at least two centuries earlier. A neighbouring ruler, Cleisthenes of Sicyon, now set the fashion of instituting other such festivals by starting the Pythian Games at Delphi. A few years later, Periander imitated him by founding the Isthmian Games to be held biennially on the Isthmus in honour of Poseidon. This festival, owing to its favourable position in the centre of Greece, was able to attract larger crowds even than the great Olympic festival, and to bring much wealth to the Corinthians while its administration remained in their hands.

Besides this, Periander was particularly interested in the new popular cult of the god Dionysus, patron of vegetation—its rebirth in springtime—and especially of the vine; leader of wild revels over the countryside. Periander instituted a great choral festival in the city of Corinth, and invited a poet from Lesbos named Arîon to write special Dionysiac odes, called Dithyrambs, for these occasions. These odes are the element that later, in the hands of Attic performers and writers, developed into the Chorus of Athenian tragedy and comedy.

Periander also instituted great building activity. During his reign the great Temple of Apollo was erected near the market-place, in the Doric style, with massive monolithic columns 23½ feet high and having a diameter of 5¾ feet at the base. Their material is not marble but a rough, porous limestone overlaid with reddish-yellow stucco. The seven remaining columns stand on a high platform dominating the market-place and the road to the port. Periander's architectural innovations were notable: he was credited with the "invention" of the pediment, the triangular space formed by the sloping roof of a temple and its entablature; this space provided a frame for groups of sculpture in the round, and remarkable use of it was made in the great days of Greek architecture. Periander's encouragement of this art caused Corinthian architects to become famous; when the Temple of Apollo at Delphi was burnt down in 548 B.C. the plans for rebuilding it on a grander scale were entrusted to Spintharus of Corinth.

Corinth was never a breeding-ground of literary artists. Periander, however, remedied this deficiency by inviting noted writers to his court. As well as Arîon, he entertained Aesop the fabulist and others of the so-called Seven Sages of Greece, among whom his own name was often included by those who had no objection to dictators. In later life he seems to have been troubled by family quarrels, in particular with his favourite son Lycophron, who, believing that his father was responsible for the death of his mother, declined all dealings with him and was finally exiled to Corcyra. Periander in his old age tried by every means to induce Lycophron to return, even offering to go himself into retirement at Corcyra if Lycophron would come back to Corinth and rule. Thereupon the government of Corcyra put Lycophron to death in order to prevent the coming of Periander. Periander in revenge seized three hundred sons of prominent Corcyreans and sent them to Lydia to be used as eunuchs; but on the voyage the ship carrying the boys put in at Samos, and the inhabitants, moved by pity, saved them. Hence a feud arose between Corinth and Samos, and the

Corinthians eagerly took part in a campaign led by Sparta against the island.

Periander died after a reign of forty years. Soon afterwards, the absolute monarchy ended. His nephew Psammetichus—so-called in compliment to the second Egyptian Pharaoh of that name—was deposed and killed by the nobles, who had returned from exile with the aid of the Spartans. Corinth now joined the league of city-states of which Sparta was the head, and continued to prosper under the rule of an oligarchy. Under the dictatorship, Corinth had reached a high position of wealth and power. The "tyrants" had shaken off the domination of the neighbouring city-state of Argos, had embarked on a bold policy of commercial expansion with the planting of colonies in the west and in the northern Aegean, and had established a religious and social life of considerable brilliance for the entertainment of the hard-working and strictly-controlled ordinary citizens.

A proof of this new prosperity is the issue for the first time of an independent silver coinage. Throughout the early seventh century, Corinth had used the coins of Argos, whose ruler Pheidon had brought this invention to Greece proper from Asia Minor. Under Cypselus a separate Corinthian coinage was issued, at first on the old model, and then a new style bearing Pegasus, the city's favourite emblem, on one side, and on the other, the reverse, an indented pattern that under Periander became a swastika. These coins were called "colts" after the Pegasus-type, just as the coins of Athens were called "owls". They were issued in great numbers by Periander, and are still found in considerable quantities, especially in Sicily and Italy, showing the expansion of trade and the way it took, westward rather than eastward. The route to the west was becoming Corinth's lifeline, as important to the preservation of her growing population as the Black Sea corn-route was for Athens.

After the fall of the tyranny, Corinth enjoyed a century of almost unbroken peace, internal and external. The empire initiated by Periander fell to pieces; but Corinth established good relations with all other city-states. She was a member of the Peloponnesian League led by Sparta, and was held in high esteem as being the only seapower of any importance in the League. She preserved friendly relations with Athens, endeavouring to mediate in a war between Athens and Thebes over Plataea in 519 B.C.; refusing a passage to King Cleomenes of Sparta who came leading an army against Athens in 507 B.C.; selling Athens twenty ships for a nominal payment of 5 drachmas (about $5) because it was forbidden by Corinthian law to give the vessels. Internally, Corinth was now ruled by an aristocracy, though no longer by one family; there was a Council of eighty members, as at Argos, ten from each of the eight tribes into which the Corinthians were divided for purposes of administration. The city was an outstanding example of order and good government at this time.

The busy market-place, always one of the largest in Greece, was now adorned with a number of new buildings, including a courtyard and Doric edifice with steps leading down to the famous spring called the Lower Peirênê. Here water flowed into a basin through two bronze lions' heads, and was used by all. The "Spring-house" was a favourite meeting-place for recreation and gossip, and remained so throughout Corinthian history. It is used by the villagers to this day. On Acrocorinth was another spring called the Upper Peirene, supposed to have been engendered by a blow from the hoof of Pegasus. Corinth, thanks to this limestone mountain on the south side, was endowed with plentiful springs.

Besides the great Temple of Apollo on the terrace to the south, there were several lesser temples in the neighbourhood of the market-place. But the most important shrine, though very small, was the Temple of Aphrodite on the top of Acrocorinth. The mountain had always been held sacred to Aphrodite. Her worship was maintained by the establishment in the city below of a house of official prostitutes, destined to become one of the chief attractions for visitors and a great source of wealth. So far as is known this is the only such establishment existing in a Greek city-state, with one possible exception in Sicily; elsewhere in Greece the worship of Aphrodite was as pure and decorous as that of any other of the goddesses. Temple-prostitution seems to be an oriental custom, being found in Babylon, in Lydia and in Cyprus. In later times, Aphrodite's slave-girls at Corinth numbered over a thousand, most of them being dedicated to the goddess by men and women as a thank-offering for favours received. The route to the summit of Acrocorinth, 1,800 feet above sea level—a climb taking over two hours on foot—later became lined with shrines nearly all dedicated to female deities: to Iris and Serapis, to Demeter and Persephone, to Hera, the Fates, Destiny and others. The Temple of Aphrodite herself, exceedingly wealthy though it must have been, remained always tiny; today only a few blocks of marble remain to show where it stood.

The Corinthians, in spite of their prosperity, had not lost their fighting spirit, and could show vigour where their interests were threatened. In 492 B.C. they sent an army to Sicily to help their daughter-city Syracuse against a neighbouring ruler, Hippocrates of Gela; their action prevented the city's destruction. Then came the Persian invasion of Greece under Xerxes, and all external enterprises were forgotten.

Corinth was chosen as the headquarters of the Hellenic League, and there was talk of abandoning all Greece north of the Isthmus, including Athens, to the invader. The part played by the Corinthians does not appear to have been glorious, though one must allow for the pro-Athenian bias of Herodotus, who is our only contemporary authority. Certainly the 400 Corinthians sent to help to defend the Pass of Thermopylae departed with most of the other allies before the battle, leaving the defence to the Spartans; but this may have been by order of the commander, King Leonidas. When the news that the Persians had broken through at Thermopylae reached the Greek fleet, the first to set sail in the retreat southwards was the Corinthian contingent of forty ships, while the Athenians were the last; but the retreat was orderly, and it may be that the Corinthian position necessitated their leading the retreat. At the Battle of Salamis, the same forty ships were present, among a total of 378 triremes; but their commander Adeimantus opposed vigorous action, and in a sharp exchange of words with the Athenian commander Themistocles, remarked: "In the Games, those who leave the starting-post too soon get whipped." Themistocles retorted: "Those who start too late lose the victory-crown." When Themistocles urged that the fleet should stand and fight there, Adeimantus objected, reminding the Athenian that as Athens was now occupied by the enemy, he was a stateless man and should have no vote. Themistocles, never at a loss for an answer, replied, among much abuse of Adeimantus and the Corinthians: "My state is bigger than yours while I have a fleet of 200 vessels under my command."

The Corinthian squadron was forced to remain. The Greek fleet was now surrounded, and had to fight its way out or perish. The Athenians said afterwards that Adeimantus fled in terror at the first onset, and was followed by the rest of the Corinthian ships; but their withdrawal was stopped by a miracle. They were intercepted by a skiff, thought to be a divine apparition, and told that they were betraying Hellas, and that the Greeks were victorious. The Corinthians, at first unconvinced, then turned about and arrived after all the fighting was over. This spiteful Athenian version was not confirmed by the rest of the Greeks, who supported the Corinthian claim to have had a major share in the victory.

At the land-battle of Plataea in the following year (479 B.C.) the hard fighting was done by King Pausanias and the Spartans against the Persians. Corinth sent 5,000 heavy-armed infantry; these, with three other small contingents from elsewhere, were given the easier task of confronting the Medes, who were known to be less formidable than the Persians. The Corinthian troops seem to have taken little or no part in the struggle. When the news came through that the Spartans were winning, the Corinthians were waiting under the city walls of Plataea, near the Temple of Hera, and they merely transferred themselves in some disorder to another position, so Herodotus says. There is a story that the prize of valour was afterwards disputed by the Spartans and the Corinthians; during the discussion, a Corinthian named Cleocritus rose, and to everybody's surprise and delight, instead of claiming the prize for Corinth as the third city-state of Greece, he proposed that it should go to the small but courageous city of Plataea.

In the same year, a naval battle took place between the Greeks and the Persians off Cape Mycalê on the coast of Asia Minor, and the Persian camp on shore was captured. It was agreed that here, though the Athenians distinguished themselves most, the Corinthians came second in valour. Incidentally, Corinth provided the Chief Seer to the Greek army: this was a very responsible post, which involved reading the omens before a battle. Corinth, as the headquarters of the League, was also the scene of the punishment of traitors: the leaders of the city-state of Thebes, which had sided with the Persians, were sent to Corinth, tried there and executed.

After the defeat of the Persians in Greece and Asia Minor, and of the Carthaginians in Sicily, Corinth shared in the general prosperity of the Greek world. Her trade was mostly with the west, to Sicily and Italy by way of the Gulf of Corinth. The Aegean Sea, and therefore trade to the east, were coming more and more into the hands of Athens. In Syracuse Corinth had a powerful ally; and as the demand for Corinthian wares increased, so did her population increase also. It is reckoned that at this time there was a free population of between 40,000 and 50,000 in Corinth—considerably more than at Athens—and there were also great numbers of slaves. Some placed the number of the slaves as high as 460,000, but nowadays this is considered an exaggeration; perhaps 100,000 would be nearer the fact.

We get a glimpse of the wealthy and flourishing city-state in a Victory Ode of Pindar, written in 464 B.C. for a Corinthian named Xenophon, a member of the aristocratic family Oligaethidae, once the rivals of the Bacchiadae for supreme power, and now devoted to hospitality and sport. "I have a splendid theme," writes Pindar, "and a bold candour bids me speak." He had good reason to be pleased with his commission, for not only his client Xenophon had been victorious in the Games with a double triumph at Olympia—in the footrace and the five-event contest—but his father Thessalus had won the chariot-race there, and his grandfather and other members of the family had carried off a total of over sixty prizes at the various athletic festivals held throughout Greece. Pindar, in eulogizing the family, says that he is acknowledging Corinth herself; the family are:

> *"Thrice victorious at Olympia,*
> *Kindly to their fellow-citizens,*
> *Serviceable to strangers."*

And their city-state:

> *"Porch of Poseidon of the Isthmus,*
> *Grace with noble youths,*
> *Where dwell Good Government and her two sisters,*
> *Justice and Peace,*
> *Her companions in nurture,*
> *Dispensers of wealth for men,*
> *Golden children of wise Piety.*
> *They are ready to ward off Insolence,*
> *The mother of bold-tongued Excess."*

Pindar praises Corinth for the versatility of her citizens: they have often been victorious in the Sacred Games; and among their many inventive devices must be placed the eagle which adorns the finial of temple-pediments; the dithyrambic ode to Dionysus; and the horse's bit. Moreover, the arts and martial valour both flourish there. The Corinthian heroes of legend meet with nothing but praise from Pindar: Sisyphus was a man of godlike resourcefulness, Medea was the saviour of the ship *Argo* and her crew, Bellerophon who tamed Pegasus was the protégé of the goddess Athene. On whichever side Corinthians fight in war, they decide the issue, he says, thus rebutting the slanders of the Athenians—the Ode being composed, of course, for performance at Corinth.

This Ode was a processional song. Another, composed for the same occasion, was to be sung at the Temple of Aphrodite, to whom the victor Xenophon had vowed a hundred slave-girls as prostitutes. Pindar's rather fulsome opening hardly conceals his dislike of the subject. As the girls dance at the Temple, they are thus addressed:

"Maidens whose embrace welcomes many strangers,
Servants of Persuasion in wealthy Corinth,
Ye who burn the amber teardrops of fresh incense
While your thought flits often to Aphrodite,
Divine Mother of Loves!

She has granted you, girls, license to cull without blame
The fruit of your tender beauty on lovely couches:
Everything done under compulsion is fair and good.

Yet I wonder what the Lords of the Isthmus (the Corinthians)
Will say of my composing such a prelude as this for my song,
A prelude to accompany women who are at the service of all . . .

Oh Mistress, Queen of Cyprus!
Xenophon has brought hither to thy sacred precinct
A troop of a hundred herded girls,
In his delight at the fulfilment of his vows."

Nothing could better express the Corinth of this time: on the surface, wealth, order, enterprise; underneath, a commercialism willing to exploit any source, and the insensitiveness that goes with it. But the first epoch of Corinthian prosperity was already drawing to an end.

Before the middle of the fifth century B.C., the relations of

Athens and Sparta were deteriorating. Corinth was bound to be drawn into the quarrel. The Corinthians were becoming anxious about their trade-route to the west, at which the Athenians were already casting covetous eyes. They were therefore extremely irritated when in 462 B.C. the Athenian general Cimon marched his army through Corinthian territory without permission. When challenged by the Corinthian government on the ground that one does not enter another man's house without first knocking and obtaining leave, Cimon replied that the Corinthians had done the same elsewhere. In the struggle which followed, Corinth in spite of some successes was defeated at sea. By 450 B.C., Athens, now under the vigorous leadership of Pericles, had seized almost all the important points on the Gulf of Corinth, so that the trade of Corinth was virtually ruined; worse still, the Athenians had obtained the alliance of the Megarians at the north-east end of the Isthmus, and had not only planted garrisons in Megara's two ports but had caused walls to be built so as to block the coast road: the chief cause, so Thucydides says, of the hatred felt by the Corinthians against Athens. The source of this hatred was intense and justified fear.

A thirty years' truce between the Athenian Empire and the Peloponnesian League caused Athens to give up Megara; but the other reasons for fear remained, above all the Athenian domination of the western trade-route. Athens developed her relations with the western states, founding a new colony (Thourioi) on the south coast of Italy in 444 B.C., and forming an alliance with Segesta in Sicily. The truce did not last. The Peloponnesian War between Athens and Sparta broke out in 431 B.C., and the immediate causes of it were Athenian action against Corinth: Athenian support of Corcyra against her mother-city, Athenian pressure brought to bear on Potidaea in the northern Aegean—an Athenian ally but a Corinthian colony, which now turned to Corinth for help.

The Corinthians were frantic with fear. It was plain that

Athens had no intention of giving up her westward expansion, and that her sense of power under Pericles had steadily grown. Also it had been revealed in a naval battle at Sybota near Corcyra that the Corinthians, once foremost in naval architecture and strategy, were now employing out-of-date tactics: instead of manoeuvring, they preferred to crowd their decks with soldiers and grapple with the enemy vessels, thus fighting a sort of land battle at sea; and though on this occasion they were victorious, these tactics had proved clumsy and wasteful of lives. The Athenian naval commanders who were present no doubt noticed this, and the knowledge served them well in later battles when Athens herself was at war with Corinth. The Corinthians on their side were furious at the presence of Athenian ships, and at the part played by them in the battle, the largest which up to that time had ever been fought between Greeks. Ninety Corinthian ships were engaged; intensive shipbuilding had been going on at Corinth for the past three years.

When in addition to interference at Corcyra the Athenians ordered Potidaea to raze her fortifications, dismiss her Corinthian magistrates and in future receive no one sent from Corinth, Corinthian fury knew no bounds. Potidaea after an attempt at negotiation revolted from the Athenian Empire; Corinth despatched 1,600 infantry and 400 light troops, many of whom were volunteers serving under a favourite commander named Aristaeus, son of Adeimantus. This Aristaeus was destined not only to fail to save Potidaea but also to be betrayed into Athenian hands, sent to Athens, and executed.

An Assembly of the Peloponnesian League met at Sparta in 432 B.C. Here the Corinthian delegates detailed their wrongs, accusing Athens of aggression and Sparta of lethargy. Their case was forcibly presented, and in the main true; it was successful against that of the Athenian envoys who were present, and the conference voted for war. The Peloponnesian War began. Sparta headed a confederacy of free city-states against

Athens with her subject-allies: a land power against a sea power, with Corinth, also a sea power, in the vital central position between them, controlling the routes from north to south and from east to west.

What was Corinth like at this period?

To all appearances, it was as prosperous as ever. The two terraces on which the city was built were now enclosed by an impressive fortifying wall with towers and gates, except where the steep slopes of Acrocorinth made fortification unnecessary; Acrocorinth also was partly enclosed. From the city to the coast, two high walls running parallel north and south at a distance of a couple of miles from each other protected the great road from the city to the harbour of Lechaeum on the Gulf of Corinth three and a half miles away (this harbour is now obliterated). The spacious market-place was now adorned with other buildings, porticoes and statues; and there was a theatre (this too has altogether disappeared). There was plenty of space within the city, in spite of the large population; there were fields and groves, and room was found for a small cemetery inside the walls, in addition to the larger one outside. On the west side, in a valley formed by two streams, was the busy Potters' Quarter: Corinthian pottery was famous, and constituted one of her chief exports. The town was full of manufacturing and commercial activity. In the market-place, the bankers sat at their tables of exchange; the elderly and the leisured met at the Spring-house to gossip and play draughts in the shade; workers in gold, silver and bronze, weavers of cloth, stone-masons and others, plied their craft and cried their wares. The docks at Lechaeum were a hive of activity: Corinth, long expert at shipbuilding, laid down war-vessels not only for her own use but also by commission for others. Sea-captains and sailors came and went, paying transit tolls, loading and unloading goods, going up to the town to see the sights and visit the famous Temple-house of prostitution, or the many expensive private practitioners of this art. Lais of Corinth was accounted the most beautiful woman of her time, and her well-known rapacity and capriciousness did little to deter lovers. In later times her tomb was one of the sights pointed out to tourists. Every other year, the Isthmian Games drew vast crowds to the Temple of Poseidon on the Isthmus, and brought additional wealth to the Corinthian organizers of the Festival.

Yet in spite of all this prosperity, the shadow of the Athenian menace was already falling on Corinth. Three years before the outbreak of the Peloponnesian War, when Epidamnus on the Adriatic was being blockaded, the Corinthian government offered their own citizens a chance of going at once to settle there, or if they preferred to wait, of reserving this privilege by paying a deposit of fifty drachmas ($50). This seems to show that Corinth was overpopulated; and this again suggests that the Athenian interference with Corinthian trade was proving effective. At the outset of the Peloponnesian War, Corinth could put between 3,000 and 4,000 infantry in the field, instead of the 5,000 she sent to Plataea fifty years earlier. True, she entered the war with ninety triremes; but the Peloponnesian fleet, of which Corinth supplied the greatest part, grew less every year, and the Corinthian ships completely failed to protect her trade-routes and her colonies in the west.

Almost everything she attempted, by land or sea, was unsuccessful. In 429 B.C., twenty Athenian ships under the brilliant admiral Phormio defeated forty-seven Corinthian ships by superior tactics. The Corinthians were still behindhand in naval strategy, and were using vessels which were more like troop-carriers than war-galleys. In a second battle in the Gulf of Corinth, Phormio, after an initial setback, again secured the victory and drove the Peloponnesian fleet back to Corinth. Two years later, the Athenians boldly descended on to Corinthian shores some seven miles from the city, and inflicted a sharp blow on the forces that came out against them; but they were not strong enough to attack the city walls, and contenting themselves with laying waste the countryside, they then sailed away.

In 421 B.C., Sparta and Athens came to terms.

The Corinthians refused to sign the treaty; and after its completion, Corinthian envoys went from city to city in the Peloponnese, accusing Sparta of having betrayed the allied cause, and trying to get others who were equally discontented to join in a fresh combination against Athens. The anger of the Corinthians was justified: in the treaty there was no mention of the return of the Corinthian colonies Anactorium and Sollium, captured by Athens, in the west; and the fact that these remained in Athenian hands as bases of operation against the Corinthian trade-route to Sicily and Italy was her chief grievance, though the envoys kept this to themselves. They managed to detach Argos from the League; but not being successful elsewhere, they grew afraid and relaxed their activities. After some further half-hearted negotiations, they agreed to an armistice with Athens. But the grievance and the fear remained.

War soon broke out again. Corinthian hatred of Athens was kept alive by small forays; it flared up furiously when Athens in 415 B.C. sent her great expedition against the Corinthian colony and ally in Sicily, Syracuse. Corinth sent all the help she could afford. She was the only city-state outside Sicily which sent both land and sea forces, though the commander, Gylippus, was supplied by Sparta. Among the Corinthian seamen was one Ariston, accounted the best of all the pilots in the fleet; his name is preserved in history because he proposed a trick which misled the Athenians into thinking that the fighting was over for the day, and so enabled the Syracusan fleet to inflict a defeat on the besiegers.

Just before the final conflict at Syracuse, in 413 B.C., the Athenian commander Nicias in his address to his forces appealed to them to show their contempt for the Corinthians, "whom you have so often conquered," but in the ensuing sea battle the Corinthians under their commander Pythên were given the centre position, while the Syracusans took the wings. The result was a complete and overwhelming defeat for the Athenians: as Thucydides says, "the greatest achievement of any in Hellenic history, at once most glorious to the victors, most disastrous to the vanquished".

After the terrible retreat of the Athenian army by land, and their surrender, the Spartan Gylippus wished to spare the lives of the two Athenian commanders; and certainly if he had been allowed to take them back with him to Sparta, Nicias at least would have been saved. But there were many who opposed this plan, among them the Corinthians, who feared he would escape by means of bribes and live to do them further harm. So he was put to death—a man who, Thucydides says, least of all the Greeks deserved such a fate, since his whole life had been regulated with strict attention to virtue. To the Corinthians his virtues were of no interest; he was merely a dangerous foe.

In the year after his victory, Corinth was the scene of a Congress of the Peloponnesian allies at which certain operations in the Aegean were decided upon. Twenty-one vessels from the west were conveyed for this purpose across the Isthmus by road where the ground is lowest (the line of the present Corinth Canal), this method being used whenever possible in order to avoid the long and stormy passage round the Peloponnese. But the Corinthians, no doubt elated by their success at Syracuse, and interested as always in money, would not go with the ships until the Isthmian Games had been celebrated, and would not let the Spartan commander King Agis take the expedition upon himself, it being a rule that during the Festival a general truce was to be observed. The Athenians got wind of the expedition therefore. They too were invited to the Games, and went; they used this opportunity to gather information about the plans of their enemies, and so when the Peloponnesian ships at last set out, the Athenians, lying in wait for them, inflicted a sharp defeat and drove them ashore: a small but no doubt welcome revenge for the great disaster at Syracuse.

During the latter part of the war, little is heard of Corinthian activity. Corinth was less concerned now that the war was transferred to the Aegean, where her interests were few. After the surrender of Athens in 404 B.C. a Congress of Peloponnesians was held at Sparta to decide on the terms to be imposed on the vanquished. The Athenian envoys were given audience; and among the many who spoke against them, the most violent were the Corinthians and the Thebans, who urged that no peace terms should be offered and that Athens should be utterly destroyed. The Spartans, however, refused to annihilate the city-state that had once deserved so well of Greece; and peace-terms were offered.

This second rejection of their case turned Corinthian feeling against Sparta. There seems to have been a change of government, from oligarchy to democracy. The Spartans were accused of ingratitude. Corinth refused all further aid to Spartan military enterprises, and again became the focus of anti-Spartan feeling among the Greeks. Soon a new alliance was built up: Corinth, Argos, Thebes, and the late arch-enemy Athens. It is said that the Persians sent an envoy to Greece to stir up war against Sparta, and that he distributed fifty talents ($300,000) in Corinth, Argos and Thebes, but that the Athenians would not accept any bribe. The new allies held a conference at Corinth in the midsummer of 395 B.C. War was declared against Sparta, a war in which Corinth, used as a base, was to suffer severely.

There was, however, a pro-Spartan party in Corinth which was working for peace. These were the aristocrats, now out of power. Their cause was strengthened by the obvious damage to Corinthian property and the loss of Corinthian lives while the other allies lived more or less untouched by the war. The peace-party began to combine and to discuss plans for the overthrow of the government. But those interested in the continuance of the war, especially those in receipt of Persian money, became aware of the combination growing up against them; and they in their turn began to plot to get rid of the aristocratic party. The method chosen was thorough-going massacre; the scene, the market-place; the time, a certain festival, probably held in honour of Artemis, in the month of February. The last day of the festival was chosen, because the market-place would then be most crowded.

Careful instructions were given to the assassins. At a given signal, each one drew his sword and killed the appointed victim. One man was murdered while he stood talking to a group of others, another in the theatre, another while sitting as judge at the dramatic competition. When the rest of the intended victims realized what was happening, they fled to the altars and the statues of the gods which adorned the market-place; but this did not help them. The assassins struck them down even on the altars, to the horror of the onlookers, who could do nothing to interfere.

In this blood-bath, many of the older generation of the oligarchical party lost their lives. The younger men had received a warning not to come to the market-place, and they stayed quietly in a cypress-grove just outside the city-gates. When they heard the uproar, and the first fugitives began to reach them, they rushed out from the grove and made for Acrocorinth, beating off attacks on the way. On the mountain-top they held a council of war.

At first they were inclined to leave Corinth to their enemies, the democratic party; and various omens favoured this plan. Then they were visited on the mountain by their mothers and sisters, with a message from the government promising them immunity; and some of them returned to the city. But their position was intolerable, especially as the war-party was supported by the troops of Argos and Athens; and they again began plotting to overthrow the government or die in the attempt.

Two of their number slipped away down the mountain, along the watercourse through the Potters' Quarter, and out on to the road to Sicyon, the nearest city-state to Corinth, nine miles away to the north-west. Here the Spartan commander

Praxitas was lying in wait with his troops. The messengers from the oligarchs on Acrocorinth offered to give the Spartans a chance to attack Corinth by admitting them inside the Long Walls leading from the city to the harbour at Lechaeum.

The Spartan commander, after a preliminary reconnoitring, agreed; and the entry of the troops inside the walls was effected without interference. Nothing happened the next day. The Spartans were able to take up their position with their backs to the harbour, and to make a long ditch and stockade to cover their front, between the two Long Walls. Next day, the troops from the city sallied forth, and a battle was fought in which the Spartans, the Sicyonians and the Corinthian oligarchs, about 150 in number, faced the Corinthian democrats, the Argives, and the Athenian mercenaries under their able commander Iphicrates. The troops were disposed as follows:

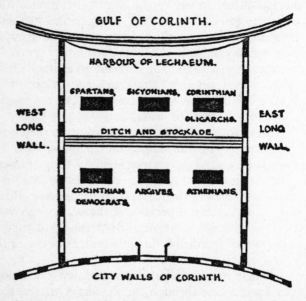

The battle that followed was fierce. The Argives beat the Sicyonians, and bursting through the stockade drove them to the sea with great slaughter. The leader of the Corinthian oligarchs, a cavalry-officer named Pasimachus, seeing the plight of the Sicyonians, tethered his horse to a tree, as did his few comrades, and seizing a Sicyonian shield which had been thrown away, went against the Argives. The Argives, seeing the letter S for Sicyon on the shields, were deceived, and thinking little of the Sicyonians confronted Pasimachus and his friends boldly. Pasimachus, calling on the Twin Gods Castor and Pollux in his broad Doric, charged and fell fighting against superior numbers. Those of his comrades who survived broke through the ranks of their Argive opponents and reached almost to the city walls.

Meanwhile the Spartans had gone seaward to the aid of the defeated Sicyonians; and the Argives, afraid of a Spartan attack in their rear, turned and fled back to the stockade. Thus they were trapped between the Corinthian oligarchs and the returning Spartans, and unable to escape because of the two Long Walls. Some climbed up the ladders which stood against the East Wall, jumped over and were killed; others were caught beside the ladders and struck down; others were trampled to death in the mêlée. The Spartans had an orgy of killing. Xenophon the Athenian, who was pro-Spartan and pro-oligarchic, thus describes the event, doubtless from the tales of eyewitnesses:

"God granted the Spartans an undreamt-of opportunity. The delivery into their hands of an enemy in the mass, terrified, panicking, defenceless, showing no fight, all contributing to their own destruction, could only be called heaven-sent. On that occasion so many fell in such a small space that the heaps of corpses were like the familiar sight of heaps of corn, logs or stones."

Such was the Battle of the Stockade outside Corinth in 393 B.C. It was indecisive. The Spartans were not strong enough to take the powerful city-walls, though they captured the harbour of Lechaeum. The Athenians and Argives continued to garrison Corinth, and the oligarchs remained in exile.

Three years later, in a second campaign against those holding Corinth, the Spartan King Agesilaus descended on Corinthian territory during the celebration of the Isthmian Games, control of which had now been usurped by the Argives. These, hearing of the approach of the Spartan army, dropped the ceremonies and fled back to Corinth along the south coastal road. Agesilaus did not pursue them; he encamped in the Temple of Poseidon where the Games were held, and stayed there until the Corinthian exiles had performed the sacrifice and held the athletic contests. After his departure, the Argives came out again and celebrated the Festival a second time; so that in this year sometimes the same prize was won or lost twice by the same competitor. News of the destruction of a Spartan escort outside the walls of Corinth by the Athenian troops attacking from the city caused Agesilaus to withdraw. The fighting was then transferred elsewhere, and was ended by the Peace of 387 B.C., one of the terms of which was that the Corinthians should dismiss their Argive garrison.

These terms were not at first carried out. Naturally the democratic government of Corinth were not willing to send away the troops on which their power depended. But the Spartans threatened to use force, and at last the Argives left. The assassins of the market-place and their accomplices fled, the exiled oligarchs returned, and the city-state under its new government rejoined the Spartan League. After eighteen years' estrangement, Sparta could count on Corinthian loyalty again.

This loyalty was soon to be tested.

In 371 B.C. Sparta was at war with Thebes under Epameinondas, and suffered a serious defeat at Leuctra in Boeotia. The Corinthians among others joined the Spartan reinforcements that were sent northwards, and not only manned ships themselves but asked their neighbour Sicyon for transport vessels. But there was no fighting, as a truce was arranged before the reinforcements arrived. In 369 B.C., when the

Thebans invaded the Peloponnese, the Corinthians sent reinforcements south to help to defend Sparta. When the question
of help for Sparta was debated in the Athenian Assembly, it
was a Corinthian who turned the scales in Sparta's favour, reminding the Athenians of Theban ravages on neutral Corinthian territory. The Athenians agreed to send Iphicrates with
troops to watch the Isthmus, using Corinth as a base; and so
this commander, who had taken part in the Battle of the
Stockade against the Spartans, found himself on familiar ground
again, though on the other side.

Unfortunately for his allies, Iphicrates chose a bad position
from which to watch the route; and the Thebans, retreating
from Sparta at the onset of winter, slipped past on their homeward march. Moreover, a Theban contingent, after ravaging
the neighbourhood, were passing Corinth when they decided
to make a rush against one of the western gates, near the
Potters' Quarter, in the hope of finding it open and getting
in. When they were about 400 feet from the wall, they were
met by some light-armed troops, who climbed on to the tombs
and other vantage-points near by and hurled darts at the at-
tackers. These suffered heavy losses and withdrew, hotly pursued. After that, the Thebans left the allies of Sparta alone.

But this fresh contact of the Corinthians with the Athenians
brought out the underlying antagonism between the two city-
states: the one Dorian and governed by an oligarchy, the other
Ionian and democratic. In 366 B.C. a speaker in the Athenian
Assembly expressed doubts regarding the attitude of Corinth
to the Athenian democracy, and suggested that steps should be
taken to ensure that there was no treachery. The Corinthian
government, deeply offended, sent troops to every post in
Corinthian territory where there was an Athenian garrison,
and ordered them to leave as they were no longer needed. The
Athenians had to obey. They were instructed to assemble inside the city of Corinth prior to their departure; and when
they did so, they were faced with a hostile reception. The
Corinthian government had issued a proclamation inviting

anyone who had a grievance against any member of an Athenian garrison to put in a claim for damages and had promised reparation. Fortunately for the Athenian troops, their admiral Chabrias arrived with the fleet off the other Corinthian port of Cenchreae, pretending that he had heard of a revolutionary plot against the Corinthian government and had come to the rescue. The Corinthian government thanked him, and refused to admit the Athenian navy into the harbour; but they let the Athenian troops in the city go without further interference.

The Corinthians were now in great danger.

They were allied to Sparta, which was at war with Thebes, and were therefore liable to further damage from the Thebans. They had incurred the enmity of Athens, whose troops had formerly been helping them against Thebes. They therefore mobilized their forces, and then sent to Thebes offering to make peace. Next they sent envoys to Sparta, advising the Spartans likewise to make peace with Thebes, or if they would not do so, at least to allow Corinth to make a separate peace, since otherwise Corinth would be destroyed.

The Spartans somewhat scornfully granted Corinth this permission, but said that they themselves would fight on. And so the Corinthians made their separate peace with Thebes in 366 B.C. and for the rest of the war remained resolutely neutral, allowing both armies a passage through their territory and taking as little notice as possible of either.

A period of prosperity followed for Corinth under the oligarchic government. There was one brief interruption, when a war with Argos enabled the military commander Timophanes to assume dictatorial power. But he was killed by his own brother Timoleon, who did this deed in order to restore constitutional government. Some said that Timoleon slew Timophanes with his own hand, after having tried to make him resign his power voluntarily; others said that Timoleon employed assassins, who did the work while he turned his back and even shed tears.

At this time relations between Corinth and her colony

Syracuse were particularly close. When Dion of Syracuse, an ardent disciple of Plato, and uncle of the tyrant Dionysius the Younger, expelled his nephew from the throne in 356 B.C., he sent to Corinth for advice on the framing of a new constitution. Those who disliked Dion accused him of using Corinthian advisers to help him to maintain absolute rule at Syracuse; Dion's friends said that his wish was to establish a constitution after the Spartan and Cretan model, a mixture of popular and monarchical government in which only "the best" held office. Dion, like Plato, disliked democracy, and the Corinthian tendency towards rule by the few naturally attracted him. The Corinthians did very little of their public administration in the democratic manner; and certainly their experience of democratic rule during the estrangement with Sparta had not been happy. The democratic government had always had to rely not on popular support but upon foreign troops; and during their ascendancy the massacre in the market-place had occurred, leaving behind bitter memories.

Dionysius the Younger, after an exile of twelve years, regained power in Syracuse in 346 B.C.; henceforward Corinth became the starting-point of the attempts to dislodge him. In 344 B.C. Corinth sent Timoleon against him with ten ships and a thousand men. Some say that Timoleon was called out of retirement to undertake this task—a retirement which had lasted since the assassination of his brother twenty years earlier. Others say (with less probability) that the assassination had only just occurred, and that the government, not knowing what to do with Timoleon, sent him on the expedition to Syracuse to get rid of him.

Timoleon, helped by a reinforcement of another thousand men, was successful in the following year. Dionysius was al·lowed to depart unharmed to Corinth, where he was an object of interest to visitors, whom he used to entertain with stories of his rule.

Meanwhile Timoleon, having liberated the other Greek city-states of Sicily, organized the resettlement of Syracuse, which under the tyrant had become so depopulated that grass was growing in the streets in sufficient quantity to feed horses. Timoleon brought in 10,000 settlers, mostly from Corinth, offering a division of the land; and he introduced democratic laws, including freedom of speech. He then became engaged in a war with Carthage, which ended in a huge victory for him on the River Crimissus in southwest Sicily, in the spring of 339 B.C.

Timoleon sent some of the richest of the spoils to adorn his mother-city and other cities of Greece. Two years later he died. He was undoubtedly the greatest man Corinth ever produced, combining as he did high ideals of liberty and good government with remarkable executive ability in peace and in war.

.   .   .   .   .

In the year 338 B.C., Philip of Macedon by his victory over Athens at Chaeronea gained the mastery of the Greek mainland.

Corinth, being busy with the resettlement of Sicily, took no part in the war against Philip; and he naturally chose the city as the meeting-place for his newly-formed Hellenic League, which was ostensibly directed against the Persian Empire. Here the delegates from the Greek city-states met their new master, in the autumn of 338 B.C.; and a year later they met again to declare war on Persia and elect Philip general-in-chief.

Two years later, Philip was assassinated. The Council of the Hellenic League met at Corinth to choose Alexander as Leader and Supreme Commander. We hear little of their activities throughout Alexander's reign; they were completely subservient, and were allowed only certain judicial functions, no doubt a carrying out of Alexander's wishes.

The Macedonians had now many friends in Corinth. Among these was Demaratus, who during Philip's lifetime was sufficiently influential with the royal family to reconcile Philip and Alexander when they quarrelled. Philip had repudiated his wife Olympias, Alexander's mother, in order to marry a niece of one of his generals; Alexander, who was devoted to his mother, left his father's court, and might have taken part in hostilities against Philip if the Corinthian had not acted as mediator and persuaded him to return. Another Corinthian, also called Demaratus—the name was common—wrote a work in which he said that the Greeks who had not lived to see Alexander sitting on the Persian throne missed a great pleasure. Plutarch, quoting this, says:

"I disagree. I think rather that they would have been right to weep when they thought how they had bequeathed this legacy to Alexander and the Macedonians by throwing away the Greek generals at Leuctra, at Corinth and in Arcadia."

He is referring to the wars between Sparta and Thebes which weakened Greece still further after the Peloponnesian War, and made its subjugation by Philip and Alexander possible.

When Alexander visited Corinth in person, he wished as usual to see the interesting sights. Among these was the philosopher Diogenes, a native of Sinopê on the Black Sea, who had migrated to Athens and had spent most of his life there. While on a voyage, he had been captured by pirates, and carried off to Crete to be sold as a slave. He was bought by Xeniades of Corinth, and very soon acquired his freedom; he was given charge of the education of Xeniades' children, and spent his old age in Corinth in Xeniades' house. The story of his living in a tub belongs to his Athenian period, as do many other tales of his eccentricities. He had no special philosophical system of thought to propound, but rejoiced in displaying extreme austerity combined with violent rudeness, which earned him the nickname of "the mad Socrates". His master Xeniades, however, compared his coming with the advent of a good genius to the home. The famous story of Diogenes' encounter with Alexander may be an invention, but it well illustrates the character of both:

ALEXANDER: I am Alexander the Great.
DIOGENES: And I am Diogenes the Cynic.
ALEXANDER: Can I do anything to oblige you?
DIOGENES: Yes, you can step out of the sunlight.

· · · · ·

ALEXANDER (*later*): If I were not Alexander, I should wish to
be Diogenes.

Diogenes must have been nearly eighty at the time. He died
at Corinth in the same year as Alexander died at Babylon—
some said on the same day—and was buried near one of the
gates in the east wall of the city.

But Corinth played no part in the brilliant discoveries of
Greek science and metaphysics. The only native Corinthian
philosopher whose name is preserved was called Xeniades—
perhaps a relative of Diogenes' host—and he is known only as
the exponent of a complete and self-destructive nihilism. He
said that everything is illusory, both appearances and opinions;
there is no truth, and all is nothingness.

Corinth was now the political capital of Greece, and her
prosperity increased, though her freedom was nominal only.
New buildings rose in and round the city centre: a large new
market was built to deal with the increased trade made possible by the conquests of Alexander. In the cellar of this building, excavators in modern times found fifty-one gold pieces of
Philip and Alexander, and a gold necklace of the same period.
Athens was now in decline, Rhodes was not yet a rival, so
that Corinth profited, owing to her position, by the traffic
with both east and west. Her chief imports were grain and
wood, especially wood for shipbuilding. Her exports were,
besides pottery, roof-tiles, rough bricks for building, stone
carved for architectural purposes, wooden planks for doors,
metal-work, weapons of war, and woollen rugs.

A new theatre was now built, with thirty-six rows of seats,
large enough to accommodate 20,000 people. This was used

for important public meetings as well as for entertainment. On festival occasions, special seats were reserved for the temple slave-girls of Aphrodite. This theatre was in use until it was destroyed by the Romans in 146 B.C.; it was rebuilt and enlarged after the hundred years' desertion of Corinth, when the Romans recolonized the place. Its remains can still be seen. Besides this, the whole north side of the city was rebuilt on a uniform plan, and a new temple erected on the site of the old Temple of Asclepius. The new Asclepieion was longer and wider, and had colonnades, large rooms for priests, dwellings and storage, and sacred dormitories for patients seeking a cure, as well as many other buildings. It escaped the Roman conquest of 146 B.C. and was finally destroyed in the fourth century A.D. by the Christians, to whom it represented demonology.

Corinth was busy, wealthy and populous; but she was not free, in spite of decrees renewing her freedom, for she was now saddled with a Macedonian garrison. The city was too important for the control of Greece to be left unguarded; and constant attempts were made to capture it by Alexander's warring generals.

For a time it came under the control of Polysperchon, who had once been entrusted with important duties by Alexander the Great, and who had a son named Alexander, to whom he handed over the governorship of Corinth. This Alexander was assassinated at Sicyon in 314 B.C.; but his widow Cratêsipolis proved a match for his enemies. She took over her husband's command, crushed a rising of Sicyonians and executed their ringleaders, who numbered thirty, and having restored order, governed Sicyon and Corinth for six years, until the arrival of Ptolemy of Egypt, to whom she handed over her command. This remarkable woman, famous for beauty as well as for administrative ability and courage, was adored by the troops for her benevolence to all in distress, and while she held power, was able to call upon numbers of men who were ready to face any danger. After her retirement to Patrae on the Gulf of

Corinth, she was visited by Demetrius Poliorcêtês, who risked capture in order to spend a night with her; his enemies heard of his presence, and he had just time to flee, wearing only a light cloak, leaving his tent and equipment to fall into enemy hands.

This Demetrius, surnamed Poliorcetes, "the Besieger", for his prowess in war, and destined to become the first king of Macedonia of that name, was the son of Antigonus, one of Alexander's generals, King of Asia after Alexander's death. Demetrius was devoted to his father, and first saw service under Antigonus' orders. One of his tasks was the freeing of the cities of the Peloponnese, including Corinth and Sicyon; this he accomplished in 303 B.C., proclaiming the freedom of Corinth but placing a garrison on Acrocorinth, at the request (so it was said) of the Corinthians themselves, who did not feel strong enough to ward off any further attacks from those who coveted the site. Demetrius then proclaimed the revival of the Hellenic League instituted by Philip and Alexander; and he was thereupon, like them, accorded the title of Leader. He also revived the shipbuilding industry of Corinth. In about 290 B.C. he began to build a huge fleet of five hundred ships, some of them with fifteen or sixteen banks of oars, the like of which had never before been seen; some of the keels were laid down in the Corinthian dockyards. Demetrius superintended the building himself.

The object of this fleet was to try to recover his father's dominions in Asia; but the campaign ended in failure, and Demetrius, taken prisoner, died in captivity. His ashes were sent to his son Antigonus, who escorted them back to Greece with magnificent pomp. A procession of ships was formed. The golden urn containing the ashes was placed on the leading vessel. As the procession crossed the Aegean from Asia to Greece, it called at the islands and everywhere received additions. When it sailed into Cenchreae, the Aegean port of Corinth, the whole population gathered on to the shore. The funeral urn was seen high on the poop, conspicuous in royal purple hangings and crowded with a diadem. Young men armed with spears stood on guard, while the most famous flute-player of the day sat near and played his most solemn tunes, to which the rhythmic beat of the oars kept time. Antigonus himself, weeping, with bowed head, stood by, arousing pity in the beholders. After the Corinthians had brought wreaths and other gifts to honour the dead king, the remains were taken on from there to Thessaly for burial.

Antigonus succeeded Demetrius Poliorcetes as King of Macedonia. Corinth remained loyal to him. He entrusted its control to his brother Craterus; but Craterus had a son named Alexander, who established himself as absolute ruler there. This Alexander was poisoned, it was believed, by order of Antigonus, who thus obtained control of the city of Corinth. But the citadel of Acrocorinth was firmly held by Alexander's widow Nicaea, who, emulating the famous Cratesipolis, refused to surrender it. Macedonian women were not lacking in vigour and strength of character. Antigonus knew that he could not dislodge Nicaea by force; yet he passionately desired to possess Acrocorinth, which gave whoever held it the mastery of the district and indeed of the Peloponnese. "Antigonus' passion," declares Plutarch, "was no less violent than the most insensate of loves. He was wholly preoccupied with calculations as to how he could remove its occupiers by guile," since direct assault was impossible. Then he hit upon the plan of using his son Demetrius (later Demetrius II of Macedonia) as a bait.

Demetrius was young and attractive. Nicaea was past her prime. She consented to the match; but still she refused to give up the citadel. Antigonus therefore arranged huge wedding festivities in Corinth, with entertainments and feasting day after day, and appeared to be giving himself up to leisure and enjoyment. At the moment he judged right, when a well-known singer was performing in the theatre, he went in person to Acrocorinth, wearing royal attire, and persuaded Nicaea to allow him to escort her to the show.

Nicaea was deceived. When they reached the place where

the mountain road emerges on to the highway, Antigonus asked her to proceed to the theatre without him, saying that he would follow; and no longer bothering with the singer or the wedding, he rushed back to the Acrocorinthian gates. He found them shut. Beating on them with his staff, he induced those inside to open; and immediately rushing in with his men, he gained control of the citadel.

What happened to the unfortunate Nicaea is not related; but Antigonus in his joy indulged in orgies of drinking and revelling in the streets of Corinth and in the market-place, wearing garlands and accompanied by a troupe of flute-girls. "Old though he was," writes Plutarch, "and past such things, he gambolled about, accosting passers-by and shaking hands with them, showing how a mind not steadied by reason is easily agitated and unbalanced by joy even more than by grief or fear." But he did not fail to place his own most trusted troops in the citadel, and to appoint his friend Persaeus the Stoic philosopher over it as governor.

But the sixty years' rule of the House of Antigonus was coming to an end.

Arâtus, a native of Sicyon, had for some years been the most formidable leader of the anti-Macedonian forces in the northern Peloponnese, who had formed what was known as the Achaean League for the liberation of the city-states garrisoned by Macedon. When he was only twenty years of age, Aratus had freed his own city-state Sicyon from a tyrant-usurper and had brought Sicyon into the League. He had now for some years been trying to win over Corinth also. He had made one attempt during the rule of Nicaea's husband Alexander, but had given it up when Alexander joined the League. After the capture by Antigonus, Aratus formed a new plot. The story of this conspiracy is told by Plutarch, in one of the best narratives in the Greek language. It is worth telling in full.

There were in Corinth at this time (243 B.C.) four brothers, Syrians by birth, one of whom, named Dioclês, was a mercenary soldier in the garrison on Acrocorinth. The other three brothers, having stolen some gold from the royal treasury, came to Sicyon to dispose of it. They hid some of their haul; the rest was taken by one of the brothers, called Erginus, to a certain banker named Aegias, who happened to be also Aratus' banker. While Erginus was exchanging the stolen gold, Aegias drew him into conversation. After a while, Erginus told him that when climbing up the cliff-side to visit his brother Diocles on Acrocorinth, he had seen a transverse cleft leading to a place where the wall of the fortress was lowest.

Aegias said jokingly, to test him: "You steal the King's property piecemeal, when you could sell it for a huge sum in a single hour? Or isn't it true that even robbers and traitors can die only once?"

Erginus laughed, and promised to sound Diocles, as he did not altogether trust his other brothers; and a few days later he returned to Sicyon and agreed to conduct Aratus to the place in the wall which was no higher than fifteen feet: Diocles and he would collaborate throughout.

Aratus promised them sixty talents ($360,000) if the attempt were successful; if it were a failure and he, Aratus, got away with them, he would give them a house and one talent ($6,000) each. But Aratus did not possess sixty talents, nor could he borrow such a large sum without letting someone else into the secret; so he took most of his own drinking-cups and his wife's jewellery, and deposited these with the banker Aegias as security.

The attempt, already dangerous, was made still more so by a mistake at the outset. Aratus sent his slave Technon to meet Diocles and inspect the wall. Technon had never seen Diocles, but he expected to recognize him from Erginus' description, which was that he was curly-haired, dark-complexioned and clean-shaven. Technon went to the meeting-place arranged, a spot outside the city of Corinth in the suburb called "The Bird's". Here he was to wait for Erginus to meet him with Diocles. But it so happened that the first arrival there was another of the brothers called Dionysius who knew nothing of the plot, but who was like Diocles. Technon, misled by the resemblance, asked him if he had any business with Erginus. Dionysius replied that he was Erginus' brother. Thereupon Technon assumed that he was speaking to Diocles; and without asking his name, he shook hands with him and began talking freely about the plot.

Dionysius soon grasped the mistake. Revealing nothing, and without arousing suspicion, he began leading Technon gradually back towards Corinth, keeping him engaged in conversation. When they were nearly there and Technon was almost caught, luckily Erginus came along. He saw the deception and the danger, and gave Technon a sign warning him to flee. They both sprang away, and escaping at a run reached Aratus again in safety.

Aratus did not give up. He despatched Erginus to Dionysius with gold and a plea for silence. Erginus fulfilled his mission, and brought Dionysius back to Aratus for an interview. Aratus seized him and imprisoned him in a small house while the conspirators continued their preparations.

When all was ready, Aratus led out his troops by night. He gave orders to the main body to spend the night under arms, and taking four hundred picked men, led them to the gates near the Temple of Hera, on the west side of the city. It was high summer. The moon was full and the night was clear, so that there was a danger lest the arms of the assaulting party should show up in the moonlight and alarm the guards. But when the vanguard had almost reached the gates, clouds came up and cast the whole city and district into shadow.

Here the men, all but a few, sat down and took off their shoes, partly to prevent noise and partly to get a better hold on the scaling-ladders. Erginus with seven youths slipped in through the gates and killed the captain of the gate and his guard; at the same time the ladders were placed in position, and Aratus and a hundred men climbed up and over with all speed; ordering the rest to follow, he proceeded through the city towards the citadel, delighted at having slipped in, and sure of success.

As they made for the citadel, a guard of four men who had not seen them happened to come that way on patrol. The intruders hid in the shadows, behind houses and other buildings, and lay in wait for them. Three they killed, but the fourth escaped with a sword-blow on the head, and at once raised the alarm: "Enemies within the gates!" A moment later the trumpets gave the signal, and the whole city was roused; the streets were filled with men running, and countless lights blazed out, some in the lower town, others above on the hilltop, while on all sides there was a confused outcry.

Meanwhile Aratus, keeping to the path along the cliff, struggled up, slowly and with difficulty at first, missing the path, which was hidden and overshadowed, as well as being rough and winding. Then a miracle happened: the moon broke through the clouds, and its light revealed the most difficult part of the way, until he reached the wall at the desired spot. He and his men climbed over and began to engage the garrison.

The soldiers who had been left outside the gates near the Temple of Hera, about three hundred in all, climbed over; but as soon as they were inside the city they found it seething with men and noise. They could not find the path taken by Aratus and their comrades, so they crouched all together in the shadow of one of the cliff-gorges, and waited with the greatest anxiety. By now the sounds of fighting on the citadel above were reaching them; the shouting was magnified and distorted by the echo among the cliffs, so that they could not tell from what quarter it came.

While they waited, in doubt which way to proceed, the commander of the royal Macedonian troops came by, climbing up with a large band of soldiers and trumpets, making for the citadel and Aratus' men. He passed by the three hundred crouching men without seeing them. They sprang up as if from an ambush, killed some of his men, routed the rest, and pursued them till they were dispersed in the city. Their victory had only just been won when Erginus arrived from above to say that Aratus and his men were engaged in battle with the garrison, who were fighting strongly and defending themselves bravely: there was a great struggle at the wall itself, and help was needed with all speed.

The three hundred, under Erginus' guidance, hurried up the mountain side. As they climbed, they let their coming be known by shouting. Their friends were cheered; and again at this moment the moon shone out, showing up the arms of the newcomers and making them seem more numerous than they were, because of the length of the path. The night echoes, magnifying the shouting, added to this impression of greater numbers and helped to daunt the enemy. At last the three hundred joined their friends. The height and the citadel were captured as dawn was breaking; and the sun shone forth immediately on the accomplished deed.

The main body of the troops from Sicyon now joined Aratus. By now the Corinthians were eagerly welcoming them at the gates, and helping to arrest the Macedonian king's men.

When all was securely in his hands, Aratus came down from Acrocorinth to the theatre in the city. Here a huge crowd had collected, eager to see him and hear his first address to the citizens of Corinth. When he arrived, he halted his attendant troops in the entrances at each side, and himself stepped on to the centre of the stage. He was still wearing his armour, and his features were haggard with fatigue and lack of sleep, so that physical exhaustion overlaid his joy. On his appearance, the whole audience demonstrated their friendship in tremendous applause.

When the applause ceased, he collected himself, and made a speech suitable to the occasion, urging the Corinthians to join the Achaean League. He handed over the keys of the city gates to the authorities—the first time since the days of Philip of Macedon, a century before, that they had been in Corinthian hands. This was surely the most impressive scene ever witnessed in the theatre of Corinth.

Immediately afterwards, Aratus took over the harbour and dockyards at Lechaeum. He captured there twenty-five Macedonian ships, five hundred horses, and four hundred Syrian troops. The Achaean League garrisoned Acrocorinth with four hundred heavy infantry, and fifty hounds each with its keeper, all kept in the fortress.

"In my view," Plutarch concludes, "this is the most notable achievement of the Greeks, both in daring and in the good luck that matched its courage." As a result, Aratus won not only Corinth but many other cities to the Achaean League. He was not above using assassination as a means of conquest. An early attempt to "liberate" Argos from a tyrant involved the manufacture of numerous small daggers in Corinth and the smuggling of these, sewn into bags, on mule-back among other merchandise. But the conspirators fell out among themselves, and the attempt failed.

Antigonus of Macedonia died four years later (239 B.C.) and was succeeded by his son Demetrius, the second Macedonian king of that name, the man who had been used as a bait for the widow Nicaea. During the ten years of his reign, Aratus used Corinth as a base for operations against the Macedonians everywhere, taking great personal risks and meeting sometimes with success, sometimes with failure. At one time rumours of Aratus' death were so persistent that the commander of the Macedonian-held Peiraeus, the port of Athens, sent a message ordering the Achaeans to quit the city; but when the letter arrived, Aratus himself was there to receive it, so that the messengers were driven off with ridicule.

Demetrius II died in 229 B.C. and was succeeded by his cousin Antigonus Dôsôn as king of Macedonia. But Aratus had now a new enemy to fear. King Cleomenes of Sparta set himself up as "liberator" of the cities who had joined the Achaean League; and he found many adherents in the cities themselves, including Corinth, in which a growing number were estranged and exasperated by Achaean rule. Aratus' attempts to extirpate the pro-Spartan party ended in a movement of revolt against him. A meeting was called at the Temple of Apollo, and Aratus was summoned to attend.

He came alone, leading his horse, as if without suspicion or mistrust. When many leapt up to accuse him, he answered mildly, telling them not to shout but to sit down in an orderly manner until those outside had had a chance to enter. As he spoke, he walked gradually to the entrance, as if to hand over his horse to a servant. Thus retreating, he spoke to the Corinthians he met coming in and directed them to the meeting at the Temple. In this way reaching the citadel gates, he mounted his horse, ordered his garrison commander to guard the place strongly, and rode off to Sicyon. Thirty soldiers accompanied him; the rest deserted him and slipped away.

When the Corinthians discovered his flight, after a vain pursuit they handed over the city to Cleomenes, a prize which the Spartan king considered of less importance than the loss of Aratus himself. Cleomenes built an encompassing stockade round Acrocorinth, hoping to take it by siege; but privately he sent messengers to Aratus asking for the joint guardianship of Acrocorinth and the leadership of the Achaeans, in return for an annual payment of twelve talents ($72,000). Aratus, though now deserted, refused. His house and money were in Corinth; but Cleomenes forbade the Corinthians to touch them, sending for Aratus' friends and ordering them to administer the property in Aratus' interest. Then he set out to besiege Aratus in his last stronghold.

Aratus held out; but he knew that further resistance was useless without help. Reluctantly therefore he turned to the old enemy: Macedonia. The price of King Antigonus Doson's help was the coveted citadel of Acrocorinth. Aratus sent messengers with hostages, including his own son, to make the offer.

The Corinthians, hearing the news, were furious at the betrayal. They fell upon Aratus' property, and after plundering it, gave the house to King Cleomenes. But they themselves had driven Aratus to this extreme, and he could not draw back. After the preliminary negotiations, he met the young King

Antigonus at Pegae on the Corinthian Gulf; and they became great friends. Battles were fought around Corinth, in which Cleomenes defended himself well; but he was forced to leave, on receiving reports of trouble elsewhere. Antigonus entered Corinth and took over the citadel. Thus one of the "shackles of Greece" came once again, after twenty years, into Macedonian hands.

After the capture, Antigonus held a banquet at Corinth in which he gave Aratus the couch above his own at the table. On hearing Aratus say that he felt cold, the king caused a servant to lay one coverlet over the two of them, thus fulfilling a prophecy that Aratus would be reconciled to his greatest enemy. Nevertheless Antigonus, once in power, did not spare Aratus' feelings: he set up in the Corinthian market-place the statues of the tyrants of Argos which had been thrown down, and pulled down the statues set up by Aratus to celebrate the taking of Acrocorinth. Further, Aratus had to face the censure of his friends for having handed back Corinth to Antigonus as if it were some unimportant village. Aratus defended himself in his *Memoirs*, a history of his own times down to 220 B.C., which he composed during his retirement, and from which the vivid stories of his feats are taken by the historians.

In spite of disagreements, his friendship with Antigonus lasted until the latter's death in 221 B.C. But when Antigonus was succeeded by Demetrius II's son Philip V, Aratus' prestige proved irksome to the new king, who eventually, so it is said, arranged to have him poisoned in 213 B.C. Aratus was one of the greatest of the Greeks. After his death he was given divine honours by his fellow-countrymen; these included an annual festival named after him, the Arateia.

.   .   .   .   .

The second release of Corinth from Macedonian rule came from the Romans.

In the year 197 B.C. Philip V of Macedon was finally defeated at Cynoscephalae in Thessaly by the consul T. Quintius

Flamininus; and in the following year Flamininus proclaimed the freedom of Corinth at the Isthmian Games, through a herald speaking in the name of the Senate and People of Rome. But the Corinthians had sided with Philip, and were suspicious of Rome. Their liberation meant that Corinth again became the headquarters of the Achaean League, which often held its conferences there, and a base for any movement of resistance to Rome.

In 191 B.C. the elder Cato was sent to oppose an invasion by Antiochus of Syria, and to prevent Corinth from siding with the invader. Throughout the first half of the second century B.C. antagonism to Rome increased to hatred; and the Roman Senate, recognizing the danger, began to take steps. Envoys were sent demanding a reduction in the status of the Achaean League and the resignation of Corinth therefrom. They met with abuse and even violence: some of the Corinthians threw mud at the Roman envoys as these passed their houses, an insult soon to be cruelly avenged.

In the summer of 147 B.C. L. Sextius Caesar arrived with modified proposals. This time there was no disturbance, but the Corinthian government contrived to send him away with nothing settled. Envoys were again sent by the proconsul of Macedonia, Q. Caecilius Metellus; and these again met with severe insults.

The Romans waited no longer.

The final subjugation of Greece fell to the lot of the consul L. Mummius. He easily defeated the army of the Achaean League, and entered Corinth without opposition. The garrison and the chief inhabitants had fled. There followed a frightful punishment. L. Mummius handed over the city to pillage and destruction, and gave most of its territory to Sicyon. Any man who remained was put to death, and the women and children were sold as slaves. The city was set on fire, many of its buildings were razed to the ground, and the site was cursed.

We have a contemporary account of what happened. Polybius, an Arcadian Greek, who for many years had been in exile in Rome, had returned to the Peloponnese in 151 B.C. to advise his fellow-countrymen against a conflict with Rome. His advice was of no avail. In the summer of 146 B.C. he was with his friend Scipio, and witnessed the destruction of Carthage. Polybius then hurried to Greece in the hope of acting as mediator. He probably arrived soon after the fall of Corinth, and visited the deserted city.

He was shocked by what he saw: not only at the devastation of what had been one of the finest cities of Greece, but at the disrespect shown by the Roman army towards its works of art and religious offerings. He saw, he says, soldiers playing draughts on valuable paintings, and mentions in particular a painting of the god Dionysus by Aristeides, and one of Heracles in the fatal robe sent by Deianeira. The picture of Dionysus was saved and sent with many others to Rome, where it adorned the Temple of Demeter; it was seen there two centuries later by a traveller, but was later destroyed in a fire. Most of the other votive works went to Rome, though neighbouring cities acquired some of them: Mummius, generous but indifferent to art, gave them to anyone who asked.

Thus ended the long history of Corinth as a Greek citystate. No other Greek city was so treated by the Romans; its fate served as an example to all.

.   .   .   .   .

Corinth remained deserted for a century. Then, like Carthage, by a decree of Julius Caesar it was recolonized, probably after his death in 44 B.C.

The new colonists were Italian freedmen with no interest whatever in the remains of the Greek city, except in so far as these had a money-value. They rummaged among the ruins and dug up the tombs in search of terracotta and bronze ware, which they sent to Rome in such quantities that though at first, like most things of Corinthian workmanship, they were prized, their price soon declined. But when once the colonists settled down the city began to flourish; not only Greeks but also Jews and other orientals began to gather there.

Shortly before the battle of Actium (31 B.C.) Corinth was occupied by Octavian's general Agrippa. After Actium and Cleopatra's desertion, Antony wrote to the governor of Corinth, Theophilus, asking him to give his, Antony's, friends shelter until they could propitiate Octavian; but Theophilus had already gone over with all his family to Octavian. Later, under the new organization of the province, Corinth was made the residence of the proconsul.

When St. Paul came to Corinth in A.D. 51 after his visit to Athens, he stayed first with two Jews named Aquila and Priscilla—who like himself were tentmakers—and preached in the synagogue daily; but failing to convince the Jews, he began preaching to the Gentiles and made many converts. From Corinth he wrote his earliest extant letters, to the Thessalonians. When Gallio became proconsul of Greece, the Jews attacked Paul, bringing him before the court with accusations of religious heterodoxy; but Gallio dismissed them, saying that he had no jurisdiction in matters of Jewish law. They then set upon Sôsthenes, the chief of the synagogue, and beat him before the tribunal, a proceeding viewed by Gallio with complete indifference. After a stay of eighteen months in Corinth, Paul left for Syria, taking Priscilla and Aquila with him.

The Christian church at Corinth grew and flourished in spite of opposition and the presence of many other cults, Greek, oriental and Egyptian. Paul's letters to the Corinthian Christians show the great anxiety he felt for them, because of their internal dissensions; and his earnest exhortations against immorality and licentiousness show that the city offered the same temptations as before. The Christians laid out their own cemetery on the city terrace, inside the walls; the great pagan cemetery lay outside to the north-west, and had been in use from earliest times, before the arrival of the Greeks, as well as throughout the history of the city. These are the tombs which were rifled after the recolonization in 44 B.C.; nevertheless, they have yielded numerous vases, Corinthian and Athenian, to the modern investigator.

Two descriptions of Corinth survive; unfortunately both of these describe the city after the devastation, so that we have no eye-witness account of the Greek city-state in its heyday, but must build up a picture from scattered references and archaeological evidence: the terraced lower city with its market-place, temples, theatre and commercial buildings; the many springs for which Corinth was famous, protected with their porticoes and ornamental entrances; the great walls surrounding both the lower city and the mountain behind; the numerous fine gates and towers; the houses of the rich, the cypress groves, the statues, the tombs; the industrial quarters for the potters, metal-workers, stone-workers and other skilled craftsmen; the twin walls protecting the great highway to the harbour of Lechaeum on the Gulf, with its busy shipbuilding industry, its export and import trade and customs-houses; and most impressive of all, the mountain of Acrocorinth towering up to the south of the city, its winding way lined with sacred shrines; the little Temple of Aphrodite on the top, and the famous spring of Upper Peirene on the east side, where once the residence of King Sisyphus had stood.

Strabo visited the city early in the first century A.D. "soon after the destruction by the Romans", as he says. He was also drawing on books by two other travellers who knew Corinth in the days before the destruction. When Strabo toured the site, the results of the conquest were still evident; as he climbed Acrocorinth, he saw traces of the fortifying wall which had been pulled down. He remarks on the Temple of Aphrodite, and the spring Peirene which never overflows but is always full of clear drinking-water; from it and other subterranean channels is collected the water which gushes out at the foot of the mountain and gives the city a sufficient water-supply. Standing on the summit, he admired the view: Parnassus and Helicon with snow-covered summits, the sea and the shore, the territory of Corinth and Sicyon and their ports, Attica beyond.

The city's trade was already beginning to revive, in spite of the deplorable ravages of the conquerors, soldiers and settlers alike.

After the recolonization, building began again; sometimes on the sites of the Greek buildings, sometimes enlargements of these, sometimes entirely new. The theatre which had seen the triumph of Aratus was rebuilt and enlarged, and eventually turned into an amphitheatre for gladiatorial shows, the first of these to be introduced into Greece. The front seats were removed, and a surrounding wall ten feet high, painted with pictures of the combats, was built to protect the spectators from the dangers of the arena. An Odeon or music-hall was built for ordinary entertainment. But the reconstructed Greek theatre proved too small for the gladiatorial combats, and it was allowed to revert to its original purpose when a great new amphitheatre was built on the east side of the town. The city had indeed become as Roman in spirit as its new official name: Laus Julia Corinthus ("Praise-Julius Corinth").

Under the Emperor Gaius (Caligula), A.D. 37–41, earlier attempts to cut through the Isthmus were resumed; this is said to have been the only project that defeated Alexander the Great. These attempts were continued under Nero, who visited the Isthmian Games in A.D. 67 with his usual display, and entering Corinth, proclaimed the freedom of the city in person in the market-place. But the Isthmus was never cut in ancient times, though traces of the Roman workings were visible to the modern engineers who carried out the project in the last decade of the nineteenth century.

Later emperors continued to treat Roman Corinth with benevolence. Vespasian, though he annulled the rights granted by Nero, helped the city after an earthquake. Hadrian built baths, repaired the roads, and arranged for an increased water-supply drawn from the Stymphalian lake. When Pausanias visited the city in the second century A.D. it was again one of the finest and most modern cities of Greece. He devoted a whole book of his *Itinerary* to Corinth and its neighbourhood, and in the course of his extremely interesting description, he mentions twenty-three temples, as well as numerous statues, paintings, tombs and other buildings. Of these, the modern excavators at Corinth had revealed (up to 1935) eight temples (five Greek and three Roman); three theatres, five springs or reservoirs, with a giant network of subterranean canals; five markets with booths, five market-places or squares, five hot baths, two Roman basilica, a gymnasium, the Potters' Quarter, three cemeteries (two ancient, one early Christian), the wall-circuit with its many gates and towers, and various roads.

Of the city's intellectual life we know little, except that schools of study existed. Galen, the most important medical writer of antiquity except Hippocrates, began his studies at Corinth; and the Emperor Julian patronized scholarship there.

A terrible invasion of Goths in A.D. 267 wrecked the lower city and devastated the land; but another century of peace allowed prosperity to rise again. In the middle of the fourth century, the Christian population destroyed many of the pagan buildings. Forty years later, in A.D. 395, Alaric the Goth invaded the Peloponnese, and Corinth was burnt down. Again the city was rebuilt; but in the early sixth century another terrible earthquake again laid it in ruins. In the reigns of Justinus (A.D. 518–527) and Justinian (A.D. 527–563) it was for the last time rebuilt and refortified; but it was not strong enough to resist the barbarian hordes, who, stamping on the last sparks of ancient Greek civilization, made an end of the city of Corinth also.

5. MILETUS

"Miletus once was mighty, long ago."—GREEK PROVERB.

THE CITY-STATE of Miletus was one of the most remarkable communities of antiquity or of any other age. Small in extent and in population—its citizens numbered between 20,000 and 30,000 when it was most flourishing—it produced some of the men and women whose genius have reshaped civilization, and whose work still affects the whole world.

Miletus was the first Greek city-state to use the invention of coinage, which transformed commercial activity; the first to see an electrical experiment—though of course this was merely observed and speculated upon, not understood; the home of the first thinkers to propound a scientific explanation of all natural phenomena, as opposed to the religious and superstitious beliefs of the time, and to suggest an evolutionary theory of life; the place of origin of the first tentative map of the known world, and of the first writings on navigation. Yet this city, rearer of seamen, craftsmen, musicians, politicians, merchants, architects, lovers of good living; herself an offshoot of old Greece, and mother of half-a-hundred colonies: this city, once the greatest seaport on the coast of Asia Minor, is now a malaria-ridden, almost deserted mass of ruins surrounded by uninhabitable swamp. Throughout the centuries, the river Maeander was piling up its silt into the Latmian Gulf on which Miletus stood, turning the serviceable shipping-route into the muddy waste that was to cut the city off from her source of wealth: the sea.

The people of Miletus retained a fairly accurate knowledge of their city's origins. The Greek population which arrived there some ten centuries before the birth of Christ were men from the Greek mainland, who at that time were flocking oversea to escape the pressure of new immigrants, the Dorians. The initiative was taken, apparently, by the Athenians—legend says that the leaders of the colonists were the sons of King Codrus of Athens—but many men from other parts of Greece joined these expeditions. Those who adopted the site of Miletus for their new foundation were a mixed band of Athenians and Ionians from other parts of Greece. Nevertheless, in later times Athens regarded Miletus as her colony.

The immigrants found the site already inhabited by a non-Greek population. These too were of mixed origin. There were Carians, who had probably come from the Aegean islands and now had spread all over the district round Miletus; and there was a Cretan strain, derived from men who had fled from Crete for political reasons centuries before in the days when Crete was the leading power in the Aegean. These Cretans perhaps had already given Miletus its name: there was a Miletus on the coast of Crete also. They had intermarried with the Carians, and had established themselves on a hill overlooking the sea, the hill now called Kiliktepe, where their remains have been found by archaeologists in the present century.

The Cretan immigrants settled down peacefully; perhaps they were not strong enough to use force, and were glad to receive sanctuary. The Greek immigrants under King Codrus's son Neileus came in strength, overpowered the inhabitants, killed all the males who did not escape, and having brought no women with them, kept the Carian females for their wives. Thus the next generation of Milesians were of mixed blood.

To the Greeks—to Homer, for instance—the Carians were a "barbaric-tongued" tribe who fought against them in the Trojan War, and who were led by a chieftain who went into battle "wearing golden ornaments like a girl". But it was the Greek strain that prevailed: Greek thought, Greek religion, sentimental ties with the Greek mainland; so much so that the Carian strain was soon forgotten by all but the Milesians themselves. The immigrants used the Carian women as concubines, breeders of children; and they seem to have kept them in complete subjection. There was a tradition in Miletus down to the fifth century B.C. that Milesian women did not eat with their husbands or call them by name; but the explanation given to Herodotus was that the custom originated with the Carian women themselves, who refused to eat with or speak to the men who had taken them by force after killing their husbands and sons.

Meanwhile the other Ionian Greek immigrants were settling all along the coast. Miletus was the furthest south. Opposite Miletus on the Latmian Gulf was founded Priênê, and further inside the Gulf, Myous. The other Greek cities included Ephesus, Phocaea and Teôs; the Greeks also took the islands of Samos and Chios. Altogether the Ionian city-states then founded were twelve in number. After they had had time to settle down and fortify their settlements against the attacks of those whom they had displaced, they founded on the north slope of Cape Mycalê a meeting-place which they dedicated to Poseidon and called Panionion (All Ionia) to symbolize their racial union. The whole coastal district thus peopled by the Greeks came to be called Ionia. It was from here—perhaps from Chios—that the Homeric poems originated: those telling of the Trojan War, including the quarrel between Agamemnon and Achilles (the *Iliad*), and those telling of the return of the chieftains after the fall of Troy, including the adventures of the ruler of Ithaca, Odysseus (the *Odyssey*).

The site chosen by the founders of the new Miletus was on a small peninsula jutting north-north-eastwards into the Gulf

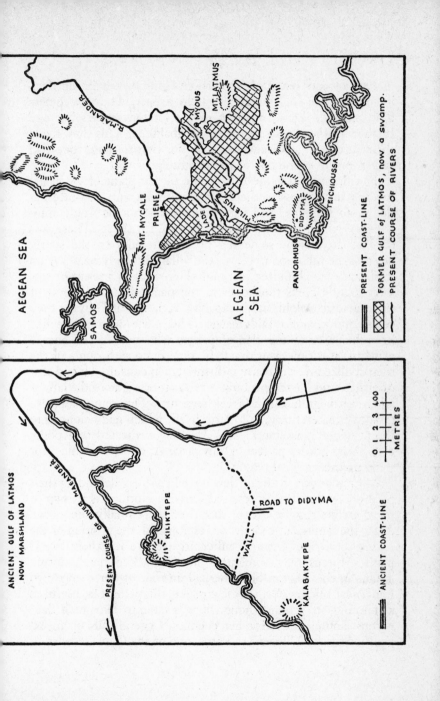

AEGEAN SEA

R. MAEANDER

MT. MYCALE

PRIENE

MYOUS

MT. LATMUS

LATMUS

SAMOS

LADE

MILETUS

PANORMUS

DIDYMA

TEICHIOUSSA

AEGEAN SEA

PRESENT COAST-LINE

FORMER GULF OF LATMOS, now a swamp.

PRESENT COURSE OF RIVERS

ANCIENT GULF OF LATMOS
NOW MARSHLAND

PRESENT COURSE
OF RIVER MAEANDER

KILIKTEPE

ROAD TO DIDYMA

WALL

KALABAKTEPE

ANCIENT COAST-LINE

N

0 1 2 3 400
METRES

of Latmos, and having four harbours, one of which ran deep inland and was big enough to hold a fleet. The newcomers first occupied a hill, not that of the Cretan settlers but one further south, nowadays called Kalabaktepe. This they made their acropolis, as Greeks liked to do. Before long, they had spread out over the rest of the peninsula.

The situation was ideal, from the Greek point of view: affording easy access to the sea, yet within a gulf and offering shelter to shipping; and having behind it, to the south, hilly country which gave excellent pasturage for sheep. There was another attraction: some ten or eleven miles to the south, beyond the hilly country, was the village of Didyma, itself on a hill some two hundred feet high. Here was an ancient oracle, which the Greeks took over in the name of Apollo, god of the oracle at Delphi; in his capacity as patron at Didyma they called him Apollo Didymaeus. The place was also called Branchidae, after the clan of priests who were given charge of it. In later times this oracle became famous throughout the then civilized world; many influential men consulted it and sent offerings, and the temple built on the site was one of the largest and most magnificent in Greek territory. The immigrants also took over a sanctuary, in Miletus itself, which had belonged to the previous inhabitants. This too they dedicated to Apollo, calling the god as patron of this place Apollo Delphinius, for some unknown local reason.

At first, however, the settlers were kept busy defending their position against the dispossessed Carians. Nothing is known of these early struggles except that they were finally successful. After the Panionian League was established, the position of the Greek city-states became sufficiently secure for them to expand. Miletus may sometimes have attacked neighbouring islands in the Aegean Sea. She had an islet of her own called Ladê, just off the north-west coast of the peninsula, useful as a jumping-off ground though it was later to become a dangerous landing-point for her enemies. Legend tells of an expedition of the Milesians to Paros, one of the Cyclades islands.

This ended in disaster: the ship, carrying fifty men, was wrecked near Paros, and all were drowned except one, who through the intervention of Poseidon was placed on the back of a dolphin and brought safely to land; the friendly creature remained loyal to him for life, and even came to his funeral. The Greeks dearly loved tales of dolphins: in Greek animal-myth, it is the dolphin, the lover of music, who is the friend of man. But this is fiction; the first Milesian enterprise to which we have historical reference is a voyage to Egypt in the middle of the eighth century B.C. when Miletus was already a considerable sea-power; and even this is uncertain.

In earliest times, Miletus was probably ruled by kings, descendants of the original leader: but somewhere about 900 B.C. the monarchy was replaced by an oligarchy. It was under the rule of a few noble houses that Miletus began to develop into the metropolis of the eastern Aegean. The citizens were divided into six tribes, four of which bore the same names as those at Athens; but beyond this we know nothing of their internal organization until much later.

By 700 B.C. the great days were beginning.

Miletus was established as a busy maritime trading-state, ruled by an oligarchy of merchants whose principal object was to protect their commerce and to keep out of wars. The chief occupation of the countryside was sheep-rearing: Milesian sheep were exported to the islands, and the objects manufactured from their wool, especially quilts and blankets, were and remained famous throughout seven centuries. At about the same time, coinage was invented by the inland state of Lydia: pieces of electrum, a natural alloy of gold and silver, were stamped with an official device guaranteeing their weight, and used in exchange for goods; thus trading received an enormous impetus, when the clumsy system of barter was superseded by a new and convenient method of payment.

The Milesian merchants quickly realised the importance of this invention, and they too began striking electrum coins which could be exchanged for those of the Lydian kings. At first the coins of Miletus bore many different devices. The upper side (called the reverse) bore a crude pattern of two squares and an oblong indented; but on the under side (the obverse) a variety of animal-types was used: stag, ram, cocks, lion, horse, goat, eagles, bull, ibex, bitch, hare. The obverse side probably represented the seal of the official in charge of the Mint, who was annually elected: one coin carries a stag with the words, "I am the badge of Phanês", Phanes being evidently the Controller of the Mint for that year. This is the most ancient inscribed coin known.

We speak of a Mint; but actually only the simplest apparatus was needed for the production of these early coins. There was an anvil, in which was inset a die engraved with the pattern to be produced on the under side of the coin. For the upper side, a punch engraved with the required pattern or device was used. Hot metal of the correct weight was laid on the anvil, the punch was laid on the lump of metal and struck with a hammer, and a coin impressed on both sides was thus produced. The art of coin-making lay in the engraving of the dies; this became, in the great days of the Greek city-states, a highly-skilled profession, and some Greek coins are miniature works of art of the greatest beauty and interest. Famous engravers were lent by one city-state to another, and their styles and methods copied. But this came later: the early coins of Miletus, imitated from those of Lydia, were crude lumps of metal compared with those of later times; but they were the first Greek coins, and that gives them a special interest. The invention soon spread to Greece Proper, where a silver coinage began to be minted in about 670 B.C. on the island of Aegina; but Athens did not begin to strike coins until over half a century later. At this time the wealth and importance of Miletus far exceeded that of Athens, which was still a weak state struggling with poverty and internal dissension.

Once, for a brief while, danger threatened. Early in the seventh century B.C. Asia Minor was invaded by hordes of barbarians from the northern shores of the Black Sea; they were known to the Greeks as Cimmerians, and were believed to live in a land swathed in mists and darkness. They conquered the Phrygians in the north, and swept southwards, burning and destroying. As the menace came nearer, the Milesians prepared, building a wall round their acropolis—the modern Kalabaktepe—within which they could retire if their territory were invaded. But fortunately for Miletus, the Cimmerians, before they reached there, met with stronger opposition than that of the Greeks; after overthrowing Phrygia they came into collision with the wealthy and powerful inland kingdom of Lydia, and a long struggle began.

The insecurity of the hinterland made the Milesians look more than ever to the sea for their salvation; and so began what a modern writer has called "the wonderful flowering" of Milesian colonization, an object of admiration and astonishment even in ancient times.

During the seventh century Miletus sent out band after band of explorers, throughout the Mediterranean, to Egypt, and above all, over the length and breadth of the Black Sea, whose coasts until then had been lands of legend. Milesians took over Abydos on the Dardanelles, thus gaining control of the Aegean entrance. On the Bosphorus they were forestalled by other settlers, probably from Megara, who planted first Calchêdon on the Asiatic side, and then, on the European side, Byzantium, destined to be the greatest of them all. Nevertheless, the Milesians, daring the difficult winds and currents of the "Inhospitable", as the Greeks called the Black Sea, passed through to plant city after city on its shores, as far as the extreme east end, Phasis, once the home of the Golden Fleece, according to the legend. In fact, the Milesians planted, it is reckoned, no less than forty-five colonies during this century—ancient writers give double this number—and as one of them says, changed the Inhospitable to the Hospitable Sea. In about the middle of the century, they also sent colonists to the joint

Greek foundation of Naucratis on the mouth of the Nile, and dedicated a Temple of Apollo there; part of the fortifications was called "the Milesian Wall".

The kingship of Lydia was usurped in 687 B.C. by Gygês, round whose name legend has gathered. His gifts so much impressed chroniclers that they credited him with the possession of a magic ring by which he could make himself invisible. He fought the Cimmerians, and was inclined to be impressed by Greek civilization: after his usurpation, he sent a huge treasure to the Temple of Apollo at Delphi. But he coveted the Greek seaports on the coast of Asia Minor, and made a number of attempts, some successful, on them during his reign of nearly forty years. Among others, he attacked Miletus; but the city's defences proved too strong for him, and he was diverted by the inroads of the Cimmerians, against whom he fell fighting in about 650 B.C.

His son and successor Ardys renewed the attempt to capture Miletus; but he too had to give it up, in the face of furious attacks by the northern barbarians, who at one time took and burnt his capital, the city of Sardis. Ardys' son Sadyattes, inheriting both these wars from his father and his grandfather, was successful against the Cimmerians, whom he drove out of Asia Minor, but found himself with a new war on his hands, against the kingdom of the Medes. Nevertheless, he still found time to carry on attacks against the Greek coastal cities. For twelve years, he and his son Alyattes tried to capture Miletus, invading the surrounding country every year at harvest time and destroying crops and trees, but—with great cunning—not the houses, so that the farmers would return and retill and resow, only to have their labours laid waste again.

The Milesians did not despair. They had command of the sea, and so they kept alive and defied the land-invaders from their walls. The Greek story was that during the twelfth year of these inroads the Lydian soldiers set fire to a Milesian temple dedicated to Athene, in one of the suburbs. This act of sacrilege was immediately punished, so it was said: King

Alyattes fell ill. He sent to consult the oracle at Delphi, and was told that he must rebuild the temple that his soldiers had destroyed. Before Alyattes had received this message, it had been conveyed across the sea to the ruler of Miletus by his friend Periander of Corinth, so that when the Lydian envoys arrived to ask for the necessary truce, the Milesians arranged to let them see heaps of corn and other supplies. The envoys carried away the impression that Miletus could hold out indefinitely. Alyattes was convinced. He made peace with Miletus, and built two temples to Athene in place of the one destroyed.

This was the story told to Herodotus, probably by the priests, who liked to show the avenging power of their deity. The truth probably is that peace with Lydia was secured by the new ruler of Miletus, a man named Thrasyboulus, who seized dictatorial power after a revolution in about 630 B.C. This was the period when, in many of the city-states, a long-established oligarchy of privileged families was overthrown by an enterprising leader, usually himself of noble family, who placed himself at the head of the discontented masses. Absolute rule by one man was on the whole alien to the Greek mind; but oriental kings always encouraged it where they could, because they found "tyrants" easier to deal with and more after their own mind than constitutional governments, especially democracies.

Little is known of the rule of Thrasyboulus of Miletus, apart from his pact with the King of Lydia and his friendship with Periander; but we do know that during his time colonization continued and commerce flourished. One of his reforms was the abolition of the annual office of Master of the Mint; the private badge on the coinage was abolished, and a state device was adopted, which was retained on Milesian coins as their chief symbol from now onwards until the time of the Flavian emperors of Rome, over a thousand years. This device was a lion with reverted head, and it was so popular that some of the Milesian colonies used it in their new city-states on the Black

Sea; it too had been borrowed from Lydia, where the first type was the forepart of a lion with open jaws; but Miletus adapted it to her own liking, as she did everything that she took from her non-Greek eastern neighbours. Later, the Milesians set up a stone lion at the entrance to their naval harbour; modern archaeologists, finding it there, called the harbour "Lion Bay".

The eastern nations were stirring. In 612 B.C. the great city of Nineveh, capital of the Assyrian Empire, was captured and looted by the Medes. In 590 B.C. the Lydian king Alyattes, afraid of the growing power of the Medes, went to war with them. Five years later the two armies confronted each other on the eastern boundary of Lydia, which was the river Halys, and a battle was imminent when an eclipse of the sun began, and so much frightened the inhabitants that they separated without a blow. This eclipse is perhaps the most famous in history. It had been foretold by Thales of Miletus, the first scientific observer of the heavens whose name is known to us. It took place on May 28th, 585 B.C.

Thales did not know the true explanation of eclipses; he foretold this eclipse by some means of calculation known to the Chaldean astrologers, and the fulfilment of his prophecy at such a time was a matter not of science but of luck. Yet he was and is accepted as the father of Greek philosophy. We know little about him. He seems to have been the most outstanding of a group of investigators at Miletus, who, observing nature for themselves and studying the observations of others, were convinced that the phenomena of the universe can be explained by natural causes: that no other cause, either magical or religious, enters, and no other kind of explanation is admissible. In detail, their explanations were far from the truth; it was their attitude to phenomena that changed the course of knowledge and therefore of human destiny. Thales observed not only that the magnet attracted iron, but that amber also, when stimulated, could attract objects to itself; he remarked, "All things are full of gods", and thus recorded the first observation of an electrical phenomenon. The word "electric" is derived from *electron*, the Greek for "amber", and was given to these phenomena by William Gilbert, physician to Queen Elizabeth, in homage to Thales and his observations.

Thales was not an unpractical dreamer, though a story was invented in later times, when philosophers had come to be regarded as cranks, that he fell into a well while looking at the stars. Actually, he was as much concerned with the application of his knowledge as he was with general speculation. He is said to have "discovered" that the Little Bear gives the north, a fact useful to seamen; and to have helped King Croesus to get his army across the river Halys by diverting the stream. He was also a shrewd business man. Once, it is said, he was able to predict, by meteorological calculations, a good olive-harvest. Keeping this knowledge to himself, he set about renting all the local olive-presses. The harvest proved to be as good as he had foreseen, so that he was able to re-let the olive-presses on his own terms, and thus made a fortune. His object was to prove that a philosopher, though not interested in money, can make money if he chooses.

Thales' greatest achievement is that he originated the science of metaphysics by postulating that "things are not what they seem". He suggested that all material objects and substances, however different they may appear to our senses, can really be reduced to one basic substance. He also suggested that this basic substance or element was water, and in this he was wrong; but the pursuit of the one substance underlying all phenomena has occupied science ever since, and is only now beginning to yield its full results. It is odd that the wheel has come full circle: that the force on which the composition of matter depends, and that which Thales saw at work when he watched the magnet and the amber, should turn out to be the same.

The name of Thales became famous all over the Greek world, and in ancient times was always included among the list of the Seven Wise Men of Greece. A pleasant story was told, sometimes about Thales, sometimes about Solon of Athens, concerning a golden tripod. The story was told in several versions. One of these, to which Thales' name was attached, was that some fishermen of Miletus one day drew up a golden tripod in their nets. Not knowing who could be the owner, they sent to Delphi to ask advice of Apollo's oracle. The oracle replied: "Give it to the wisest of all." They therefore gave it to Thales; but he in his modesty handed it to Bias, a fellow-philosopher of Priene across the Latmian Gulf. Bias passed it on to another wise man, until in the end it came back to Thales; and he, at last realizing the meaning of the oracle, dedicated it to Apollo himself, as "the wisest of all".

Thales was no isolated thinker. He was one of a band of men at Miletus who studied the stars, the weather, the sea, the effect of water on land, the causes of growth in plant and animal life, and all other natural phenomena open to them to observe, as well as information brought to them by their adventurous fellow-countrymen who sailed the seas and travelled to strange lands. This work flourished throughout the whole of the sixth century, down to the fall of Miletus in 494 B.C. when the inhabitants were scattered abroad. The name of the most important thinker at Miletus in each of four generations is known to us, and some of his speculations. Thales' pupil was Anaximander, who succeeded him as the leader of scientific thought there. He believed that man derives from a different species, a fish-like creature which in the early stages of creation left the water for the land when the sun's warmth began to dry up the sea. His pupil, Anaximenes, believed that all apparent differences in substances are due to difference of density; he was impressed by the changes of solids into liquids and liquids into vapour, as with water. The last generation of the Milesian school of thought bred Hecataeus, a historian with a special interest in geography, who elaborated the first map of the known world which had been drawn by Anaximander.

During this century, Miletus produced also a poet, one of the very few from this city-state whose name has been preserved. This was Phocylides. His verse is not of a high standard, and his sentiments are undistinguished; but he had a gift of expressing sensible opinions in pithy phrases which lent themselves to quotation, and so have survived. He thought that the middle status in society was the best; that high birth had ceased to give a man influence in public affairs; that it is better to be a small well-run community built on a rock than reckless Nineveh; that night is the best time in which to reflect; that youth is the time for education; and that women are of four species, deriving from the bitch, the bee, the sow and the mare. The mare-woman, he says, is swift, energetic, handsome; the sow-woman is neither good nor bad; the bitch-woman is bad-tempered and fierce; but the bee-woman is the best worker and makes the best wife. One of his lines says: "Seek your living first and virtue afterwards"; but this may not be his own sentiment, since another of his lines says: "All the virtues are summed up in honesty", and he proudly claims: "I am a true friend, and I know my friend as such. I utterly loathe all the bad. I am no hypocritical flatterer. Those whom I respect, I love from first to last." He was not a great poet; but he was an honest man. He is the author of a rude couplet which has been adapted to suit national prejudice down the ages:

"The men of Leros all—yes, all—are bad
Save Procles; and he too's a Leros lad."

. . . . .

While Thales and his friends were studying the stars, and Milesian commerce was still expanding, the internal politics of the city-state were extremely disturbed. After the death of Thrasyboulus, a violent struggle for power led to the rise of other "tyrants". The two chief parties were called "The Wealthy" and "The Handworkers". Blood was shed, and outrages were committed on both sides. It was said that the leaders of the upper class held their deliberations on board ship, to avoid attack, and so were nicknamed "The Permanent Sailors"; but this is probably a mistake by the historian, who misread a word that really means "Permanent Templar", and occurs elsewhere as a title of a religious official. The dispute was finally settled by the friendly government of Paros, who were called in by the Milesians to arbitrate. When this took place, or what settlement was arrived at, is not known. The story was that the arbitrators asked to inspect the district. As they passed through the countryside, they made a list of all landowners whose estates were well kept, and on returning to the city they called a meeting and proposed that these landowners should rule, thinking that the men who best managed their own affairs would best administer those of the community.

During the struggle of the Milesians with King Alyattes of Lydia, none of the other eleven Ionian city-states helped them except the island of Chios. When Alyattes' son, the famous Croesus, came to the throne in 560 B.C. he rose to great power. The Ionian Greek cities, unable to resist him, had to accept his overlordship and to pay him tribute. Miletus was spared any invasion or attack, because of her pact with Croesus' father; and Milesian trade probably benefited from the connection now that the hinterland was pacified.

Croesus, like his father, had a great respect for Greek religion, though he understood little of the Greek way of life. He consulted Greek oracles, and sent gifts both to Apollo of Delphi and to Apollo of Didyma. Thales, it seems, would have liked his city to resist Croesus and repudiate the pact with Lydia; to this end he advised a revival of the Panionian League, but this time with new headquarters at Teos, and with the proviso that each city should forgo some of its state sovereignty, in order to make unity possible. This idea, however (Herodotus remarks), pleased no one, and was abandoned. Thales himself seems to have given up further resistance as hopeless. In his old age, we find him with the Lydian army directing the diversion of the river Halys which enabled Croesus to get his army across during his campaign against Persia.

By now the Persians, who had formerly been a tribe subordinated to the Medes, began to get the upper hand under their powerful ruler Cyrus. Croesus, alarmed at this development, which threatened his eastern frontier, considered the advisability of a preventive war. The advice that he received encouraged him. The Greeks say that he consulted many of their oracles, including Apollo of Didyma and Apollo of Delphi. What Apollo of Didyma advised is not recorded; Apollo of Delphi gave the equivocal answer that Croesus would overthrow a great empire. Croesus interpreted this according to his desire. His armies marched. The war went against him. Finally he was besieged in his capital at Sardis, which fell after fourteen days. Croesus was taken prisoner. To the Greeks, this represented a most solemn object-lesson on the uncertainty of life, and the uselessness of material possessions. They liked to think that Solon himself had advised Croesus to "look to the end", that is, to believe that no man can be called fortunate until he has reached the end of his life without disaster. Croesus, they said, recognized this truth when by Cyrus' orders he had been placed on the pyre on which he was to be burnt alive; three times he called on Solon's name, and was overheard by the conqueror who, on learning the story, reprieved the victim. However that may be, Cyrus deposed Croesus and kept him prisoner. The Greek city-states along the coast of Ionia had now another master.

In the early days of his victorious march, Cyrus had sent to the Greek coastal cities offering them favourable terms if they would revolt against Croesus. The cities refused. After the defeat of Croesus, they in their turn sent to Cyrus asking for the same terms which they had earlier rejected. Cyrus told the envoys a cruel little story. There was once, he said, a piper who, seeing some fish in the sea, began to play his pipe to them, thinking that they would come out on to the land. He was disappointed: they paid no heed. So he took a net, cast it, and drew in a big haul of fish. While the fish were leaping in the net, he addressed them thus: "You can give up your dancing now, since you would not come out and dance before, even when I played for you."

The envoys went away, each to his own city. The city-states began their preparations for defence—all except Miletus. The Milesians had the doubtful distinction of having accepted Cyrus' offer of a pact, so that they alone had nothing to fear. The oracle at Didyma also behaved equivocally.

A Lydian named Pactyês had been given a position of responsibility by Cyrus at Sardis; but as soon as Cyrus left, Pactyes revolted and fled to the Greek city-state of Cymê, on the coast near Phocaea, ninety miles north of Miletus. The Persian king sent his officer Mazarês to arrest Pactyes. The government of Cyme sent to the oracle of Apollo at Didyma to ask what they should do. The oracle's advice was to surrender the fugitive. When the reply was carried back to Cyme, the people in their fear of Cyrus wished to obey; but one of their leading citizens named Aristodocus, not being satisfied that the answer was genuine, insisted on the sending of a second delegation to Didyma to question the oracle again; and he himself went with them. The oracle repeated its advice.

Aristodocus said nothing. Instead, he began walking round the temple dislodging the sparrows and other birds of various sorts which had built their nests there. A voice came out of the oracular chamber: "Most impious man, how dare you treat my suppliants so outrageously?" Aristodocus replied: "Lord, thus thou helpest thine own suppliants; and dost thou then bid the men of Cyme hand over their suppliant?" The oracle, unabashed, explained that the advice had a hidden meaning: the people of Cyme were to be led into committing a sin, which would bring retribution; and so they would learn not to consult the oracle of Apollo about the betrayal of suppliants. When the people of Cyme received this message, they were in a fright: if they kept Pactyes, Cyrus would attack them; if they handed him over, the oracle said that they would be committing a deadly sin. So they compromised by sending him to the island of Lesbos. The Lesbians were about to hand him over to Cyrus themselves; but the men of Cyme, still afraid that the responsibility would be theirs, sent a ship and fetched him back. Then they sent him to Chios—and the men of Chios delivered him over to the Persian Mazares.

The Ionian city-states were now conquered one by one, in spite of their newly-built fortifications, and the appeals they sent to Greece Proper, particularly to Sparta. Cyrus entrusted the conduct of the campaign to his general Harpagus; and the cities all resisted him bravely, except Miletus, which, enjoying the security of its treaty, remained quiescent while Ionia was enslaved for the second time: formerly to the Lydians, now to the Persians. When all resistance was at an end, and even the island Greeks had submitted through fear, the Panionian Festival was held none the less. There, Bias of Priene addressed the assembly with advice which, if it had been taken, would have given the Ionians freedom and prosperity. He exhorted them to migrate in a body to Sardinia, and found there a new all-Ionian state, warning them that if they stayed at home they would all be Cyrus' slaves. His advice came too late, and was unheeded, like that of Thales before him. The only Ionian Greeks who escaped slavery were the men of Teos, who moved to Abdêra on the Thracian coast; and the men of Phocaea, who went to Sardinia. They failed, however, to establish themselves on the island, not being numerous enough to resist the attacks of the Etruscans who ruled these waters; and after getting help from the Greeks of southern Italy and Sicily, they settled at Elea on the west Italian coast, where they found peace and prosperity.

The Milesians, having remained neutral, sacrificed nothing of their wealth and suffered the minimum of interference. At about this time, they seem to have reorganized their constitution. Records show that in about 525 B.C., after the Persian conquest of Ionia was completed, there was an annual magistrate called Aisymnêtês or President, who was also the Chief Priest of Apollo of Didyma; there were also officials called Molpoi (Psalmists), from whose number the President was elected; these too were priests of Apollo, and lists of their names were kept at the two temples of the god, at Didyma and in Miletus.

They were assisted by three officials called Associates, who were elected biennially from the six Tribes into which the population was divided. Finally, there were subordinate officials called Onitadae, which probably means "Assistants", though some modern writers are prepared to believe that it means "Donkey-men", the donkey (*onos* in Greek) being in some places sacred to Apollo. The whole new arrangement shows that after decades of civil strife in which the workers tried to wrest privilege from the merchants and landowners, Miletus now settled down to a régime in which power remained in the hands of the wealthy, with the strong support of the priestly class. The Persians probably encouraged this development, since it made their task easy: no freedom-loving democracy would tolerate the rule of an oriental despot, and the Persians knew that the priesthood was on their side in frowning on ambitious national movements, because they could endow Apollo with more treasure than any Greek city-state possessed.

King Cyrus died far away fighting the Scythians, in 529 B.C. He was succeeded by his son Cambyses, whose cruelty was equalled by his folly. He died in 522. A struggle followed, resulting in the seizure of power by Dareius in the next year. His accession made no difference to the Greek cities at first; they lived on under Persian rule as before, and Dareius contented himself with seeing to it that they were administered by petty dictators, not by popular governments. The more important rulers delegated authority to the lesser: the small town of Teichioussa in Milesian territory on the coast to the south of Didyma was ruled by a man named Charês, of whom nothing is known except that he must have been held in high honour, since a number of his statues were set up along the Pilgrim's Way to Didyma. One of these, a seated figure bearing the inscription "I am Chares, ruler of Teichioussa" is now in the British Museum. Later, they served as milestones or landmarks.

The worship of Apollo at Didyma, originating in the distant

past, was now in its prime. The priesthood throve on the gifts made by visitors who came to consult the oracle, as at Delphi, and to admire the huge temple of Apollo with its groves and sanctuaries, and its alley-way lined with seated figures and couchant lions in the Egyptian manner. The route from Miletus to Didyma, about eleven miles, led over hilly country, unlike the Sacred Way from Athens to Eleusis, and must have required considerable endurance in those who walked, though there were resting-places. The procession left the city by the Sacred Way, through a gate called the Didymaean, southward over the hills; the last stretch of road bent coastwards to avoid another climb of six hundred feet. Somewhere *en route* the pilgrims were met by a procession of dancers and singers. When they reached the coast at the harbour of Panormus, they were joined by other pilgrims who had made the journey by sea. From Panormus the road wound upwards past the seated figures and lions, to the hill-top, which was about two hundred feet above sea-level. The pilgrims made their offerings, and consulted the oracle. They were probably entertained, as at Eleusis and elsewhere, with a miracle-play: at Didyma, one showing scenes from the life of Apollo and his friend Branchus, a beautiful youth who was said to have founded the oracle, and from whom the Branchidae who administered Didyma traced their descent. A statue of Apollo in bronze could be seen at this time inside the temple, which was now more than two centuries old. Both the temple and its treasures were filled with works of art from Egypt, Lydia, Persia and Greece.

But now, at the end of the sixth century B.C., the acme of Milesian greatness was almost over when the full flowering of Athens had not yet begun; and the oracle at Didyma was soon to be silenced for over a hundred and fifty years. A melancholy interest attaches to the story that when in about 510 B.C. Sybaris in south Italy was destroyed by its neighbour Croton, all male Milesians, young and old, shaved their heads in mourning, because (Herodotus says) these two city-states were bound by closer ties than any others he had known. He does not say why. The connection was probably racial, Sybaris being a colony from Achaea in the Peloponnese which was also the motherland of some of the original settlers at Miletus; and the two cities may have kept up trade-relations as well. Less than twenty years after the fall of Sybaris, Miletus too was laid in ruins and its population scattered, after having brought disaster on the other cities of Ionia.

From about 520 onwards a man of noble family named Histiaeus ruled as dictator at Miletus with the full approval and support of King Dareius. Of all the "tyrants" favoured by Dareius, Histiaeus stood highest in his confidence. The other Greek city-states of the coast were restive under Persian rule; and when Dareius went on a campaign against the Scythians, there was talk of revolt. Histiaeus of Miletus advised his fellow-rulers against this, pointing out that they held their positions in virtue of Dareius' patronage, whereas their subjects wanted democracy. He prevented the others from carrying out a plan to help the Scythians by destroying a bridge over the Danube and cutting off Dareius' retreat; he even guarded the passage until Dareius and his men had made a safe crossing. For this he earned Dareius' gratitude. When asked to name a reward, Histiaeus asked for and obtained the gift of a fortified town in Thrace; but Dareius soon afterwards retracted the gift on the advice of one of his officers, who said that it was dangerous to put such a stronghold into the hands of one of those cunning, clever Greeks. Dareius accepted his advice. Histiaeus, already busy fortifying his new outpost, received a friendly message asking him to join the King at Sardis; and when he arrived, he was invited to accompany Dareius to the Persian capital, Sousa, as Dareius could not do without his constant presence as counsellor. Histiaeus, flattered, went gladly, unaware at first of the deception. His son-in-law Aristagoras was given the governorship of Miletus.

Miletus was now at the height of its prosperity. The new ruler, Aristagoras, anxious to distinguish himself in the absence of Histiaeus at Sousa, planned an attack on Naxos, the wealthiest of the islands, where a revolution had recently substituted government by the people for the rule of the propertied classes. Many of the aristocrats had been driven into exile. When they arrived at Miletus and asked for help, Aristagoras saw a chance of increasing his own power while pleasing the Persians. He set off to Sardis, and proposed to Dareius' representative there that if Naxos were captured, the Persians should proceed to the conquest of the other islands and even Euboea, a stepping-stone to Greece Proper. Dareius' consent was obtained, and Persian help was given: troops, two hundred ships (twice the number asked for by Aristagoras) and a Persian general named Megabatês, a cousin of the King's.

The combined forces were assembled at Chios. Here, Megabates and Aristagoras quarrelled over a question of authority; and (so the Greeks believed) the Persian in his annoyance sent a secret message to the government of Naxos warning them of the impending attack. The Naxians prepared for a siege; and the attacking force found them impregnable. After four months, the Persian contingent withdrew; and Aristagoras also, aware that he had failed, was soon obliged to withdraw. Fearing that his failure would bring punishment from Dareius, who would hear a very unfavourable report from Megabates, Aristagoras decided on revolt.

He called a meeting of the leading citizens of Miletus. All agreed to the project except Hecataeus, whose special subject was geography; he advised against a conflict with the Great King, on the ground that Persia was strong and Miletus was weak. He failed to dissuade the others. He then said that if they were determined to fight, they must have control of the sea. He advised them to take the treasure of Apollo of Didyma and use it to equip a fleet; in this way they would help their own cause and prevent pillage by the enemy. This second counsel also was rejected, as was to be expected in a state in which the chief officials were also priests of Apollo; and it argues great courage on the part of Hecataeus to have made a suggestion that must have seemed highly sacrilegious. The revolt was decided upon, with far-reaching consequences for the whole of Hellas. The story was that Histiaeus also was in favour of it: tired of being kept in attendance on Dareius at Sousa, and having no means of sending a letter to Miletus as the roads were watched, he took his most trustworthy slave, had his head shaved and tattooed with a message urging revolt, and as soon as the hair had grown again, sent him to Miletus with an oral message for Aristagoras to shave the speaker's head. Aristagoras did so, and read the message. With this final encouragement, he proceeded to carry out energetic plans for the revolt not only of Miletus but of all the Ionian city-states from Persian rule.

But first, unity was essential. The rulers of the Greek cities were all men favoured by Persia. Aristagoras' first act was to relinquish his own government, and proclaim "equality of rights" for all citizens of Miletus—that is, a democracy. Next, he carried out similar measures throughout Ionia, expelling some of the pro-Persian Greek rulers and capturing others; he handed the captives over to their former subjects, who either executed or banished them. Then, having won the confidence of his own people and of the other Ionian cities, he set off to Greece Proper to ask for help, taking with him a map of the known world engraved on bronze, with all the seas and rivers marked—a map no doubt derived from that of Hecataeus.

First he went to Sparta.

Sparta was ruled by two kings. At this time the dominant king was Cleomenes I, a crafty and ambitious man who had already interfered in the politics of other city-states, including Athens, where he had narrowly escaped with his life. When Aristagoras came before him and displayed his map, the King was interested but cautious; after hearing Aristagoras' case, he postponed his answer for three days, and when Aristagoras returned at the appointed time, asked him how long was the voyage by sea from Ionia to Persia. Aristagoras, usually a clever man and well-skilled in deception, this time made the mistake of telling the truth; he said that the land journey took three months. Cleomenes cut short any further explanation by ordering Aristagoras to leave Sparta before sunset. Nevertheless, Aristagoras pursued the King to his palace, and having learnt his lesson, offered a bribe, which he increased at each refusal. Cleomenes was tempted, and (so the Spartans told Herodotus) might have succumbed, if his little daughter Gorgo who was present had not said: "Father, if you don't go away, the foreign visitor will corrupt you." Cleomenes, delighted at her shrewdness, did as she advised, and Aristagoras left Sparta for ever.

He went from Sparta to Athens. Here the atmosphere was more favourable. The Athenians, having got rid of their own dictator, were flourishing, and ready to listen to an appeal for help against a tyrannical non-Greek power. Aristogoras' speech to the Assembly was well received: he called on Athens as the mother-city of Miletus to save her and the other Ionians from slavery, pointing out that this was her duty as a great power, and made all manner of promises besides. He succeeded in convincing them. Herodotus, who disapproved of the enterprise, remarks that it is evidently easier to deceive thirty thousand (the Athenian Assembly) than one (the Spartan king).

The Athenians voted twenty ships in aid of the Ionian revolt. Aristagoras then returned to Miletus, to set on foot other plans meant to harm Dareius—for this, Herodotus says, and not the good of the Ionian Greeks, was his objective. When the Athenian ships arrived at Miletus, they brought with them five triremes from Eretria in Euboea; these had come, not to please the Athenians, but in gratitude to the Milesians, who had helped them in one of their own wars.

At Miletus, therefore, all was activity, as the ships and men assembled.

Aristagoras planned that the army should march straight to Sardis, the former Lydian capital, and now the Persian headquarters in Asia Minor; but he did not go himself. He sent two other Milesians as generals, one of them his brother. The army marched. Sardis was attacked and partly burnt, but not captured. The Persian army pursued the retreating Greeks towards

Ephesus, and inflicted a severe defeat. The Athenians then deserted the Ionians, in spite of Aristagoras' messages of appeal —an ignominious end to their campaign of liberation. But their desertion did not save them from the undying hatred of Dareius. When he received the news of the burning of Sardis and was told that this was the work of the Athenians and Ionians, he inquired: "Who are the Athenians?" Having been told, he took his bow and shot an arrow into the air, saying: "O Zeus, grant me vengeance on the Athenians!"; and he gave orders that one of his servants should say to him three times, as he sat at dinner each day: "Master, remember the Athenians!"

His wrath fell also on Histiaeus, who was still with him; but Histiaeus defended himself boldly, saying that this had happened because he himself had been absent, and asking to be allowed to return to Miletus and restore order. Dareius, rather strangely, consented; he retained always a tenderness for Histiaeus, and seems to have been unwilling to mistrust him. It is quite uncertain what part the Milesian really played.

The Ionians, though deserted by their allies, had no thought of surrender. They continued their preparations, and were joined by other city-states, though the Persians were now actively engaged in crushing the rebels. Soon they regained control of the Hellespont; then they marched southward into Caria, where the natives had joined the Greeks. On the river Marsyas, a tributary of the Maeander, the Carians were heavily defeated. They fled to one of their sacred precincts, dedicated to the God of Hosts—they were the only people known to Herodotus who worshipped him—where there was a fine grove of plane-trees. Here they were holding a meeting, to discuss whether they should leave the country or surrender, when the Milesians arrived and persuaded them to fight on. Again there was a battle, and again the insurgents were defeated, more heavily than before. The brunt of the fighting fell on the Milesians, who suffered the greatest losses. The Carians lived to fight again and to win a notable victory.

It was now clear to Aristagoras that his attempt to resist

Dareius could not succeed, and he decided on flight. Herodotus condemns his cowardice: he had upset all Ionia, and had undertaken a huge enterprise, yet when disaster threatened he turned renegade. Aristagoras did, however, suggest a refuge, in case Miletus should be taken: he would either conduct a colony to Sardinia, as Bias of Priene had formerly advised, or else they would migrate to Myrcinus, the stronghold in Thrace which Histiaeus had been fortifying when Dareius summoned him away. Hecataeus the geographer spoke against both these proposals, and suggested a temporary withdrawal to the nearby island of Leros, which they could use as a base for a subsequent descent on Miletus. Once again his advice was rejected. The Milesians voted for the proposal to go to Myrcinus; and Aristagoras then left, with all those who wished to accompany him. Not long afterwards he and all his army were wiped out by the Thracians while fighting for the possession of Myrcinus.

Histiaeus, though he had somehow persuaded Dareius to let him go to Sardis, failed to convince the governor (who was Dareius' brother Artaphernes) that he had had no part in encouraging Aristagoras to rebel. Realizing his danger, Histiaeus fled to Chios, and from there to Miletus; but the Milesians, having tasted freedom, and happy to have got rid of Aristagoras, were quite unwilling to admit another "tyrant" into their territory. Refused entry, Histiaeus made an attempt to force his way in by night; but he was wounded in the thigh by one of the Milesian guards, and had to return to Chios. From there he went to Lesbos. Here he obtained a number of ships, and sailed to Byzantium, where he carried on piratical attacks on shipping passing out from the Black Sea.

A great Persian fleet and army were now concentrating on Miletus, as the largest of the rebel city-states. The Ionians held a council of war at Panionion. They decided not to send an army, but to let the Milesians defend their own city, which was strongly fortified, while the other states manned every available ship and took up their station off the islet of Ladé, to fight for the sea approach to Miletus. This former islet is now a hillock rising above the surrounding mud among the sluggish windings of the river Maeander; it is strange to consider that it was the scene of one of the most momentous naval battles in history.

Herodotus gives us the exact disposition of the combined Ionian fleet. The Milesians were on the right wing with eighty ships, covering Miletus itself. Priene came next with twelve ships, and the little town of Myous at the far end of the Latmian Bay came next with three. Then came Teos with seventeen ships, and Chios with a hundred, the largest contingent of all. The left wing was held by Erythrae, Phocaea, Lesbos and Samos, the latter two states bringing seventy and ninety ships respectively. The total number, according to Herodotus, was three hundred and fifty-three ships. But the component parts were not all of equal value.

There had been discontent and indiscipline during the period of training for this battle; and the Persians had been trying to create dissension and disloyalty, using the previously-expelled rulers as envoys to the separate contingents, each of which thought that they alone were being approached. The Persians, having conquered Cyprus three years earlier, now had a huge fleet of six hundred ships, made up of Cypriot, Phoenician, Egyptian and other vessels. During the great battle which followed, massive desertions turned the scale against the Ionians, though most fought bravely. Herodotus admits that he cannot give the facts because afterwards they all blamed each other; but so far as he could ascertain, the Samians were the first to desert, all except eleven vessels which remained loyal. The Lesbian contingent followed. The men of Chios fought the most bravely; but their efforts were vain, and they all perished either before or after the battle, some of them at the hands of the Greeks at Ephesus, who refused admittance to the refugees.

After the battle of Lade, the Persians besieged Miletus by land and sea. They undermined the walls, and brought up every kind of siege-engine. The inhabitants, with the sea approaches cut off, could not hold out long against hunger. Miletus was captured, six years after Aristagoras' rising. Vast numbers of men were slain; the survivors were reduced to slavery, and transported first to Sousa, then, without further injury, to a place called Ampê on the Persian Gulf at the mouth of the river Tigris. Herodotus' words suggest that their treatment by Dareius was comparatively merciful, in that the men escaped maiming and the women a life of concubinage.

Thus Miletus was emptied of the Milesians.

The city and its environs were occupied by the Persians. The hilly regions were given over to one of the Carian tribes, who had refrained from helping the Milesians. These had consulted the oracle at Didyma, and had received the answer: "Miletus once was mighty, long ago." This they rightly interpreted as forecasting a Persian victory. The oracle became a proverb to express vanished glory.

The temple at Didyma also was pillaged and burnt, and the treasures were taken to the Persian capital Sousa, with the concurrence of the priests, so it is said. These treasures included the bronze statue of Apollo, which remained at Sousa for nearly two hundred years, until it was restored to the rebuilt temple at Didyma by King Seleucus I of Syria.

The fall of Miletus caused a sensation throughout the Greek world. The threat to Greece Proper from the Persian Empire now became unmistakable; but an awareness of danger was not the only nor even the predominant feeling, at any rate in Athens. When in the spring dramatic festival a tragedy by Phrynichus called *The Capture of Miletus* was performed, the audience burst into tears, the dramatist was fined a thousand drachmas ($1,000) for having reminded the Athenians of a disaster they considered as their own, and a repetition of the performance was forbidden in perpetuity. Not a single fragment of this drama survives.

Histiaeus, when he heard the news, left Byzantium with his ships borrowed from Lesbos, and began raiding the Greek islands in the north, taking cruel advantage of their weakness after the naval defeat of Lade. In particular he sacked Chios, already on her knees after the disaster to her men at Miletus. But retribution was at hand. Histiaeus was captured and sent to the King's brother Artaphernes at Sardis, the man who had refused to believe him innocent of complicity in Aristagoras' revolt. If Histiaeus had been taken to Dareius at Sousa, he would have been pardoned, Herodotus thinks; but Artaphernes, probably knowing this, had him executed without delay, and sent his head to Dareius. The King was angry and grieved. He ordered that the head should be honourably buried, as that of a great benefactor of himself and the Persians. Histiaeus was indeed an enemy of his own countrymen, being governed solely by his own interest. In Herodotus' narrative, it is Dareius, not Histiaeus, who shows greatness. The Milesian was, like Alcibiades, perfectly willing to help either side or both according to his immediate objective, and his duplicity was such that it was impossible then as now to tell what was the exact purpose of his particular moves. The opinion held of him by Greek posterity was mildly expressed by Pausanias the traveller who, writing six centuries later, said:

"The Milesians were destroyed because of the temperament of Histiaeus, which was swayed this way and that by violent desires: first for the castle in Thrace, then to be Dareius' adviser, and then again to return to Ionia."

The Persian fleet spent the winter at Miletus, no doubt in the long inlet now called Lion Bay. The following spring they sailed out, and easily captured the islands nearest the continent, as well as many other city-states. They treated the Greeks with all the cruelty they had threatened; and so, Herodotus says, for the third time Ionia was enslaved.

Thus ended the great period of Milesian history.

The rest of Dareius' exploits do not concern Miletus, which remained deserted except for the Persian occupiers and their attendants for fourteen years. In 480 B.C. the battle of Salamis saved the Greek mainland from the Persian invasion under Xerxes. In 479, the battle of Cape Mycalê freed Ionia. In the latter, Milesians played their part. Probably these were prisoners taken at the time of the capture or in earlier battles, and retained by the Persians as guides. Mycale is the long mountainous cape running westwards into the sea above the Gulf of Latmos. Here the Persians had made a naval camp near the sanctuary of Demeter of Eleusis which had been constructed by the first band of immigrants when they came with Neileus on the expedition for the founding of Miletus. The Persians, not being at all sure of victory in the forthcoming sea battle with the Athenians off the cape, had assigned the guarding of the wild mountain passes on Mycale to the Milesians, who knew the country well and could act as guides: a strange miscalculation if, as Herodotus says, they already distrusted the Milesians and wanted them out of the camp. The Milesians naturally took full opportunity of revenge. After the naval defeat of the Persians, the guides took the fugitives along paths which led back to their enemies; and in the end, the Milesians also turned on the Persians and helped to slaughter them.

.   .   .   .   .

Now that Ionia was liberated, Miletus was repopulated and its rebuilding was begun.

Who the new inhabitants were is not known; the historians at this point leave Miletus for events in Greece Proper — the after-effects of the Persian defeat, the failure of Sparta to take the lead which she had won by her military prowess, the rise of the Athenian Empire. Miletus, broken and in ruins, with her ships destroyed and her population gone, lay outside the main stream of events for many a decade. Whether the new citizens were returning Milesian refugees from other Greek cities, or from Ampê, or whether they were a mixture of Greeks from every part of Ionia, cannot be said for certain; but it seems likely that there were a good many Milesians among them, because an attempt was obviously made to restore the life of the city-state on the earlier lines. The Kalabaktepe, "old Miletus", which had been laid waste by the Persians—traces of burning have been found in modern times—was again occupied, and a good deal of building began on the lower land to the east of this hill. A new temple of Athene was built on a thin stratum of ashes.

It is not surprising that all this activity gave much training to architects and builders. Miletus produced at this time or perhaps a little later the famous town-planner Hippodamus,[1] whose services came to be in demand all over the Mediterranean. He was called in by Pericles to re-plan the Peiraeus-district, and also by the Thourians in 444 B.C. What he did at Miletus cannot now be traced; but there is no doubt that his expertness was derived from the opportunity afforded to him in the reconstruction of his native city. It was fitting that a man from Miletus should restore the Athenian harbour, wrecked by the Persians in 480 B.C. and should rebuild Thourioi on the ruins of Sybaris, for the destruction of which an earlier generation of Milesians had mourned.

The old constitution also was restored. The priestly guild of Psalmists was reconstituted, and a yearly President was chosen from their number to give his name to the year. The Associates were abolished, and their work was taken over by the other officials. The annual procession to Didyma was instituted afresh, although the temple was in ruins, and Milesians were too much occupied with restoring the city itself, and too poor, to begin rebuilding at Didyma as well. No doubt there was some temporary substitute, a chapel where the pilgrims could meet for worship; but the oracle was not resuscitated.

In the city, the population was divided as before into six Tribes. By the middle of the fifth century B.C. there existed, as records show, officials acting "for the month"; their duties are not fully known, but seem to have included certain ex-

[1] See pp. 29-30.

ecutive functions connected with legal sentences. For instance, when there was a question of the return of certain men who had been exiled and the annulment of the price set on their heads, the officials "for the month" had to see that any decision was carried out. Their title, unlike that of the Psalmists and the President, suggests for the first time secular, not religious officials. Miletus was drawing away from Apollo. Can it be that their bitter experience of his helplessness to protect his worshippers had shaken their faith? This faith may also have been undermined by their own school of scientific philosophers. Thales, referring to the latent forces in inanimate objects, said: "*All* things are full of gods", and his successors explain the universe entirely without reference to divinities, while Hecataeus could even propose using Apollo's treasure to pay for an efficient navy. Now, the oracle was silent; and the temple had to wait until more urgent matters had been attended to.

After the liberation, Miletus, like the other Ionian cities and islands, became a member of the new alliance against Persia, under the leadership of Athens. In the early days, when the treasury of the League was kept on the sacred island of Delos, Miletus was probably in no position to contribute anything to the common resources, either in ships or in money. In the spring of 454 B.C. the treasury was transferred to Athens, and the League became openly, as it had long been tacitly, an Athenian Empire. A reassessment of annual contributions was made; from these, a quota of one-sixtieth was abstracted for the goddess Athena, and the accounts, inscribed on marble blocks and slabs, were kept on the Athenian Acropolis, where many fragments have been found and pieced together by modern archaeologists.

The result of these labours has given us six of the marble slabs, showing the annual payments to the League from 454 B.C. to 412 B.C. with a few gaps. From time to time, further reassessments of the payments due from each member-state were made; a marble slab recording one of these revisions made in 425 B.C. has been pieced together out of thirty fragments found on the Acropolis at different times. Taken as a series, these records in marble show the finances of the Athenian Empire throughout its most vital period, under the leadership of Pericles, up to the middle of the Peloponnesian War, and thereby reveal the changing fortunes of each of the member states, or, as they were after 454 B.C. the subject allies. In the first of the quota-lists (454 B.C.) the city-state of Miletus is not mentioned at all, though "Milesians of Teichioussa" and "Milesians of Leros" are listed separately, the latter paying half a talent ($3,000). This shows that the population of Miletus was still scattered, and that the city itself was too weak to contribute, a generation after the liberation. This was perhaps due to internal strife.

The trouble caused by political dissension in restored Miletus was severe. Athens, contrary to her usual practice, which was to favour democracy, had made an exception in the case of Miletus, allowing the upper class to govern. But the rulers soon took advantage of their position to inflict a devastating blow on the workers. A punitive expedition was sent from Athens to restore order; an Athenian garrison was put in, and a commission of five was appointed to revise the constitution. The result was that Miletus received a new constitution something like that of Athens. There was a Council; there were a number of superior magistrates called Wardens (*Phylakes*) as in Plato's *Republic;* there were also assistant-magistrates called Colleagues (*Proshetairoi*). The right of jurisdiction at Miletus was, however, curtailed: important cases had to be sent to Athens for trial. From now onwards, the Psalmists retained only their priestly functions, and the state was no longer identified with Apollo, though it took responsibility for his worship, providing some of the sacrificial animals from the public funds. There was still a President (*Aisymnêtês*) who was also Apollo's "garland-wearer" and who gave his name to the year. The Guild of Psalmists still kept certain records and had their own communal residence at or near the Temple of Delphinian

Apollo in the city, where they took their meals. The habit of communal meals for the men at Miletus went back to ancient times, when the women of the conquered race did not eat with their husbands; Plato compared it to the common mess at Sparta, and remarks (or makes his Athenian character remark) that this custom, like that of physical training, may be a good thing in many ways, but it conduces to civil strife, as is shown by the sons of the Milesians among others. Evidently, therefore, it was still usual in Plato's day, in the fourth century B.C., for the males at Miletus to dine together instead of in their own homes. The whole reorganized constitution, however, was democratic. Athens regarded this, one of her few experiments in allowing government by a privileged class in one of her tributary allies, as a failure.

Miletus now began slowly to rise again.

In 450 B.C. she was assessed at ten talents' tribute ($60,000), which though not high, was an advance on the previous lists, where the city did not appear. In 434 B.C. the tribute had to be halved. The reason for this is not known; but in the following year Miletus was involved in a quarrel with the islanders of Samos over the control of Priene on the opposite side of the Latmian Gulf, so that probably the Samians were trying to interfere with the revived Milesian sea trade, and were succeeding. The Samians, who had at that time an anti-democratic government, had no doubt received some of the exiles from the deposed Milesian government, and these had suggested retaliatory measures. Priene was at that time entirely depressed: the little city-state had never recovered from the effects of the Persian conquest, and in 450 B.C. could pay only one talent ($6,000) to the Athenian League.

The Milesians were unsuccessful in the war with Samos. They took their complaints about Samian behaviour to Athens, where their case convinced the authorities. An expedition was sent against Samos, and a democracy was established there under the protection of an Athenian garrison; hostages were taken off the island and deposited further north on the island

of Lemnos. The Samians did not submit easily to this interference. Refugees of the opposite political party fled to the
mainland of Asia and journeyed to Sardis to get help from the
Persians. They then returned, and with this foreign aid over-
threw the democracy, recovered their hostages from Lemnos,
sent the captured Athenian guards to Sardis, and began preparations for an attack on Miletus.

This, from the Athenian point of view, was a major crime
against Hellas. Persia was the late enemy, defeated with such
effort only forty years earlier. This time the Athenians sent a
contingent of sixty ships against Samos. Forty-four of these
under the command of Pericles defeated the Samian fleet as
it was returning from Miletus; the Athenian troops then landed
on Samos and began a siege. Pericles, leaving the siege to his
officers, went away for a time; and during his absence the
Samians managed to sally forth and deal a sharp counterblow.
For fourteen days they retained the mastery of their own seas,
and imported and exported whatever they pleased. But the
return of Pericles put a stop to all this; and soon afterwards
another forty ships arrived from Athens. After a nine months'
siege, the Samians surrendered. They were made to destroy
their fortifications, to hand over their fleet, and to give hostages
again; they also had to pay reparations by agreed instalments.
Their interference with Milesian trade-recovery was at an end.
This was in the year 440 B.C.

At the time, gossip alleged that the strong action taken by
Pericles was due to a desire to please Aspasia, who came from
Miletus. This remarkable woman was a source of wonder to
the Greeks of her own time and afterwards; they found it
almost miraculous that a woman should be sufficiently intelli-
gent to influence men; only the most outstanding gifts made
them excuse this phenomenon. Miletus, where women were
segregated in the Ionian manner, had nevertheless already produced one remarkable woman: this was Thargêlia, who lived
in the time of Dareius, and was a convinced pro-Persian. She
was outstanding in beauty and wit, and married fourteen

times, each of her husbands being men of eminence, and one at any rate a king. Her political influence through these men, all of whom she imbued with pro-Persian sentiments, was prodigious. Plutarch, mentioning Thargelia in his *Life of Pericles*, says that she served Aspasia as a model.

Pericles, virtual ruler of Athens from the middle of the fifth century till his death in 428 B.C., must have met Aspasia at some time before the Samian War—probably in or about 450 B.C. when Athens reorganized the Milesian constitution. He was already married to a widow who had borne him two sons; but it is said that he divorced her in order to live with Aspasia. He could not legally marry Aspasia because, by one of his own decrees, marriage of an Athenian to a non-Athenian was prohibited; but virtually she was his wife, and their son Pericles was legitimized by special decree. Plutarch, in writing of her influence, apologizes for the digression, but remarks: "As these things have come into my mind, it would perhaps be inhuman to banish them from my essay and ignore them." He records as amazing that Pericles loved Aspasia so much that he used to kiss her whenever he went out or came in. Her position was unique for a woman at Athens, where the Ionian custom prevailed of keeping the women segregated in their own quarters; freedom to mix in male society belonged only to wealthy courtesans. Aspasia associated on equal terms with the most brilliant men of the day. Plato in one of his dialogues makes Socrates deliver a Funeral Oration which, he pretends, he was taught by Aspasia and made to learn by heart. Socrates professes to be afraid of her, and to have incurred her wrath by his stupidity. This, of course, is irony; nevertheless, as Plutarch admits, it shows that she had a reputation for high political intelligence and for skill in expression.

Like all prominent personages of the day, she came in for the satire of the Athenian writers of comedy, as well as for much scurrilous talk. For instance, she held educational classes for women; but the comic writers preferred to depict her as keeping a school for prostitutes. After Pericles' death, she married Lysiclês, whom Plutarch describes as a sheep-dealer and a man of low birth; probably he had trade-connections with Miletus, since the export of sheep and of articles manufactured from wool was one of Miletus' principal activities. Lysicles was killed the following year near Miletus, on the plain of the river Maeander, where he was ambushed by a band of Carians and others. What happened to Aspasia after this is not known. She left no writings, and the few sayings attributed to her have no authenticity.

It was perhaps after the Samian War that Miletus made further changes in her constitution, on the Athenian model. The number of Tribes was doubled, from six to twelve, each Tribe comprising a number of demes or village-units as at Athens. Miletus was now a democracy depending on the Athenian fleet for its existence; and its government could therefore be counted upon to serve Athenian interests when war broke out between the Athenian Empire and the Peloponnesians led by Sparta in 431 B.C. This remained true for the first nineteen years of the war: the Athenians collected funds, used the Milesian harbours for their shipping, and imported Milesian products such as the famous blankets, cloaks, beds, and preserved fish.

In 424 B.C. the tribute payable by Miletus to Athens was doubled, from five talents to ten ($30,000 to $60,000). The Milesians briefed the Athenian statesmen Cleon to appeal to the Athenian Assembly against this assessment, but without success; the appeal was dismissed, much to the delight of the comic dramatists. From then onward, nothing is heard of Milesian affairs for a number of years; but the long war between Athens and Sparta and the severe defeat of the Athenians in Sicily revived the hopes of the anti-democratic party in Miletus, who were, of course, also anti-Athenian. In 412 B.C. Alcibiades, who had been exiled from Athens since 415 B.C., visited Miletus with proposals that the city-state should revolt from the Athenian Empire. He was already on friendly terms with the leading citizens; and he managed to persuade them. Immediately afterwards, Sparta concluded a treaty with Persia, so that Miletus was once again within the orbit of Persian power. The Athenian fleet arrived at Miletus too late to prevent the uprising. The ships anchored off the island of Lade, and later in the summer the troops, landing at Panormus further south, encountered a small band of Spartans and overwhelmed them, killing the Spartan general. They then set up a trophy of victory which, as soon as they had gone, the Milesians removed as having been illegally erected on their territory.

The Athenians rightly took the revolt of Miletus very seriously. Their other subject-allies in the Aegean were deserting them, and they believed that if they could regain Miletus, the rest would return. They therefore sent an expedition at the end of the summer: 3,500 troops—Athenians, Argives and other allies—and forty-eight ships, which made Samos their base. The defence of Miletus was undertaken with vigour; Alcibiades himself was present, and also the Persian governor Tissaphernes with a contingent of cavalry. The Milesians themselves put 800 men in the field.

In the battle that followed, the troops from Argos, underestimating the Milesians as "Ionians, who would not stand firm," were defeated and lost nearly three hundred men out of a thousand; but the Athenians were victorious against the Spartans and Persians. The Milesians, after their own success, withdrew inside the city walls, so that the Athenians did not come into contact with them but were halted at the gates. They set up a trophy, and proceeded to build a wall across the base of the peninsula, so that Miletus would be cut off on the inland side. But on that same evening, news came that some Sicilian ships were on the way. These, hearing that the Athenians were at Miletus, turned aside and anchored in Teichioussa Bay.

Alcibiades, energetic as ever, no matter what the cause, evaded the Athenian blockade and rode out from Miletus, twelve miles over the hills, to meet the Sicilians on the coast. He told them of the defeat, and urged them to come at once to the help of Miletus and not allow it to be encircled, if they did not want to lose Ionia and with it the whole war. They agreed.

The Athenian generals wanted to stay and fight; but one of them, Phrynichus, with his customary good sense, refused to take the risk. So they abandoned the siege, and the whole blockading fleet returned to Samos. The Argives, smarting at their defeat—Dorians for the first time beaten by Ionians—returned home in dudgeon. From then onwards, Miletus became the chief base of the Spartans and Persians in the eastern Aegean; and we get the impression that she was something of a tool in their hands. Nevertheless, we are told, the Milesians remained eager to carry on the war against Athens, and they readily contributed supplies.

The Spartan and Persian leaders came and went. In Thucydides' narrative we get glimpses of interesting scenes, as the war drags on, apparently never to end. We see Tissaphernes, the very able representative of the Persian king in Asia Minor, coming to Miletus to pay the crews of the Peloponnesian fleet, at the rate of one drachma (about one dollar) a day per man for a month; for the future, he wanted to halve the rate, until he could obtain the King's consent to pay the full drachma; but this proposal met with such resistance that he had to give way. We see Spartan admirals coming and going, first Philippus, then Astyochus, to take command of the fleet at Miletus, and carrying on fresh negotiations with Tissaphernes, thinking that he has not given them sufficiently generous terms. The Persian signed no less than three treaties with his Greek allies at Miletus, to keep them satisfied. An expedition was organized and sent from Miletus under a Spartan commander to engineer the revolt of Abydos, a Milesian colony on the Hellespont, from Athens. A Milesian ship took part in a sea battle in which the Athenians were defeated; this success greatly cheered those in Miletus. Then came a temporary setback. Alcibiades deserted the Peloponnesian cause, and, as he had always wanted to do since his exile four years earlier, returned to Athens, where a revolution had overthrown the democratic government and a select few held power. This was in 411 B.C.

The result at Miletus was consternation and confusion. It was known that Alcibiades had offered his fellow-countrymen, as the price of his return, an alliance with Persia: the Persians, he claimed, would join whatever side he wished. At Milesian headquarters, where Tissaphernes had long been distrusted, this new move of Alcibiades was a proof that the Persians had all along been playing a double game. The men, however, took another line: they were dissatisfied with their pay, and they blamed their commander, the Spartan Astyochus, for having annoyed Tissaphernes, who held the purse. Feeling ran high. The Syracusan and Thourian sailors mobbed the admiral, so that he had to take refuge at an altar to save his skin.[1] In the Milesians, the memory of their old wrongs at the hands of Persia flared up: in a surprise assault they seized the fort built by Tissaphernes, and threw out the garrison. The other allies all applauded; but a Spartan official named Lichas protested, saying that they all, including the Milesians, should continue to "serve" Tissaphernes until the war had been brought to a successful conclusion. This tactless expression infuriated the Milesians to such an extent that when shortly afterwards Lichas died of an illness, they refused to let his Spartan compatriots bury him where they wished.

After these unfortunate episodes, the Spartan government thought it best to relieve Astyochus of his command. He left with a number of others: a Milesian delegate; and a bilingual Carian called Gaulîtês, sent by Tissaphernes to accuse the Milesians concerning the capture of the fort, and to defend himself against the charge which he knew that the Milesian delegate would make, namely that he, Tissaphernes, had been playing a double game. All these, and certain others who had claims to make or causes to state, sailed for Sparta. At Miletus, the Spartan admiral Mindarus took up the command of the fleet. Soon afterwards, he sailed from there to the Hellespont . . . Here the masterly narrative of Thucydides, unfinished

[1] See pp. 36–37.

at the author's death, breaks off, and the pedestrian chronicle of Xenophon continues the story.

For the next four years we hear little of Miletus, which remains a Spartan base. The famous Spartan admiral Lysander touched here in 407 B.C. on his way north. But a year later Lysander was replaced by Callicratidas; and though Lysander's friends tried to stir up trouble, Callicratidas remained. The question of pay for the troops was still paramount. Callicratidas did his best: he went to see Prince Cyrus, the King's brother, at Sardis, but being asked to wait for two days, he was annoyed and left Sardis for Miletus. Here he called an Assembly of the Milesian people, and addressed them. He urged them to use all zeal in the war against Athens, and explained that although he had declined to dance attendance on Cyrus, he had sent instead to Sparta for more money for the troops. Meanwhile, he asked the Milesian people to make a contribution, which would be gratefully repaid.

At this, many of his audience—especially those who had been criticizing him—rose and made voluntary contributions, being afraid to oppose him. He took the money, and set out northward with the fleet.

The following year, 405 B.C., the long Peloponnesian War was suddenly decided in Sparta's favour by the destruction of the Athenian fleet at Aegospotami by Lysander. The admiral chose a Milesian pirate named Theopompus to carry the glorious news to Sparta. Theopompus arrived there in two days. When the Milesians heard of the final surrender of Athens, did any of them remember how, ninety years before, the Athenians in the theatre had stopped the performance of the tragic *Capture of Miletus* with their tears?

.   .   .   .   .

The end of the long war between Athens and Sparta left the Aegean world in a state of flux. Many men, used to a life of adventure, were unable or unwilling to return to a peaceful life of commerce, politics and the like. When therefore the young Persian prince Cyrus decided to try to depose his elder brother from the throne of Persia, he had no difficulty in collecting an army of Greek mercenaries to add to his other forces. Among these was the Athenian Xenophon, a pupil and admirer of Socrates. Xenophon joined the expedition on the persuasion of one of his friends, for the sake of adventure. Cyrus did not tell the troops his objective; this would have daunted them, and they would have refused to go. Instead, he chose a pretext: Miletus.

The Ionian city-states had long ago been assigned by the Persian king to Tissaphernes as his sphere of influence. These now went over to Prince Cyrus, who was popular with them, while Tissaphernes was not. The only Ionian city retained by Tissaphernes was Miletus, where in the spring of 405 B.C. shortly before the battle of Aegospotami, a change of constitution from democracy back to oligarchy had been achieved with Spartan help. A thousand democratic refugees had appealed to the Persians for protection, and had been granted a stronghold in Lydia. Three years later, these were led back to Miletus by Tissaphernes, who conquered the city and drove out the government installed by Lysander. These in their turn sought refuge with Prince Cyrus.

This now gave Cyrus his excuse for collecting an army. He besieged Miletus by land and sea, taking care to lull the suspicions of the King, his brother, by continuing to send tribute from the other city-states. The King, thinking that the loyal Tissaphernes was aiming at independence, accepted his brother's explanation; and their mother, who preferred Cyrus, helped in the deception.

When Cyrus was ready to proceed up-country on his march to Persia, he recalled the various armies he had financed, including the troops besieging Miletus. He promised the Milesian democrats that if they carried out the new campaign successfully, he would not stop until he had restored them to their native city. They gladly obeyed, because they trusted him; and all assembled at Sardis, still unaware of the nature of the new enterprise. This was in the spring of 401 B.C. But Cyrus, who prided himself on keeping his word, was not destined to fulfil his promise to the Milesian exiles: he was killed on the battlefield of Cunaxa, forty miles from Babylon, and his armies, including the Greeks, were left without an objective. How the survivors eventually reached Greek territory again is told by Xenophon in his *Anabasis*.

In the early part of the next century, at the Panionian Festival on Cape Mycale, a performance was given of a musical piece called *Persae*, glorifying the Ionians and tracing their origin to Achaea in the north of the Peloponnese rather than to Athens. The composer was Timotheus of Miletus, who was born in about 446 B.C. and was by this time famous as a creator of new fashions in music. Miletus, with its worship of Apollo, was an ideal place for the development of musical talent; and its contact with Lydia bred a taste for musical styles less austere than those of Greece Proper, where the majestic Dorian mode was most highly regarded. Music in Greece was an accompaniment to words, not a separate art, so that poets were musicians and musicians poets. Timotheus took his work to the great spring festival at Athens; but the audiences there, fond as they were of novelty, found his highly-coloured style too much for them, and his compositions were hissed off the stage. One critic complained that his notes scurried to and fro like ants in an ants' nest.

But Timotheus had found one admirer who compensated for the critics: Euripides, who not only encouraged him by saying that he would soon have the theatres at his feet, but who also collaborated with him, writing the words for some of his music, and adopting many of Timotheus' innovations. Euripides died in 406 B.C.; but by then his prediction had come true. Timotheus was famous, and for better or worse his "modern" style had ousted the older and more austere. His works, like the plays of Euripides, found their way on to school curricula; and he was once awarded a thousand gold pieces by the Ephesians for a hymn to Artemis. He lived to the age of ninety. A portion of the verses from his *Persae*, the piece played at Panionion in 398 B.C. was discovered on a papyrus near Memphis in Egypt in 1902; it describes the sea battle of Salamis, and in the concluding verses the composer names himself. The music is of course lost. Timotheus had a successor who in his youth was a prodigious flute-player, but who gave it up for oratory: Philiscus of Miletus, a pupil of Isocrates, and writer of a work on Public Speaking in two books.

* * * * *

Between 390 and 387 B.C. Miletus was engaged in a law-suit with the small town of Myous higher up the Latmian Gulf, over land in the plain of the river Maeander. The court was made up of representatives of the Ionian city-states, showing that the Union existed for other purposes than the celebration of the Panionian Festival. The judge was the Persian governor of Ionia. The Milesians won their case.

Meanwhile, the Spartans had been campaigning against Persia, now allied to Athens, in Asia Minor; but this war was ended in 386, by a peace which gave the Greek city-states of Asia Minor, including Miletus, to the Persian King. The Milesians were allowed to keep their constitution, and to manage their internal affairs by means of a Council and an Assembly of the People, as at Athens.

Then came an uprising of Persian governors (satraps) against their King (Artaxerxes Memnon). Among the rebels was Hecatomnôs, the satrap of Caria, who succeeded in making himself independent and in capturing Miletus after a long struggle; there were traitors in the city, which was taken by a stratagem. Coins were issued by the victor; these were stamped with his name and that of his son Maussôlus, who succeeded him. Maussolus, who reigned till 352, was married to his sister Artemisia, who in turn succeeded him. She mourned his death with such intensity that she spent the remaining two years of her life in perpetuating his memory. She built at Halicarnassus the famous tomb known as the Mausoleum, which has given its name to all similar memorials; and rumour said that every day she mixed his ashes with the wine that she drank. When she too died in 350 B.C. the brother of Maussolus, Idraieus, and his sister-wife Ada, succeeded her. In 345 B.C. the Milesians sent to Delphi a pair of portrait-statues of these two.

But a greater conqueror than any was on his way.

In 334 B.C. Alexander of Macedon, after a short victorious march, appeared before Miletus, which was held by the Persians under a Greek garrison-commander. A prominent Milesian citizen tried to negotiate, but in vain. Alexander attacked. The outer city quickly fell. He encamped there, and decided to cut off the inner city by a wall. At Lade, the Macedonian fleet guarded the approach by sea; the Persian fleet stood farther away, off Cape Mycale. Alexander attacked again. At first the defenders by sheer numbers and quantity of arms staved off the assault; but Alexander, pressing on with great energy, shook the walls with his military engines, and his men broke through into the town.

Many of the Persian defenders were killed. Some escaped; the rest were enslaved. But Alexander made a complete distinction between them and the Greek inhabitants, whom he treated most humanely. There appears to have been no destruction of the city; and the surviving Milesians were granted freedom. Thus Alexander was accepted at first as the liberator of Ionia from Persia. For this year he was granted the title of President (Aisymnetes) at Miletus; he was described on the list of Presidents simply as "Alexander, son of Philip", without the title of "King."

Some historians say that after Alexander had left on his march against Persia, Miletus was recaptured for the Persians, and recaptured again for Alexander; but this is uncertain. Perhaps the most sensational result, for the Milesians, of Alexander's passage was that the holy spring inside the sanctuary of Didyma, the spring which had dried up a century and a half before when Dareius came, now gushed forth again, and the prophetic voice of Apollo was heard through his priestess proclaiming the divine origin of Alexander, his coming victory over Persia, the death of the present Persian king Dareius, and the political activities of the Spartans. These oracles were duly reported to Alexander on his travels, by Milesian envoys: it was well known that the conqueror set great store by such signs and would go a considerable way to consult the oracle wherever he happened to be.

Miletus was now once more a free city; and she blossomed accordingly. Such details as we hear suggest renewed activity in every direction. The city walls were completed. Additions were made to the Temple of Delphinian Apollo in the city. A new system of regular street-planning was begun, after what was now called the "Hippodamian" method, from it inventor. New contacts were made with other city-states; there was a renewal of old ties, religious and commercial, with some of the colonies, and Miletus was again busy with her carrying trade, shipping wheat from the Black Sea to Athens. She was on good terms with her neighbour across the Gulf, Priene, now also a free city, whose sovereign Assembly voted honorary rights to one Theodorus of Miletus, possibly a relative of the Stoic philosopher of that name. The increased activity caused a shortage of labour; during the latter half of the fourth and throughout the third century B.C. Miletus was admitting new citizens, principally from Crete.

· · · · ·

After the death of Alexander in 323 B.C. his conquests were divided among his generals. The wars and intrigues of these men and their descendants against one other form a confused period in the history of Greece, Asia and Egypt.

The governorship of Caria, which chiefly concerned Miletus, fell to Asandrus, and the governorship to the north of Caria to the much more able and active Antigonus. These two soon began fighting for the possession of the whole of Asia Minor. The Milesians found Asandrus oppressive: he kept a garrison in the city, and built a stronghold called Heracleia on the Latmian Gulf to control the land-route between Miletus and Caria. But Antigonus, who had a Milesian named Aristodêmus in his service as a general, sent a force to Miletus, called on the citizens to strike a blow for their freedom, overpowered the garrison, and gave the city back its independence. In this liberation, the Athenians also helped; an inscription recording Milesian gratitude is still in existence. This was in 313 B.C. A few years later, Athens itself was temporarily liberated from the rule of the Macedonian Cassander (the murderer of Alexander's mother Olympias and of his wife Roxane with their son); on that occasion the Milesians decreed to Athens a congratulatory garland worth over 260 drachmas (about $260).

Miletus was not long allowed to remain without a "patron". In 301 B.C. the great battle of Ipsus in the north of Asia Minor put an end to the long struggle for power between the generals of Alexander. Antigonus was killed. The new ruler of the East was now Seleucus, who had originally received Syria as his province, but whose power had gradually been extending, in alliance with Ptolemy of Egypt and others. In 312 B.C. the oracle at Didyma, which Seleucus had consulted, addressed him as "King" (or so he told his troops); and the battle of Ipsus confirmed the prophecy. Seleucus did not fail to repay this friendly gesture: one of his first actions after his victory was to restore to Didyma the statue of Apollo taken away by the Persians two hundred years before.

This was only one of many favours bestowed on Miletus and Didyma by Seleucus and his family. Through their munificence, additions were made to the Temple of Apollo of Didyma; a piece of stone survives bearing the name of Seleucus' son Antiochus, who was thanked by a public decree. Antiochus also paid for a large and magnificent portico in the city itself. The Temple of Delphinian Apollo in the city likewise received its share: a new portico was added, with wooden panelling and columns, on which was a notice prohibiting the hanging of dedicatory tablets except in a certain specified place. Seleucus' queen Apama cared for the Milesian wounded who went on campaigns with her husband; for this she was thanked in a decree. Seleucus had a Milesian for his general, a man named Demodamas, whose campaigning took him into Central Asia. This man carried his love for his native city with him, and planted an altar to Apollo of Didyma somewhere beyond the Caspian Sea. On his return, he wrote an account of his travels which was still extant in Roman times.

Other influences still strove for the possession of Miletus. For a brief while, there was a resurgence of the war between the generals, when Antigonus' son Demetrius [1] tried to wrest power from Seleucus. Somewhere about 300 B.C. Miletus received an interesting new resident—Eurydice, daughter of Antipater, one of Alexander's generals. She had been married to Ptolemy I of Egypt, but he had now divorced her in order to marry Berenice; and she now came to live in Miletus with her daughter Ptolemais, whom she betrothed to Demetrius Poliorcetes. In 295 B.C. Miletus granted to Demetrius the office of Chief Magistrate. Meanwhile, Ptolemy himself had made a treaty of friendship with the city, and had set it free from severe tribute and customs dues payable to Demetrius; for this, Ptolemy was awarded a statue to be erected in the South Market, and another statue in the Temple of Delphinian Apollo.

Miletus is now swayed to and fro once again between rival claimants, each with his supporters in the city. There was Demetrius Poliorcetes, ruler of Macedonia, whose affianced bride lived in the city. There was Lysimachus, another of Alexander's generals, now ruler of Thrace and in alliance with Kings Seleucus and Ptolemy against Demetrius. There were King Seleucus and his son Antiochus, rulers of Syria. All these constantly strove to win Milesian favour by bribes and promises. Each year the balance of power shifted from one to the

[1] Demetrius Poliorcetes, King of Macedonia. See p. 118.

other of these rulers. In 289 B.C. an influential Milesian citizen managed to persuade the Council to invite Lysimachus in. In 288 B.C. King Seleucus and his son Antiochus sent by messenger a huge gift to Didyma, and a letter to the Council and People of Miletus, with an inventory attached: gold and silver vessels, a large candelabra, various cups, dishes, drinking-goblets, mixing-bowls, incense, myrrh, cinnamon, and so on. These were to be dedicated to the protecting deities by the six Temple treasurers. In 289 B.C. Demetrius landed at Miletus and celebrated his marriage with the princess Ptolemais, though he had had three wives already, as well as many mistresses.

Demetrius after the wedding went off at once on a campaign, and was captured shortly afterwards by Seleucus, who kept him in prison for three years until he died. He left four legitimate sons, one by each of his wives, and also a number of illegitimate children. After his defeat, Miletus was punished for her friendly reception of him, and made to pay a large tribute by Lysimachus. In 282 B.C. the impoverished government had to borrow money from the city of Cnidos. But finally the two Asiatic rulers, Seleucus and Lysimachus, engaged in a struggle for dominion, and Lysimachus was killed, in 281 B.C., at the age of eighty. Miletus breathed again.

The victor, Seleucus I, was assassinated in 280 B.C. He was succeeded as ruler of Syria by his son Antiochus I, whom the Milesians honoured with the title of President. He spent most of his reign warding off an invasion of Gauls from the north; and it was doubtless in one of these attacks that the Temple at Didyma was sacked and plundered in 277 B.C. so that only a few pieces of the treasure, old and new, remained. In Miletus itself, as is usual in times of danger, a dictator emerged; his name was Timarchus. But his rule was oppressive, and the people longed for a return to freedom. In 269 B.C. an embassy from the Ionian city-states asked King Antiochus to restore democratic government in Miletus; but this he did not live to do. He fell in battle against the Gauls in 261 B.C. and was succeeded by his son Antiochus II, who carried out the Milesian wish.

For this, the Milesians gratefully awarded him the title of *Theos* (God).

.   .   .   .   .

Among all these wars and political manoeuvres, it is pleasant to catch a glimpse of the life of a private citizen of Miletus at the time.

Somewhere about 270 B.C. the poet Theocritus came to Miletus on a visit to his old friend and fellow-student Nicias, now married and carrying on medical practice in the city. They had met twenty years before, on the island of Cos, where Theocritus was studying the art of poetry, and Nicias medicine. The delightful poem in which Theocritus celebrated those carefree days survives:

"*On a deep couch of fragrant leaves we lay,*
And new-cut vine-leaves, blissfully at ease . . .
The scents of summer reigned, the scents of autumn,
Rich with their harvest; pears about our feet,
Apples beside us, rolled in plenty, while
The damsons weighed their branches to the ground.
From the winejar's neck, we broke the four-years' seal . . ."

In the same poem, the poet mentions the names of stream and temple, hill and district, at Miletus, as if he knew them, calling upon:

"*Loves like blushing apples,*
Who dwell near the sweet streams,
And where stands the steep throne of blonde Aphrodite."

The famous poem in which he shows the Cyclops sighing for Galatea was playfully dedicated to Nicias:

"*No medicine exists with power to heal passion,*
Dear Nicias,
No, nor unguent either,

> *No salve,*
> *Save only one—the Muses' gift.*
> *Gentle it is and sweet for mortals,*
> *Yet not easy to find.*
>
> *So I believe,*
> *And so you too know well, I fancy,*
> *Since you are—not just a doctor,*
> *But special favourite of the tuneful Nine."*

So too the poem called *Hylas*, the story of Heracles and his lost friend:

> *"Not for us only was the Love-god born,*
> *Whichever deity owns to his begetting.*
> *We were not first, we short-lived petty mortals,*
> *To find the beauty in a beauteous setting . . ."*

So twenty years later, Theocritus comes to Miletus. He brings with him a distaff carved in ivory, a present for Nicias's wife Theugenis, and with it a poem written on the voyage:

> *"Distaff, come with me to the splendid city founded by Neileus,*
> *Where Aphrodite's holy sanctuary lies green among the soft reeds,*
> *Thither I pray Zeus to grant me a safe voyage,*
> *So that I may feast my eyes on my dear friend Nicias,*
> *And clasp him to my heart,*
> *That blest scion of the Graces who charm with their song,*
> *And so that I may give you, my gift so carefully-wrought of ivory,*
> *Into the hands of Nicias's wife,*
> *To help her to make much wool for garments:*
> *Cloaks for the men,*
> *And fine flowing robes such as women wear.*
> *The lambs' mothers in the pasture would have to be shorn twice yearly*
> *To satisfy Theugenis with the slender ankles,*
> *So industrious is she,*

So devoted to all the works of the wise.
Never would I have handed you over to a lazy, idle woman . . .

But now, you are to live in the home of a man well-skilled
In the knowledge of such drugs as protect mankind from painful
*   diseases.*
Now you are to live with Ionians,
In lovely Miletus,
So that Theugenis may be distinguished among her neighbours for
*   her fine distaff,*
And you may always remind her of her friend the poet.
Anyone who sees you will say:
'Ah, the gift may be small,
But the affection is great,
And all is precious that comes from a friend.' "

One last glimpse of Nicias the Milesian physician: he possessed a statue of Asclepius, patron of doctors, carved out of fragrant cedar-wood by a skilled artist, and to this he daily offered incense and a prayer.

. . . . .

After the expulsion of the dictator Timarchus, things went well with Miletus under the protection of Antiochus and his successors, and of the Ptolemies.

Treaties were concluded with Cnossus and other Cretan cities forbidding the sale of free Milesians and Cretans as slaves, showing that this traffic existed beforehand, perhaps through the activities of pirates. The famous Milesian sheep were now being exported to Egypt, and the merchant fleet grew. At the end of the third century B.C. Miletus was rich enough to float a state loan for the citizens, at an interest of ten per cent, payable in monthly instalments. Individual citizens amassed wealth; one, named Eudêmus, is recorded as having made an educational endowment of ten talents ($60,000).

During this period, literature also flourished. Miletus had never been productive of writers. During her early period, she had produced in poetry only Phocylides the gnomic poet; and in prose, besides the scientists, only a few obscure writers such as Cadmus, named with Hecataeus as one of the three earliest prose-writers, and a certain Dionysius, who wrote a book on Persia probably used by Herodotus. Now, in her latter period, she again began to produce a school of prose-writers; but this time they wrote fiction, not history or science. The "Milesian story" was erotic, even obscene, rather than romantic. Originating in the third century B.C. it became famous as a genre all over the Greek world, in Roman times. Apuleius and others consciously imitated it; and so it may be said to be the forerunner of the novel.

.   .   .   .   .

After the end of the third century B.C. the influence of Rome in Asia Minor was paramount, though Miletus remained nominally free.

In 188 B.C. the inhabitants of Myous higher up the Gulf were forced by a plague of mosquitoes to leave their city and join with Miletus. The site of Myous remained deserted, the river having surrounded it with an unhealthy swamp and cut it off from the sea. Thus the fate of Miletus itself was foreshadowed; but of this the citizens remained unaware.

Their energies were spent in building. A new and magnificent temple was begun at Didyma; and Miletus itself was endowed by King Antiochus IV (Epiphanes) with the money to build a new Council Chamber. Two fine sports-grounds (gymnasia) were laid out. But nothing could stop the decline of Miletus in importance, as the influence of Rome ever increased; and when in 133 B.C. King Attalus of Pergamum bequeathed his realms to the Romans, Miletus was soon reduced to the status of a small provincial town in Roman Asia. There was still a certain amount of bickering with Priene opposite: one lawsuit refers to the silting up of the Gulf with the mud of the river Maeander.

In the years 84 to 82 B.C. Miletus built ten ships for the

Roman fleet. The rapacious Verres,[1] then in Asia, took one ship away from the Milesians and sold it, as well as robbing them of wool from the state storehouses and grossly insulting the magistrates.

In 77 B.C. Julius Caesar, then a young man of twenty-two, was on his way to Rhodes to complete his education when he was captured by pirates. He was taken to the small island of Pharmacousa, some twelve or thirteen miles off Miletus, and kept a prisoner there. A ransom of twenty talents ($120,000) was demanded; but Caesar told them that they had set his value too low, and made them raise their price to fifty talents ($300,000). During his captivity, Caesar's personality, like that of the Admirable Crichton, gave him the ascendancy over them, to such an extent that he used to send messages telling them to keep quiet when he wished to sleep. He used also to sport with them and take exercise, so that in the end they were not his guard but his body-guard. He wrote poems and speeches, and made use of the pirates as his audience; if they did not appreciate his performance, he would call them savages and threaten to hang them. They enjoyed his frankness, thinking it a joke.

But Caesar was not joking.

The ransom from Rome arrived at Miletus, and thence at the pirates' camp on Pharmacousa. Caesar was set free. He immediately manned vessels from the Milesian harbour (Lion Bay) and set out on a punitive expedition. He caught the pirates still on the island, captured them, confiscated their property, including the ransom, and sent them to Pergamum to be imprisoned. Later, he went in person to Pergamum and saw to it that they were all executed. That was what it meant to take liberties with a noble Roman.

During the wars of Rome with Mithradates—King of Pontus, the territory to the south of the Black Sea—Miletus suffered as usual: the city was occupied, and finally liberated by Pompey in 63 B.C. Pompey was honoured by the Council and people of

[1] See pp. 80–81.

Miletus in a decree; but a Milesian orator named Aeschines was exiled for speaking too freely against him, and the city's freedom was not legally restored by the Romans, apparently through mistrust.

In 54 B.C. the reigning Ptolemy (XII, surnamed Aulêtês), who ruled under Roman protection, sent a present of thirty-four elephants' tusks to Didyma for the adornment of the Temple, as well as some ivory doors. In 38 B.C. Miletus received back its freedom, as a reward for loyalty, from the Romans, and was allowed its own Assembly and its own laws. An embassy was sent to Rome to plead this cause, and their success is praised in a decree.

Not long afterwards, Strabo the geographer visited Miletus on his way to Rome, and has left a brief account. He speaks of the enormous temple at Didyma, the circumference of the sacred precinct as large as a village, the richly-adorned groves, the oracle and the other holy places within, all expensively equipped with offerings, the products of the ancient crafts. "From here to the city," he says, "is only a short distance by road or by sea," and he mentions the four harbours, one large enough to accommodate a fleet, the small islands (still infested with pirates), the Latmian Gulf, with Mount Latmos at the eastern end, where the traveller was shown Endymion's cave; the site of Myous, now deserted; the city of Priene opposite, and to the north Cape Mycale, well-wooded and stocked with animals. He does not mention the precinct of Poseidon, once the scene of the splendid Panionian Festival of the Twelve City-states; all this had vanished under the rule of Rome.

And now, Miletus had acquired the venerable status of an ancient monument in the eyes of the Romans. The Emperors, from Augustus onward, bestowed favours and received the honorary title of President. Under the Emperor Claudius, hot baths and an open-air swimming-pool were built. Under Trajan, there were new roads, and improvements to the theatre that overlooked the middle of the three western bays. The traffic with Athens increased; it seems that the citizens of Miletus were migrating, returning to the mother-city, and were marrying Athenian citizens. Many grave-stones of this period bearing the names of Milesians are to be found in Athens. The mud from the Maeander is piling up rapidly now, robbing Milesians of their means of livelihood, and the mosquitoes and malaria increase as the sea recedes. Yet still Miletus is to travellers the capital of ancient Ionia; the culture-loving Emperor Hadrian, and the Antonines, show generosity towards the dying city. In the reign of the Emperor Commodus (A.D. 180 to 192) the festival of Didyma was still being celebrated, and under the Emperor Alexander Severus, in A.D. 228, Apollo of Didyma was a protégé of the Roman State.

In A.D. 263 when the Goths came, they destroyed the Temple of Artemis at Ephesus; but the citizens of Miletus who took refuge in the temple courtyard were saved from thirst by a miraculously rising spring.

Under Constantine (A.D. 306 to 337) Miletus was Christianized, and Apollo's functions were ended. The Emperor Julian (A.D. 361 to 363) tried to restore the old glories, and even made improvements at Didyma by having some of the outbuildings cleared away from the vicinity of the Temple. He was decreed a complimentary pedestal by "the glorious Metropolis of the Milesian People and Nurse of Apollo of Didyma", and a milestone four miles from the city bears his name. But the end of his brief reign put a stop to this movement for ever. Theodoret, Bishop of Antioch, writing in the first half of the fifth century A.D., triumphantly proclaims that all oracles are silenced, including that at Didyma. Gradually the whole district became a centre of Christianity, and a monastery was built on Mount Latmos.

Earthquakes, the silting up of the whole Latmian Gulf, and the destructive activities or neglect of man, continued their work throughout the centuries. The enormous Temple at Didyma, worthy to be ranked with the wonders of the ancient world, with its double rows of Ionic columns sixty feet high, enclosing an area of 350 feet by 150; with its majestic flights of steps and its entrance, its stairways leading up to the roof and down to the oracular chamber: all this was laid low, reduced to a mass of rubble among which, when the archaeologists came, only one column was still standing. On the site of the city of Miletus itself, the confusion was even more heartrending: the temples of Athena, Aphrodite and Asclepius, and of Delphinian Apollo with its records on stone; High Street and Sacred Gate, Council Chamber and courtyards, stadium and gymnasia, market squares with their storerooms for wine, figs and olives; monuments and fortifying walls, theatre built to seat an audience of 30,000, with entrance-tickets of ivory and bone; buildings of various dates throughout the long centuries from the foundation of the Greek city-state a thousand years before the Christian era, were all mixed up together owing to movements and rebuildings, and the task of sorting out this heap of masonry in the face of every difficulty of situation and climate was carried through with enthusiasm, patience and skill.

Miletus, surrounded by malarial marsh, is still "full of gods".

6. CYRENE

"Sweet garden of Aphrodite."—PINDAR.

IN THE southern Aegean Sea lies a group of three islands, of which the largest, Thêra (the modern Santorin), is still famous for its wines. The group forms the edge of the crater of a huge volcano, which erupted at some time in the second millennium B.C., allowing the sea to pour in; Thera is its eastern edge. The island is now a precipitous, sickle-shaped mass of volcanic rock only three miles across at its widest point; but it is the product of still further eruptions, which have reduced its size, and have caused neighbouring islands to appear and disappear. In ancient times, when Thera was somewhat larger, it offered a home first to the Phoenicians, and then to a colony of Dorians from Sparta and Minyans from Lemnos. The island is completely waterless: all water has to be collected in cisterns.

Thera soon proved too small for its inhabitants. During the seventh century some of them had to emigrate. Under a leader whose name was probably Aristoteles, a band of men set out to seek a new home to the south. They had been advised by the Delphic oracle to look for a site on the hitherto little-known coast of North Africa to the west of Egypt.

At first daunted by the unknown, the emigrants repented of their decision and tried to return; but they were beaten off by the islanders and refused a landing. Then, under the guidance of a Cretan dye-fisher, they set out again southwards, and reached a small island called Platea. From here, still seeking the promised land, they moved to the coast, to a place called Azilis, where they stayed for six years. Then, in 631 b.c., they moved along the coast to their final home, Cyrene.

These are probably the basic facts regarding the foundation of the city-state of Cyrene, "between the sea and the Libyan desert, solitary and remote, the ancient, only colony that Europe led to Africa, a land of wealth and beauty, not without its men of genius and not unknown to fame".[1] The facts were concealed by later legend, as always, under layers of picturesque miracle. The name of the city was actually derived from the local spring called Cyrê; legend made Cyrene a princess who lived in the forests near Mount Pelion and was a huntress beloved of Artemis. Apollo saw her fighting a lion without weapons, and fell in love with her. He took her to Libya, and united with her; she became the queen of the country, and bore a son named Aristaeus, an agricultural and pastoral deity. Local legend said that Cyrene killed her lion in Libya, where the King had offered his kingdom to anyone who would rid him of the destructive beast. At any rate, the immigrant Dorians made Cyrene their patron-goddess along with Apollo, whose cult they had brought with them from Sparta and Thera under his title Carneios, and to whom their chief worship was always consecrated.

The site was well-chosen: "from its position, formation, climate and soil," says one modern writer, "the region is perhaps one of the most delightful on the surface of the globe." The whole district was a vast garden of fruitfulness and natural beauty, endowed with a fresh, cool climate. Heavy summer

[1] Farley Brewer Goddard (1884).

dews and winter showers supplied numberless springs and brooks, and the deep soil provided not only abundant crops but excellent pasturage. For the new city, the colonists chose a site ten miles inland, on a tableland bounded on the south by ravines leading to the upper plateau, and on the north by the edge of a great scarp two thousand feet above sea level. "Here, on the saddle between hills, with a full view over the blue Mediterranean . . . lie the scattered ruins of 'golden-throned' Cyrene." [1] Between the two limestone hills, whose dazzling whiteness made the poets liken them to a woman's breasts, a carriage-road wound, so that the city lay athwart and controlled the route between the luxuriant hinterland and the sea. No wonder that Cyrene and its surroundings, "by the favours of nature and by the enterprise and genius of its inhabitants, became a little cosmos of well-rounded prosperity".[2]

When the settlers from Thera arrived, they found the country near by already occupied. There were other immigrants, perhaps from Troy, on a hill between Cyrene and the sea. There were perhaps even earlier settlers from Greece—Thessaly and the pre-Dorian Peloponnese. There were also the Libyans, a fair-haired people originally from the Caucasus-region, with whom the newcomers soon intermarried.

The two limestone hills lay to the south-west and north-east of each other. The north-easterly hill, which was nearer the sea, was bare; the south-westerly one was covered with myrtles. The newcomers named it Hill of Myrtles, and myrtles are still to be seen there. From this rock issued the spring Cyre, which they dedicated to Apollo who had guided them thither, and gave into the charge of his priests; its water still flows abundantly. Here they began to build. Here, they decided, the union of Apollo with Cyrene had taken place; here perhaps she killed the lion and won her kingdom. Here, at any rate, they built the dwelling for their leader Aristoteles, who now became their first king; and on the north side they laid out a

[1] Herbert Weld-Blundell, *A Visit to Cyrene* (1895).
[2] Farley Brewer Goddard.

precinct of Apollo and erected his temple, making a highway along which all important traffic passed, including the annual procession to Apollo's shrine. The Hill of Myrtles from the first had great sanctity; it was the real acropolis of Cyrene. But the colonists soon began to build on the north-easterly hill also, and it was here that the main city grew into being; this hill had two temples, one to Artemis, who as Apollo's sister and Cyrene's friend was greatly honoured, and a smaller one to Isis, who was worshipped at Cyrene from early times. Cyrene from first to last was to feel the powerful influence of Egypt.

The leader Aristoteles, who became their first king, was given the title of Battus, and was the founder of a dynasty of kings called Battus and Arcesilas alternately. "Battus" is probably merely the Greek form of the Libyan word for "king", but the word suggested to the Greek ear "stammerer", and so gave rise to the story that Battus, before the new colony set out from Thera, had visited Delphi to ask the god how to cure his defect of speech; the god, instead of a recipe, commanded him to found a city in Libya, and when he did not at once obey, visited Thera with a seven years' drought. Battus was finally cured of his stammer (the story continued) when he reached Cyrene, and saw a lion: fright caused him to cry aloud, after which his stammer was cured. Other story-tellers, thinking this conduct unworthy of a hero, made the lion flee from Battus.

The dynasty founded by Battus I lasted for nearly two centuries, until the middle of the fifth century B.C., when monarchy almost everywhere throughout the Greek world had been superseded by oligarchy or democracy. Battus I was considered a good and mild ruler; nothing is known of him except his arrival from Thera. He was honoured in Cyrene as a hero; after his death he was buried in a tomb apart, at the farther end of the market-place, whereas his successors were buried in front of the royal palace. His son, Arcesilas I, who

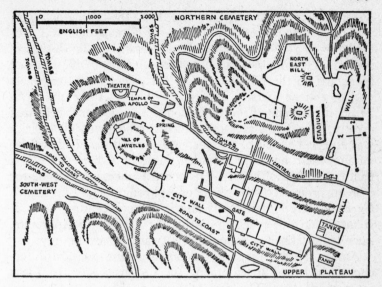

succeeded him, left no record behind, though he reigned for sixteen years.

The third of the line, Battus II, was nicknamed "the Fortunate". By now, Cyrene's potential prosperity demanded new workers. The help of the Delphic oracle was invoked to invite new citizens from all Greece to the country. They came in swarms, especially from the Peloponnese; and they began to rob the Libyans of their land. The Libyan king called on Apries, the Pharaoh of Egypt, for help; but the Egyptian army was heavily defeated by the Cyrenaeans, and Apries was deposed. The Egyptians believed that Apries had deliberately sent them to their destruction in order to weaken them and rule them more securely; and when Apries sent his officer Amâsis to reason with them, they went over to Amasis and easily persuaded him to accept the throne of Egypt. Amasis ruled jointly with Apries for six years; then he had Apries put to death, and himself entered upon a long and brilliant reign.

The advent of Amasis (Aahmes II) to the throne of Egypt was the greatest good fortune for the Greeks. He was pro-Hellenic to the extent of alienating many of his Egyptian subjects. He employed a bodyguard of Ionians. He restored Naucratis on the Nile Delta as a settlement for Greek merchants; and he married Ladicê, a noblewoman of the royal house of Cyrene. From this connection Cyrene benefited greatly; Herodotus says that Amasis, who loved all Greeks, was especially fond of Cyrene, and showed his good will by sending them not only a golden statue of Athene but also a painted portrait of himself. His queen Ladice, in gratitude for a favour granted, had a statue of Aphrodite made and sent to Cyrene; Herodotus himself saw it there a century later. It seems to have been set up outside the Temple of Aphrodite, since he speaks of it as looking outwards from the city.

Amasis, Herodotus says, composed certain political differences which had arisen among the Cyrenaeans, and made a treaty with them. This was doubtless at the beginning of his reign, when Battus II, "the Fortunate", was still king of Cyrene. But after Battus II died in 560 B.C. and was succeeded by his son Arcesilas II, nicknamed "the Harsh", internal troubles at Cyrene grew too acute for any outside intervention to be of much avail. Arcesilas's brothers quarrelled with him, and having left Cyrene, founded a new city called Barca. The Cyrenaeans attempted to conquer Barca but were defeated, losing 7,000 men, by an army of Barcans and Libyans. Soon afterwards the King was murdered by his brother Learchus; but his death was avenged by his widow Eryxo, who murdered Learchus and preserved the life of the son and heir; he then became king as Battus III, surnamed "the Lame".

The monarchy was greatly weakened by these events. Battus III, whether because of youth or physical deformity, was not strong enough to restore order; and the Cyrenaeans sent to the Peloponnese for an arbitrator called Dêmônax, giving him power to revise their constitution. Demonax divided the people into Tribes, according to nationality, a provision which when compared with the work of Solon and Cleisthenes at Athens seems unwise, as being designed to foster disunity. One Tribe comprised the Therans and the incorporated Libyans; another the Peloponnesians and Cretans; and a third, all other islanders. The royal powers were greatly curtailed; Battus kept certain estates and priestly duties, but his other functions were taken over by the people.

The reign of his successor, Arcesilas III, was stormy, occupied as it was with a struggle to overthrow the reformed constitution and regain absolute power. At first he failed and was obliged to flee; but he had a determined supporter in his mother Pheretîmê. Between them, these two collected an army from the islands of Samos and Cyprus, and returned to avenge themselves on their democratic opponents. In 525 B.C., when King Cambyses of Persia conquered Egypt, Arcesilas of Cyrene sent gifts and acknowledged Persian supremacy, as did the people of Barca and the Libyans. Cambyses accepted the Libyan gifts, but he despised those of Cyrene as being too small (they sent only five talents, about $30,000), and to show his contempt, distributed the money himself in handfuls to his army.

Cyrene was now for a time a tributary to Persia, and under King Dareius was actually reckoned, for purposes of assessment, along with its colony Barca, as part of Egypt, the whole huge domain being assessed at 700 talents' income ($4,200,000). But Dareius's son and successor Xerxes was too much preoccupied with his attempt on the Greek mainland to trouble about Africa; and Cyrene on the outskirts of that domain must have recovered virtual independence. At any rate, throughout the rule of Cambyses, Dareius and Xerxes, internal trouble at Cyrene continued.

At first the Persians were called upon to intervene when danger threatened the Cyrenaean monarchy. King Arcesilas III, who had submitted to Cambyses, was assassinated while on a visit to his father-in-law at Barca; and for this his mother Pheretime was able to take cruel vengeance on the people of Barca with Persian aid.

The murdered king was succeeded by his son Battus IV, "the Fair", of whom nothing is known except the name. Then comes the last of the line, the eighth king of Cyrene, Arcesilas IV, son of the preceding king.

According to Herodotus, an oracle at Delphi had prophesied that four kings called Battus and four called Arcesilas would rule in Cyrene. By now the city was immensely wealthy, owing to its splendid position on the trade-route from inside Africa; and the luxuriance of its own harvests drew from Pindar admiring epithets such as "fruitful", "most fruitful", "all-fruitful", "wheat-bearing". Cyrene's native poet called the city "deep-soiled", and other writers describe Libya as "lovely" and "fair-harvested". Herodotus gives a more accurate idea of Cyrene's fertility: the harvest-season lasted three months, and the most productive regions yielded a hundred-fold. Trees, especially the olive and the cypress, flourished exceedingly; but the most important of all the cultivated plants was *silphium*, a sort of asafoetida, said to be like the *hing* of modern India. Its juice was used as a medicine and as a flavouring essence; and its export was the main source of Cyrene's wealth. In the time of the monarchy it seems to have been a royal monopoly: a well-known Laconian cup now in Paris shows King Arcesilas II ("the Harsh") superintending the loading of bales, probably of silphium, on to a ship. The plant became the symbol of the city-state, and one of the main types on its coins, which were issued in abundance during the sixth, fifth and fourth centuries B.C. The plant as a whole, its stalk, its seeds and its leaves are all depicted by the die-maker's exquisite art. In later times silphium became extinct, owing to the great demand for it and also the wilful depredations of invaders.

Wine, honey, roses and saffron: Cyrene was a garden indeed. The surrounding tableland gave rich pasturage for cattle, goats, sheep, and above all, horses. Cyrene was famous for

horse-breeding, and in the making and manipulation of war-
and racing-chariots. One of Medea's prophecies was said to
have been that Battus should build on a gleaming hill a city of
noble chariots, whose citizens "instead of the short-finned
dolphins should take to themselves swift horses, and instead of
oars, should ply the reins and the chariots swift as the breeze".[1]
And in 462 B.C., the prophecy found its consummation in the
victory of Arcesilas IV's chariot at the Pythian Games, a
victory for which Pindar wrote the longest of his Odes, to be
sung at a banquet in Cyrene, as well as a shorter Ode to greet
the return of the victorious charioteer, who was the Queen
of Cyrene's brother.

In Pindar's victory Odes, through the praise of Cyrene and
its founder, its present riches and the power of its ruler, there
are, however, distinct warnings of trouble and danger. "In
spite of chequered fortune," the poet writes, "there *still* exists
the olden prosperity of Battus", and "in very truth, even
now in the latter days as in the prime of rosy spring, eighth
in the line of those descendants blooms Arcesilas". He pleads
for the return from exile of one Dêmophilus; and in his plea
there is, as often in Pindar's addresses to kings, a note of
admonition:

> *"Even for the feeble,*
> *It is easy to shake a city to its foundations,*
> *But it is a hard struggle to raise it again*
> *Unless God becomes a guide to its rulers.*
>
> *For you, the web of these fair fortunes*
> *Is now being woven out towards its end.*
> *Deign to bestow on happy Cyrene all earnest heed."*

Two years later, Arcesilas won the coveted victory in the
chariot-race at Olympia; but soon afterwards a democratic
rising in Cyrene deposed him. He fled, and was assassinated.
With him, the long dynasty came to an end. It was about this

[1] Fourth Pythian Ode, trs. Sandys.

time or shortly earlier (in 454 B.C.) that a number of Athenian soldiers, refugees from the unsuccessful expedition against Egypt, reached Cyrene after six years of warfare in which most of their comrades had perished; and it may be that their arrival precipitated the anti-monarchical revolution.

When the Peloponnesian War broke out in 431 B.C. Cyrene naturally took the side of Sparta, from which her people sprang. In 413 B.C. she helped some Spartan ships driven into her harbour by contrary winds, and sent two galleys with them against the Athenians at Syracuse. But her remoteness from the scenes of action spared her any real part in the conflict, and left her completely untouched by it. She continued to prosper, to grow crops and breed horses, and to preoccupy herself with internal party struggles.

After the fall of the monarchy, power seems to have been divided among the rich; but half a century later, in 401 B.C., there was a successful democratic revolution against a government which had attempted a too strict control of the working people. This government repression was due to fear of the working class, which now outnumbered the upper and middle classes; in this revolution, five hundred of the rich were put to death and others fled. The democratic party now proceeded to consolidate their strength by constitutional changes. Imitating the measures of Cleisthenes at Athens a century before, they created new Tribes and clan-groups, outnumbering the old ones, and they broke up the old associations, mixing the people up together as far as possible and substituting a small number of religious festivals common to all citizens for the many celebrations of family and tribal rites. Thus the arrangement into national groups within the state, which had been made by Demonax under Battus III, was abolished, and a final effort was made to establish a genuine unity under popular government.

Apart from these events, nothing is known about the history of Cyrene between the fall of the monarchy and the coming of Alexander the Great, about a hundred and twenty years.

By now Cyrene, with its port Apollonia, was the centre of a flourishing district, with several colonies of its own in the neighbourhood: Barca, the earliest of these, almost as strong as the mother-city and often her opponent; Hesperis, founded by Arcesilas IV, the legendary site of the Garden of the Hesperides, and later to be named Berenice (modern Benghazi) after the wife of Ptolemy III; and Tauchira (Tokrah), later called Arsinoê; these, with the later Ptolemais, the port of Barca, destined to eclipse it in importance, were to form the group known as the Pentapolis. But during the fifth and fourth centuries B.C. Cyrene remained the undoubted leader and queen of the land.

By this time, the two limestone hills with their temples, palaces and dwelling-houses, and the royal road running between them, are the centre of a teeming civic and commercial life. The chief religious festival of the year remains the annual procession to Apollo's temple on Myrtle Hill, where Apollo's spring still flows abundantly. Here at a certain solemn moment, the god visits his shrine. The laurel-branches tremble, the shrine itself vibrates, a knocking is heard on the door; the palm-tree brought from the sacred island of Delos waves pleasantly of a sudden, and the swan flying above sings sweetly. Apollo comes! The bolts and bars yield before him, and the young men prepare for the song and the dance . . . All hope to see the god with their own eyes; but he appears not to all, only to the good. He who sees him is exalted; he who does not is abased. Apollo is the god of archery, of music and divination, of flocks and herds; the leader of migrations, the hunter of wolves, with his sister Artemis. His promise is ever sure. Did he not swear to bring Battus and his people to a promised land, and did he not lead them across Libya to the fertile territory of Cyrene? For this, Battus built him his shrine and instituted a yearly festival, with sacrifice of bulls. As well as the song, Apollo rejoices in the armoured dance of the young warriors, which typifies their dancing with the yellow-haired women of Libya whom they found in the land on their arrival . . .

Besides this great annual festival, thus described by Cyrene's own poet Callimachus, the other gods and goddesses were not neglected: Artemis and Aphrodite, Dionysus, the Dioscuri, Isis and others. Some of the festivals were accompanied with games: there were contests in honour of Olympian Zeus at Cyrene, where in the stadium the splendid racing-steeds trained for the greater contests at Greek Olympia, Delphi and elsewhere; there were also from early times games in honour of Pallas Athene, and of Mother Earth. At all these, women as well as men were present: it seems likely that the women of Cyrene enjoyed a freedom similar to that of their ancestresses at Sparta itself.

Life at Cyrene was easy and pleasant: the soil was so fruitful and the climate so propitious that there was leisure to enjoy life as all Greeks loved to do. But in the midst of this golden existence, the Cyrenaeans did not forget the shortness of life, the imminence of death; nor did they forget the dead. From earliest times, when Battus I was buried on the edge of the market-place, they built tombs which were like houses. The oldest were situated along the original road, the Sacred Way of Battus I, as it winds round the eastern hill towards Apollonia; these were cut into the rock along the face of the escarpment. The earliest and largest, near the town, faced the Spring of Apollo. Gradually as the nearer positions were taken the whole face of the cliff for more than a mile eastwards from the Spring was honeycombed with thousands of sarcophagi, so thickly crammed together (as one visitor [1] says) that in some places they give the effect of a mountain of tombs piled on top of one another. In one group, very early, there are Doric columns at the entrance; but as a rule the cavities are hewn in the hard limestone. Further away, on the plain to the south, are a different kind: open courtyards excavated from above, surrounded by a colonnade and entered by a stairway. But the immense and intricate necropolis of the cliff faces below the town remains the chief wonder, with its miles of

[1] Farley Brewer Goddard.

catacombs recalling those of Egypt: the long lines of plastered façades, Doric and Ionic, sometimes painted and engraved, sometimes hewn in the rock or built up with masonry. This (to quote Goddard again) makes a series of terraces with miles of roadway intervening, and huge sepulchres like little temples interspersed, the whole almost clothing the hillside in marble, a veritable City of the Dead. Yet as in Egypt, the presence of the dead did not make for unhappiness; it is no accident that the first philosopher to preach pleasure as the goal of life was Aristippus of Cyrene.

Besides their athletic contests, the Cyrenaeans had also a beautifully-situated theatre, carved in the hillside above the Hill of Myrtles, so that the spectators looked out over the scene to the Mediterranean, across the richly-clad terrace below. The city itself, its temples and its best dwelling-houses, as well as its tombs, were adorned with innumerable works of art: wall-paintings of figures and animals, hunting-scenes and sacred processions, geometrical patterns; sculptures of gods and goddesses, relief-carvings of groups, architectural features coloured, as in Egypt, blue or red. The marble of buildings and statuary in the bright sunshine must have presented a brilliant spectacle; and there were also the carefully-tended groves, nourished by the plentiful rainfall which was preserved in numerous cisterns and reservoirs. Cyrene had no river, but her water-supply was second to none, thanks to the natural springs and the preservation of water both from the clouds and from the springs by artificial means, a process begun by the Greek inhabitants and developed later by the Romans.

.   .   .   .   .

When Alexander the Great, after his victory at Gaza, marched with all his forces into Egypt in 331 B.C., Cyrene had no difficulty in preferring him to the Persians who had for so long been their neighbours as rulers of Egypt. Alexander, on his way to visit the shrine of Zeus Ammon in the desert, was met *en route* by ambassadors from Cyrene bringing garlands and valuable gifts, including three hundred of their famous war-horses, and five of their finest four-horse chariots. Alexander accepted the gifts and made a treaty of friendship and alliance with the city, which, however, he had no time to visit, and so never saw. Nine years later he died in Babylon, and his death began a struggle for power from which the remote position of Cyrene could no longer save her.

At once the city found itself involved. Harpalus, formerly treasurer to Alexander, guilty of embezzlement and treachery, had fled to Crete with money and troops. Here his subordinate Thibron murdered him, took the treasure and the men, and, at the instigation of some Cyrenaean political exiles, set out against Cyrene. Helped by the exiles' knowledge of the district, he captured the port of Apollonia and fought a victorious battle in which the Cyrenaeans from the city lost many killed or taken prisoner. A blockade of the city itself was unsuccessful; but he forced Cyrene to come to terms at the price of a huge indemnity, five hundred silver talents ($3,000,000) and half their war-chariots. He plundered the merchants' property in the harbour warehouses, and let loose his army to pillage the district, hoping thus to stimulate the war-spirit in them; but he quarrelled with one of his Cretan officers, who deserted to the Cyrenaeans and persuaded them to break their treaty with Thibron when they had paid only sixty talents ($360,000) out of the total indemnity. Thibron seized eighty Cyrenaeans who were in the harbour, and also attacked the city, but in vain, although he had persuaded the neighbouring cities, Barca and Hesperis, to join him. The Cyrenaeans, in whom prosperity had never destroyed the martial Dorian spirit, sent out half their forces against Barca and Hesperis, and when Thibron went to their aid, the remaining Cyrenaeans recaptured the harbour during his absence. By various accidents and desertions, Thibron lost his fleet also; but he obtained reinforcements from the Peloponnese and fought on, winning another battle.

Meanwhile in Cyrene the continuing political unrest resulted in a victory for the democrats. The opposing leaders fled to Ptolemy, now ruler of Egypt, and obtained his help. Ptolemy sent an army under his officer Ophellas. The democratic government of Cyrene then made terms with Thibron; but Ophellas defeated and captured him, and thus the whole district with its cities became part of the kingdom of Ptolemy I (Sôtêr).

For nine brief years Cyrene was held down by force. A garrison from Egypt occupied the city, taking over the Hill of Myrtles, which now began to be fortified by a wall. Then there was a revolt. The garrison was besieged on the acropolis, and envoys from Alexandria were murdered. Ptolemy at once sent an army under Agis, and a fleet. The rebels were obliged to surrender. The leaders were sent to Alexandria, the rest of the population were disarmed, and order was restored, in 313 B.C.

    .   .   .   .   .

It was about this time that Cyrene's most famous citizen was born. Callimachus, son of Battus who claimed descent from the founder, was sent to Athens for his education, and returning to Africa, taught for a while at Alexandria. He soon attracted the notice of the reigning Ptolemy, the second of that name (surnamed Philadelphus), and may have become the head of the newly-founded library at Alexandria, though this is not certain. He is said to have written over eight hundred works in verse and prose. He was famous for his immense learning, his polished style, and his dislike of epic poetry: he preferred the short epigram, though he wrote hymns to the gods as well, including the rapturous Hymn to Apollo which describes the coming of the god to his temple on the festival day. He had several pupils who also won renown, including a fellow-citizen named Eratosthenes who specialised in mathematics, astronomy and geography, and Apollonius of Alexandria—with whom he quarrelled so bitterly over the question of epic as opposed to epigrammatic poetry that Apollonius was forced to retire to

Rhodes, and was afterwards known as "Apollonius of Rhodes"
—author of a long poem on the exploits of Jason and the
Argonauts. Callimachus's famous dictum, "A big book is a
big bore," was directed at his pupil with devastating effect. We
possess some of the work of both these poets, and can therefore, if we wish, take sides in the quarrel over the long and
the short in poetry.

Cyrene, unlike Corinth, was in spite of her wealth and
business enterprise always a home of study and thought. At a
very early date, in the latter half of the sixth century B.C., her
school of scientific medicine was considered second only to
that of Croton under Pythagoras, which then came first. In
the late fifth century B.C. Aristippus of Cyrene journeyed to
Athens, attracted by the fame of Socrates, with whom he remained until shortly before Socrates' death in 399 B.C. After
various travels, Aristippus finally returned to Cyrene, there to
found a new school of philosophy, the original hedonism. His
principal study was concerned with sensation. He taught that
the pleasant was by nature equivalent to the good, and the
painful to the bad; we should therefore seek the pleasant and
avoid the painful, but it is necessary to know which pleasures
were followed by pain, and therefore to use both judgment
and self-control. His system was further developed by his
pupils, chief among whom was his daughter Arêtê, who inherited the headship of the school, and who educated her son in its
doctrines. These doctrines were developed and modified by
a later Cyrenaean philosopher named Anniceris, who flourished
at the end of the fourth century; and they were eventually
merged into the more elaborate system of the Epicureans. Last
in the line of famous Cyrenaean philosophers is Carneades, who
flourished in the second century B.C. He became the founder
of a new school at Athens known as the Third Academy, and
he was noted for his extreme scepticism: truth, he thought,
was not supplied by either our perceptions or our intellect; he
was also noted for his hostility to the teaching of the Stoics.
He was a gifted orator: when visiting Rome on an embassy

from Athens in 155 B.C. he delivered a series of destructive orations on justice, showing that it was not a virtue but an arrangement necessary for the maintenance of communities. His oratory was so persuasive that Cato demanded his return to Athens in order that he might not demoralise the young men of Rome.

.   .   .   .   .   .

Under the Ptolemies, Cyrene continued to suffer vicissitudes.

Officers sent from Egypt to govern the city seemed to find in its remoteness and self-sufficiency a temptation to independence. First of these was Ophellas, sent to Cyrene after the crushing of the revolt in 313 B.C. This man, an old campaigner with Alexander, and now one of Ptolemy I's most trusted generals, allowed himself to be seduced by messages from Agathocles of Syracuse, who was planning the conquest of Carthage. Ophellas, now that he had control of Cyrene, was ambitious for greater power; so obtaining mercenaries from Athens and elsewhere in Greece, he set out westwards to meet Agathocles. The march proved disastrous. The army was accompanied by women and children; the country between Cyrene and Carthage was a snake-infested desert with wild coast and sea, frequented only by wild beasts and savage tribes—a country of such formidable difficulty that legend peopled it with the basilisk, a fabulous serpent that scorches the earth and pollutes the air so that no bird will fly above it. The mercenary army of Ophellas took two months to reach the rendezvous. There, after pretending to receive him kindly, Agathocles attacked his camp, killed Ophellas himself, and took over his troops.

After this, in 308 B.C., Cyrene was reconquered for Egypt by Magas, a step-son of Ptolemy I.

At first, Magas ruled Cyrene as governor, but when Ptolemy I died in 285 B.C. and was succeeded by his son Ptolemy II (Philadelphus), Magas not only assumed independence but also the title of King, and used Cyrene as a base for an attack on Egypt. The attack was so successful that he was able to make a treaty of peace with Ptolemy, the terms of which were that Magas should continue to be King of Cyrene, and that his daughter Berenice should marry the heir to the Egyptian throne. Magas died in 246 B.C. before his daughter's marriage could take place, and his widow offered Berenice's hand to Demetrius the Fair, son of the Macedonian King Demetrius Poliorcetes,[1] and with it the kingdom of Cyrene, the independence of which from Egypt she was anxious to preserve. But Demetrius not only offended the Cyrenaeans by his haughty behaviour, he also entered upon a *liaison* with his mother-in-law. This was discovered by Berenice; she arranged for the assassination of Demetrius, and he was killed in her mother's arms.

Berenice then fulfilled her original engagement to marry the Egyptian prince, who became king as Ptolemy III (Euergetês) in 246 B.C. Berenice's lock of hair, which she dedicated to Aphrodite for her husband's safe return from a Syrian campaign, was made famous by Callimachus; the poem, which is lost except for a few lines, survives in a translation by Catullus. The hair, which mysteriously disappeared from the temple, was declared by a court astronomer to have been translated to the heavens and made into a constellation; *Coma Berenîcês* is still to be found on our star-maps. But retribution overtook her. Her son Ptolemy IV (Philopator), when he came to the throne in 221 B.C., caused her to be murdered, as well as his uncle and his brother and, towards the end of his reign, his wife also.

At Cyrene, after the departure of Berenice for Egypt, inner conflicts divided the city. The Cyrenaeans had recourse to a device employed by their ancestors: they invited two distinguished practical philosophers named Ecdêmus and Megalophanes to come from Megalopolis in Arcadia and arrange a settlement of the political differences. These two men had gained a reputation as champions of democracy by ridding their native city-state of a tyranny, and helping Aratus [2] of

[1] See pp. 118, 181.
[2] See p. 120.

Sicyon to get rid of the tyrant Nicocles. Ecdemus was trained in Aristotelian philosophy, as was probably his colleague also. They set sail at once for Cyrene and were successful in restoring order and establishing an improved régime.

But the city still attracted the ambitious: in 220 B.C. the exiled King Cleomenes of Sparta tried unsuccessfully to use it as a base for an attack on Ptolemy IV, who had imprisoned him; and after the death of Ptolemy in 205 B.C. the city fell into the hands of yet another adventurer named Philammon, the murderer of Ptolemy IV's wife Arsinoe, and the friend of Agathocles. Philammon in his turn was murdered to avenge his murder of Arsinoe.

From now onwards, as the kingdom of Egypt declines under the appalling misrule of the Ptolemies, Cyrene's history is obscure. The city refused support to Hannibal. Throughout the second century B.C. it became a pawn in the struggle for power between the Ptolemies themselves, sometimes separating from, sometimes reuniting with, Egypt, until at last in 116 B.C. it passed into the hands of Ptolemy Apion, an illegitimate son of Ptolemy VIII (Physcon). He bequeathed the city to the Romans, who for a long time had shown an interest in its affairs. On his death in 96 B.C. the Romans accepted the legacy, granting Cyrene a treaty of freedom and alliance.

But Cyrene was still afflicted by civil strife, including the rise to power of a tyrant Nicostratus; and in 86 B.C. Sulla's young officer Lucullus, sent on a mission from Athens to Egypt and Crete, went on to Cyrene to rescue the city once more from dissension. The Cyrenaeans asked him to legislate for them and unite the people in the framework of some moderate constitution; but their temper was uneasy. Lucullus applied flattery: "You are so prosperous," he said, "that it is hard to legislate for you. As Plato says, no one is so hard to please as the man confident of success; no one is so receptive as the man who has sustained a blow of fate." This softened the temper of the Cyrenaeans towards him as a legislator. Shortly afterwards, Cyrenaica was constituted a Roman province, and then combined with Crete under a Roman propraetor. Cyrene's life as a Greek city-state was at an end.

.   .   .   .   .

"In the Libyan Pentapolis," wrote Ammianus Marcellinus at the end of the fourth century A.D., "is situated Cyrene, an ancient city now deserted." Under the Roman Empire, Cyrene at first lived peacefully and prosperously; but again internecine strife developed, this time between Jews and Gentiles. In Vespasian's reign (A.D. 70 to 79) five thousand Jews were massacred; and before the advent of Hadrian, the passion of the numerous Jewish population for revenge had grown to such proportions that it led to a huge butchery of Gentiles. The number killed was said to be 220,000, and the province was irreparably weakened.

Plagues, earthquakes, and invasion by the surrounding tribes completed a devastation that Rome was no longer strong enough to prevent. Cyrene was reduced to complete ruin and desolation, until as a province under the Eastern Empire it had all but ceased to exist. The desert tribes swept over it, robbing the tombs and temples, destroying the crops, carrying off flocks and herds, men, women and children. A remnant of the Greek population lived on in the other towns of Cyrenaica, drained though these were by continual depredation. Finally these too were wiped out, when the Persian Chosroes II swept over the land in the early seventh century A.D.

For centuries, even the ruins of Cyrene lay neglected and forgotten. The tombs with their pillars and gaily-painted frescoes were used by Arab nomads as shelters for themselves and their animals; the once fertile land, poorly tilled, gave only a meagre yield. Then, at the beginning of the eighteenth century, Lemaire, French Consul at Tripoli, published an account of the ruins: of a splendid town twelve miles in circuit, with a pure and abundant spring pouring continuously from the rock, of reservoirs full of water, of huge marble and granite columns, of the rock-hewn tombs which he thought were shops and houses. Thereafter, a growing number of antiquarian visitors came, made sketches and paintings, collected inscriptions, and drew plans. Vases, terracotta ornaments and finally a large collection of sculptures,[1] were found and taken away, to furnish the museums of Europe. Pleas were addressed to the Ottoman government to allow archaeologists to undertake a systematic excavation of the site before the damage became even greater; but it was not until Cyrenaica was taken from the Turks by Italy in 1911 that this long-cherished hope began to be realized. Ten years later, Gilbert Bagnani, leader of the Italian archaeological expedition to Cyrene, wrote in an English journal: [2]

"On the night of the 27th of December 1913, a torrential downpour flooded the platform of the Temple of Apollo and broke down part of the retaining wall at the north-east corner. The next morning the soldiers of the garrison found, still glistening with the element from which she had been born, the beautiful statue of Aphrodite Anadyomene. Under such favourable auspices began the archaeological exploration of Cyrene. . . .

Over a hundred statues from Cyrene are now in the British Museum, many of great merit. The sculpture from Cyrene should be studied as one indissoluble whole; only thus will we be able to understand the artistic activity of this remote Greek colony. The rise, greatness and fall of ancient civilization in Africa is a subject of equal interest to the archaeologist, to the historian and to the philosopher."

To end this tale of vanished greatness, here are two inscriptions in verse taken from marble grave-monuments. The first is on Plauto, a girl aged twenty, who died in childbirth:

"Only daughter, born Sicilian, twenty years of age was I
Plauto, twice a mother, fated at the second birth to die.

[1] See *Discoveries at Cyrene*. Smith and Porcher (1861-2). Their finds were presented to the British Museum.
[2] See *The Journal of Hellenic Studies*, Vol. XLI (1921).

Once so skilful, once so busy, spindle, wool and rod are laid
Silent with their silent mistress, her companions in the shade.
Let this tomb preserve her memory, that the world may ever know
Her incomparable virtues, and her sorrowing husband's woe."

The second epitaph is on Dionysius, who died aged ninety-eight:

"Dionysius my name is, Cyrene is my land.
Children I had, and lived to see my children's children stand
Around me in my ripe old age—a hundred years less two.
Death came at last, a peaceful end: no illness e'er I knew.
Sleeping in bed I passed away.
*   Thus virtue had her due."*

7. SERIPHOS

WHAT INDUCED men to settle on rocky, rugged Seriphos? The little island lies some sixty miles to the south-south-east of Cape Sunium, the southernmost tip of Attica; it is, in fact, like its neighbouring islands Ceos and Cythnos to the north-west, Siphnos to the south-east, a continuation of the Attic mountain range. Its small area is almost filled with a mountainous mass divided into two groups, the highest peak of which rises 1,500 feet. Between the heights are deeply-cut narrow valleys, making communication difficult. The only stream is a mere winter torrent, and its name (Harmyropotamós, Brackish River) betrays the character of its water. There are two springs; but these are insufficient for the needs of the population, and to this day the chief water-supply is rain-water collected and stored in tanks.

The first Greek settlers seem to have been refugees from Thessaly; they exchanged the only rich plain-land in Greece

213

for a mere rock in the sea. But later the island was colonized from Athens by Ionians. These too may have been refugees, part of the movement from Attica oversea during the troubled times of the Dorian invasion; but if they came in order to escape, they stayed because they found on the forbidding little island a source of wealth: not silver, as on Siphnos, nor marble as on Paros, but iron.

Legend tells one story, and one only, of Seriphos; but this story makes the island part of a famous myth, dear to the Greeks: that of Perseus the Gorgon-slayer. Perseus was one of their favourite heroes, surpassed only by Heracles and Jason; and he was especially worshipped on Seriphos. He was the son of Danaê, whose father, the King of Argos, shut her up in a brazen tower to keep men away from her, because an oracle had declared that she would bear a son who would destroy his grandfather. Danae in her tower was visited by Zeus in a shower of gold; and she conceived and bore a son—Perseus.

The King of Argos ordered mother and baby to be placed in a chest and thrown into the sea; but Zeus guided the chest across the water, and by his will it touched land on Seriphos. Seriphos was famous in later times for shipwrecks; but this precarious craft was rescued from the sea by a fisherman named Dictys ("Worker-with-the-net") and taken to King Polydectes, who treated Danae and her son kindly, and gave them shelter. When Perseus was growing up, Polydectes, who desired Danae, wanted to get rid of him; so he sent him on a dangerous quest, to bring back the head of Medusa, one of the three Gorgons, whose look turned men to stone. Perseus succeeded. He brought back the dreadful head to Seriphos, and there, finding Danae and Dictys at the mercy of the tyrant, he turned king and people to stone.

There were other versions of this story, current in Athens and Argos. In all three places there were shrines and sacred precincts in honour of Perseus; at Athens, in the Propylaeum on the Acropolis, there was a painting of Perseus arriving at Seriphos, bringing the Gorgon's head to Polydectes. There was also a story that the invention of flute-playing arose in imitation of the cries of the serpents which writhed round the head of Euryalê, Medusa's sister, as she lamented her sister's slaughter: "the many-headed tune" was called after her. The Seriphians themselves were proud of the story; they evidently regarded Perseus as their liberator from a tyrant and his supporters, and used him as one of the types on their coins. But later visitors treated the tale as a joke against the island, saying that evidently the Gorgon's head had turned the whole place into stone.

Seriphos, as it had only one legend, had also one moment of glory in historical times. The Seriphians shared with their neighbours, Siphnos and Melos, the distinction of being the only islanders to refuse tokens of submission to the envoys of Xerxes when he was planning his attack on Greece in 480 B.C. They also did their best in the ensuing sea-struggle. The other combatants sent triremes, large war-galleys with three banks of oars, to fight at Salamis. Seriphos, like Siphnos, could manage to send only a penteconter, a single-banked fifty-oared vessel.

At this time, the Seriphians must have been comparatively prosperous. At first, as members of the new naval league led by Athens against Persia, they were assessed at a yearly subscription of two talents ($12,000); but later this was reduced by half. The prosperity, while it lasted, must have been due entirely to the mining-industry. The discovery of iron in an easily-workable form had led to great activity in the south of the island, where diggings had been started all over the mountain slopes; and a silver coinage bearing a frog or toad had been issued. Seriphos in those days was free, and no doubt, like her wealthier neighbour Siphnos, which had silver-mines, divided the profits of the mines among her own citizens.

But after the Persian Wars, Seriphos, like the rest of the Cyclades, became a part of the Athenian League, and then the least of her subject-islands. From now onward her poverty increased. Why? The island was always rocky and barren,

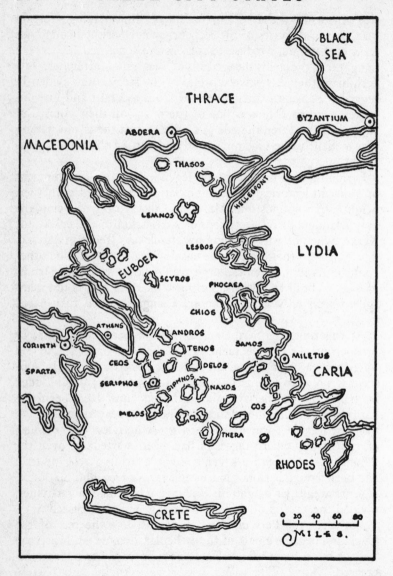

scarcely able to maintain her small population; and the supply of iron did not give out. It was mined all through the Middle Ages, and in modern times as late as 1942, when it ceased because of the Second World War. The cause of Seriphos's poverty can only have been that her population found the work too hard, and emigrated to more promising lands.

To the Athenians, their smallest ally was always something of a joke. Themistocles once was scoffed at by a Seriphian who said that he owed his fame not to himself but to his city-state. Themistocles replied: "I grant you I should not have become famous if I had been a Seriphian; neither would you if you had been an Athenian." That was the Athenian story; the Seriphians had a different version. An Athenian once treated a Seriphian with contempt because of his country's insignificance; the Seriphian replied: "My country may bring contempt on me; you bring contempt on your country."

But on the whole, the Seriphian version was no match for the pitying scorn of their mighty protectress. The Seriphian way of life was a joke because of its hardness: Aristophanes nicknamed Sparta "Seriphos" because of its austerity. Another comic poet, Cratinus, wrote a whole comedy called *The Men of Seriphos*, in which he burlesqued the exploits of Perseus with the Gorgon's head, and no doubt caricatured the islanders. An "old woman of Seriphos" was the common expression for an old maid, that is, a woman as dry and barren as the island. "Seriphian frog" was a proverb used of the inarticulate: on Seriphos, the wags said, even the frogs were dumb. In later times, savants argued about the dumbness of the Seriphian frogs: some said that this was due to the coldness of the water, and that if they were removed and placed elsewhere, they croaked just like other frogs. Modern scholars have suggested that the frogs were not frogs at all, but toads; the coinage which is thought to come from Seriphos shows a toad. Others imagine that the "Seriphian frog" was the coin itself, which "talked" without words, like all coins. The Greeks liked to call their coins after the animal used as a type, as for instance the

Athenian "owls," the Corinthian "foals", and the Aeginetan "tortoises."

By the latter half of the fifth century, Seriphos had become "the poorest of the Athenian islands." Aristophanes in his *Men of Acharnae*, produced during the Peloponnesian War, satirizes the absurdly small incidents which have led to the outbreak of war between Athens and Sparta. He makes his hero say that the Spartans have their grievances as well as the Athenians; and enumerating a number of these, he argues:

> *"What could Sparta do?*
> *If a Seriphian pup had been imported*
> *To Sparta, and then seized as contraband,*
> *Would you have sat down quietly? Not you!"* [1]

In other words, Athens was ready to take offence at anything, however trivial—even an insult to Seriphos.

The vegetation corresponded with the barrenness of the soil. The only product peculiar to the island was a species of wormwood, a wild semi-shrub called *Seriphion*, known to medical writers; and there was also a dry grass called *serphos*. The only living creatures mentioned, apart from the frogs, are an ant, winged at mating-time, called *serphos*, and a kind of grasshopper which was considered ill-omened. There was also a sea-crab, regarded as sacred to Perseus and Zeus, which if caught, had to be put back into the sea, and if found dead, had to be buried.

During the fourth century B.C. the poverty of Seriphos increased. Under the new Athenian Confederacy, the island paid 1,600 drachmas' ($1,600) subscription. We learn from a speech concerning a legacy that a native of Siphnos thought it necessary to apologise for having taken as his wife a woman of Seriphos, "from a family of much higher standing than one would expect from their nationality." In the third century B.C. an inscription reveals that Seriphos through some unspecified

[1] Gilbert Norwood's translation.

disaster lost its best and most outstanding citizens; and one hears of Seriphians working on other islands, for instance on Delos, so that evidently the struggle for existence was going against them.

Almost nothing is known of them from then onward until in 84 B.C. they came under Roman rule as part of the province of Asia. But even the Romans could do nothing for Seriphos; and it was chosen in Imperial times as the Roman St. Helena —a place of banishment. Presumably it was for the exiles and their warders that a certain amount of building was done in the reign of Augustus: a bath, a covered walk, a public square. Here came a certain Vistilia, a Roman woman banished for flagrant immorality; and one Cassius Severus, who having been exiled to Crete under Augustus, and having engaged in further intrigues under Tiberius, was more severely punished, with confiscation of property and loss of civil rights, and who "grew old on the rock Seriphos."

Yet the island remained inhabited.

Christianity reached it in the first quarter of the fourth century A.D. In the Middle Ages, the Venetians occupied it and built a fortress on one of the heights. In the seventeenth century, Italian navigators in the Aegean reported that their compass-needle swung away from the north as they passed Seriphos, owing to the presence of iron. The working of iron went on, over the ancient diggings, and continued into modern times. Seriphos could still, before the Second World War, maintain a population of about 4,000 inhabitants, now reduced to half that number. They live for the most part in the white town near the summit of the hill where the ancient city stood, overlooking the blue Aegean. Its people are still fishermen, miners and cultivators working ceaselessly to wring the necessaries of life out of the dry soil. But they have one blessing: the island, owing to the rarity of accumulations of stagnant water, is almost free from malaria.

The story of Seriphos, meagre as it is, is as much a part of the history of Hellas as that of "shining Athens" from which it sprang; and the character developed by its inhabitants well shows the working of environment on heredity. It must have been hard for the Athenians to believe that these dour miners belonged originally to their own volatile Ionian stock. No wonder they thought that Perseus with his Gorgon's head had turned the people as well as the island into stone!

Perhaps there could be no more fitting end to a story which begins with the rescue of Danae and Perseus from the sea than this Lament taken from the Greek Anthology:

"Perish the day and the fatal moonless night,
And the dread roaring of the wind-lashed sea,
That wrecked the ship on which this voyager,
Sweet soul, prayed to the gods so fruitlessly.

A breaker hurled him on Seriphos's rocks.
Fire [1] *was vouchsafed him by his country's friend.* [2]
And so, wrapped in a brazen urn, he came
Home to Abdera and his journey's end."

[1] That is, for cremation.

[2] Every Greek city-state had its "friends" (*Proxenoi*) in other city-states. A Proxenos was a native of the city-state he inhabited, who undertook to look after visitors from another city-state. For instance, there were in Athens Athenians who were recognised as Proxenoi of Sparta. Here, the Seriphian Proxenos of Abdera would see to the burial rites of a shipwrecked Abderite.

8. ABDERA

THE CITY-STATE of Abdêra, on the northern Aegean sea-board, presents one of the paradoxes of the Greek world. It was proverbial for its heavy, relaxing climate and for the stupidity of its inhabitants, so that in Roman times "Abderite" was synonymous with "blockhead"; yet it produced one of the most remarkable men in the whole galaxy of Greek thinkers: Democritus, who if not the inventor of the atomic theory of matter, was its chief exponent and the founder of a new school of thought, with consequences lasting down to our own day.

Legend attributed the foundation of Abdera to various Greek heroes in the distant past; but it seems likely that the first settlement was Phoenician, since other towns founded by them elsewhere in the Mediterranean bear this or a similar name. The Phoenicians came seeking metal: silver on the mainland, gold on the island of Thasos near by. Later, in the seventh century B.C. other settlers came from Asia Minor. One Timêsius of Clazomenae is said to have brought a colony, but this was destroyed soon afterwards by the Thracian tribes of the interior, who were always a menace to the Greek coastal settlers. One of the early legends tells how Abdêrus, a boy beloved of Heracles, was torn to pieces by the man-eating Thracian horses of Diomêdês; and this embodied the Greek view of their ferocious neighbours.

Over a century later, in 544 B.C., there came from Asia Minor the Greek settlers who were destined to retain their hold on the site. These were the citizens of Teôs, who, realising that their city was about to be captured by the Persian general Harpagus, left in a body, rather than submit to the loss of their freedom. With them was the poet Anacreon; where there is a poet, there usually is a love of freedom. The Teians are honourably mentioned by Herodotus together with the Phocaeans who founded Italian Elea, as being the only communities who took this drastic step. The rest stayed and fought and were overthrown.

The new colonists were enterprising in their desperation. It must have meant a great sacrifice for them to leave their home on the eastern Aegean and travel by sea, men, women and children, two hundred miles northward to an unknown, undeveloped site on the coast of Thrace. Yet the new position had its possibilities: a number of small hills, near the mouth of the river Nestus, on which the town could be built; two small harbours; a plentiful water-supply; and a fertile soil well-suited to the vine. The Greek city of Maroneia, Abdera's nearest neighbour to the east, became famous for its wines. Silver and gold still awaited the prospector; and near by was the large lake Bistonis, which no doubt provided plenty of fish and game.

But the liberty-loving citizens of Teos, in fleeing to Abdera, had not gone far enough. The might of Dareius pursued them, when he embarked on a Thracian campaign in preparation for his attack on Greece, and they had no recourse but to accept his domination when he chose to exercise it. Still, their fate was not as bad as it would have been if they had stayed behind. Dareius could not garrison all the Greek towns of Thrace, and on the whole he was satisfied with payment of tribute and the carrying out of any orders he might give. But as the time drew near for the invasion of Greece Proper, he became more exacting. In 492 B.C., having received information that the island of Thasos was planning "revolt", he sent a message ordering the Thasians to dismantle their fortifications and despatch their ships to Abdera. Thus the Abderites were treated to the remarkable spectacle of the whole of their wealthy neighbours' fleet, built from the proceeds of the gold-mines, sailing into their harbour at the bidding of their common enemy.

Dareius's invasion failed, thwarted by the determination of the Athenians at Marathon; and Dareius died before he could repeat the attempt on a greater scale. But Xerxes inherited the cause of "Remember the Athenians," and his proposed route lay, not across the Aegean straight to the shores of Attica, but over the Hellespont and along the Thracian coast. Many months before his coming, his envoys were despatched to the Greek city-states in that region, bidding them prepare for the reception of his huge army. In all the cities, there were anxious conferences regarding ways and means. Contributions of corn and barley were levied, prime herds of cattle were reared; the citizens were encouraged to raise land- and water-fowl in their homes and in the mines, for the satisfaction of the predatory army. Cups and bowls and all other table-utensils of gold and silver were manufactured for the king and his entourage. Huge bills of costs were submitted by the contractors to the governments of the unfortunate city-states on the route. The expense of entertaining the army even for a single night was ruinous; one contractor's bill for a banquet to Xerxes and his army amounted to four hundred silver talents ($2,400,000), and there was similar expenditure everywhere, so that the inhabitants were often reduced to the direst straits.

However, there was no escape.

When the army at last arrived, a tent had to be ready for Xerxes and his party at each stopping-place, with every luxury provided. The rest of the army slept in the open, but they too had to be waited upon and fed. When these locust-like guests had dined and taken their night's rest, it was their custom to leave next morning taking everything with them. The royal tent was pulled up, the precious vessels were collected, nothing was left behind; and the able-bodied young men were pressed into the army. Abdera suffered heavily. One of their leading citizens expressed the feelings of all the unwilling hosts when after the infliction he advised the Abderites to go in a body to the temples and thank the gods that King Xerxes did not dine twice a day, and also pray to them that he would not do the same on the return journey; for if the Abderites were ordered to prepare lunch as well as dinner, they would have no choice but to fight Xerxes and perish, or, supposing they survived, to live out the rest of their lives in the most miserable poverty.

Xerxes passed on, leaving wretchedness behind him. Accompanying him were not only his officers, but also the Magi, who advised on omens and performed the sacred rites. His baggage-animals drank the lakes dry, even in this watery country. His magicians sacrificed white horses to the river Strymon, and when they came to a place called Nine Ways, they burned alive nine native boys and girls, a Persian custom. Lucky the Greek city-states that Xerxes passed by on his left hand, not having time to stop! His route was preserved intact, not ploughed or sown upon, in Herodotus' day; and the memory of the Magi was also to remain. At Acanthus, where a canal was cut through the peninsula of Athos for Xerxes' ships, he stopped and held a review; and so the huge host marched on, into Greece and towards disaster.

Xerxes's return journey after Salamis was in striking contrast to his triumphal invading march. He fled, leaving his generals behind to fight the final battles at Plataea in the following spring. Rumours about his flight at once began to circulate. Some said that he had deserted the army and taken ship across the Aegean; and the Greeks, who could never resist a picturesque anecdote, told how the ship ran into foul weather and was in danger of sinking. The highborn Persians

in Xerxes's party, in response to the King's appeal, leapt over-
board to relieve the vessel. But (the story continued) when
Xerxes landed, he rewarded the pilot with a golden crown for
saving his life, and then had him beheaded as being responsible
for the deaths of so many Persians.

Herodotus, who records this story, also remarks that he
does not believe it. The most cogent proof that Xerxes returned by land is that he stopped at Abdera on his way home.
In fact, the Abderites said (though Herodotus does not believe
this either) that their city was the first place on his homeward
flight where Xerxes felt safe enough to "undo his belt", that
is, rest. They evidently treated him kindly, in spite of his
previous depredations, for he made a pact of friendship with
them, and bestowed on them a golden sword and a turban
made of gold tissue. Abdera, whatever her private sympathies,
was too near the Persian domain to show hostility to Xerxes
even in his defeat. The Persians had not yet been driven out of
Greece, and they still held the Greek city-states of Asia Minor.

The following year (479 B.C.) the land battle of Plataea
freed Greece Proper, and the sea battle off Cape Mycale
freed Asia Minor, including Abdera's mother-city Teos. Many

Teians then returned to their home. We possess an interesting inscription set up in that city after the return of the exiles. The departure of the Persians had left confusion; an Aisymnetes (an elected magistrate with temporary supreme powers) was appointed, and a Director to inquire into the public finances. Destruction is invoked against any citizen of Teos and his race who disobeys the Chief Magistrate, who betrays the city-state or territory, who acts as pirate or knowingly receives pirates, who plots against the commonwealth of Teos either with Greek or "barbarian" (that is, Persian), who tries to prevent the import of food, who practises "deleterious spells" against commonwealth or individual, or who destroys the pillar on which the curse is inscribed or erases the lettering. We see in this and other similar curses the temper of the Ionian Greeks who had been under Persian domination for over sixty years.

But during this period, in which a second and third generation had had time to grow up, the people of Abdera had become acclimatized to their new home. Now that they were at last free, a period of prosperity began. The colonists from Teos had brought with them, among other arts, that of the coin-maker; and on their arrival at Abdera, they began to strike coins on the same standard as that of Asiatic Greece, with the same device as that of Teos, a seated griffin. As had been their custom in Asia, they appointed an annual magistrate to take charge of the minting; and his device and sometimes his name were included in the field of the coin. They found near at hand an ample supply of silver, and their coins soon became familiar in the district, not only among their Greek neighbours, but also among the inland peoples and the Macedonians further west.

After the liberation from Persia, Abdera's prosperity is indicated by this silver coinage. The city-state during the fifth century B.C. produced one of the most interesting and varied series of coins in history, beginning with the eagle-headed griffin inherited from Teos. It is believed that the annual magistrate who was head of the Mint was also the annual priest of Apollo, who was Abdera's chief deity. Sometimes the god's own cult-statue was employed as device in place of that of the magistrate; in the following century the god's head was invariably used on the reverse. The priest of Apollo was evidently a member of some prominent family: among those whose names appear on the coins are several known to history, for example Nymphodôrus and Python, to be mentioned later, Democritus and his brother Herodotus, Protagoras and Hecataeus. The vicissitudes of Abdera's history, like those of the other Greek city-states, are reflected in the history of her coinage. The period of the silver griffins from 478 to the outbreak of the Peloponnesian War in 431 B.C. was that of her greatest prosperity and greatest achievement, intellectual as well as commercial. In this she resembles Athens whose naval League she joined in 478 B.C. When the Treasury of the League was removed to Delos in 454 B.C. Abdera's contribution to the allied funds was rated at the high figure of over twelve talents (about $72,000). This was raised to fifteen talents ($90,000) in 436 B.C.; but in 425 B.C. after the outbreak of the war, it was reduced to ten talents ($60,000). Her commercial prosperity was due partly to her position so far east, towards the Hellespont; and her coinage was cleverly devised so that its standard fitted that of Asia and that of the local Thracian coins as well. An Abderite coin which was a heavy Graeco-Asiatic four-drachma piece, for example, could also be rated as a Thracian three-drachma piece. Thus trade was facilitated at Abdera between northern Greece and Asia.

.   .   .   .   .

The passage of Xerxes, therefore, in spite of his army's large appetites and predatory habits, did Abdera no permanent material harm. Intellectually, she greatly benefited. Contact with the East always stimulated the Greek mind, which could use the strange products of Babylonian and Egyptian thought for its own rational ends. The common people of Abdera may have been dull and the climate heavy; but there were lively intellects already in the city when Xerxes came, bringing with him a number of sages, or Magi as they were called, to advise the King on his relations with the supernatural: to study omens, and to propitiate the local as well as the Persian deities.

Protagoras, the greatest of the group of teachers later to be called Sophists, cannot have been born much later than 500 B.C. though his work seems to belong to a later period. He was therefore a young man when Xerxes came and went in 480 B.C. and it is said that his father, a wealthy citizen of Abdera, entertained Xerxes on his way through, and obtained from the King the rare privilege of instruction for his son by the Magi. There is not the slightest trace of orientalism in any of Protagoras' known work: he is, in his scepticism and his expository skill, Greek through and through. One may therefore suppose that what is meant by "instruction" was the privilege of hearing a few talks by these men on the occasion of their brief visits. The result, though stimulating, was not enough to convert Protagoras to oriental magic and oriental dogmatism, but tended rather to do the reverse.

Later, he wrote a book on metaphysics, proving that there was no such thing as absolute knowledge. It began with a famous sentence: "Man is the measure of all things, of the things that are, that they are, and of the things that are not, that they are not." He also wrote a book on religion, which began:

> "I cannot know whether the gods do or do not exist, nor what they are like in form, for the hindrances to knowledge are so many: the obscurity of the subject, and the shortness of human life."

At the age of thirty, Protagoras set out on his travels as a professional lecturer on the art of speaking and on all connected with it, his special object being to train young men for public life. In this profession he amassed a huge fortune. His visits to different city-states, in later life when he had become famous, were social events of the greatest importance. At Athens, he was given hospitality by the wealthiest of the citizens, and young men of the best families flocked to hear him and hung on his words. Plato, who disagreed utterly with his opinions, has painted a lively picture of the man, charming, somewhat vain, more skilled at exposition than at argument. Plato also went to considerable trouble to refute his agnosticism. Protagoras died aged nearly seventy, enjoying high repute to the end of his days; and the influence of his views continued long after his death.

Abdera's greatest man, Democritus, was not born until twenty years after the Persian invasion, though his biographers liked to believe that he too had received instruction from the Chaldean Magi of Xerxes, the same story being told of him as of Protagoras. It is very unlikely that any Magi were left behind after Xerxes' flight; the truth probably is that Democritus as a child heard stories of their learning and their marvellous powers.

The Magi held a recognized place in the Persian system. They were descended from the Chaldees of Babylon, and were dedicated for life to the service of the gods, like the Egyptian priests. Their office was hereditary, and their lore was therefore the accumulated observation of many generations. Their studies were directed chiefly to the phenomena of the heavens, with a view to prediction; but they also claimed knowledge of purifications, sacrifices and other magic rites which would avert evil and attract good fortune. They practised augury—divination by means of the flight of birds—and the interpretation of dreams and portents. The Greek scientific thinkers used the lore of the Magi as material for their own entirely rational speculations; but there were some, even among the educated, who found greater satisfaction in the traditional lore of these seers than in the often inconclusive and unsettling speculations of their own philosophers. The Magi were a professional caste, bred and reared in the pursuit of their craft, and trained to display an authoritative and dignified bearing which impressed the layman in a way that ordinary teachers with none of these assets could not hope to do.

One of the miracle-workers who accompanied Xerxes was Ostanês, who was nearly as famous as his predecessor Zoroaster; this man sowed the seeds of the art of magic wherever he went with Xerxes in Greece, and, we are told, induced in the Greeks a rage for this kind of knowledge. The motto of the Magi was:

"Nature delights in nature, nature controls nature, nature conquers nature."

One of their chief claims was the ability to transmute other substances into gold, silver and precious stones. Many handbooks on this ever-popular subject existed, and some of them were attributed to Democritus. The Magi also taught magical recipes for curing disease in men and in animals, madness, and other plagues of nature; some of these were merely absurd, such as the prescription for getting rid of caterpillars:

"Let a woman walk barefoot with her hair down three times round an altar; the caterpillars will then fall off the trees and die."

Other prescriptions were, the ancient writers say, disgusting and wicked, such as curing certain diseases by drinking a potion made of human bones, skin and blood. This was attributed to Ostanes; and Democritus was said to have adopted it from him.

Needless to say, the attribution of such horrors to Democritus was a libel. Nevertheless, one may believe that the recollection of Babylonian lore left behind at Abdera did stimulate his brilliant mind. When he grew old enough, he set out on extensive travels, to Babylonia and Egypt, and some say even further, to India and Ethiopia. He also visited Athens; but unlike that of his fellow-countryman Protagoras, his coming caused no stir. He writes: "I came to Athens, and no one knew me." His object in travelling was not to teach but to acquire knowledge. When he had done so, he returned home to Abdera and settled down there to write a number of books on every subject of interest to scientific and philosophical speculation: the theory of matter, astronomy, mathematics, and other physical sciences; logic, psychology, the theory of knowledge; medicine; the arts of music, poetry and oratory; education, politics and citizenship. He gathered round him a large number of pupils who also wrote treatises, and conveyed his thought to others. His work, through Aristotle, Epicurus and Lucretius, passed on to Athens and Rome, and so to the rest of Europe.

His most famous theory, that matter is atomic in structure, he is said to owe to one Leucippus, his teacher at Abdera, of whom nothing is known. This revolutionary doctrine may perhaps have been suggested by the "magic" doctrine of transmutation of metals, for it means that all material substances, however much they may differ in appearance, are fundamentally of the same composition; and therefore, logically speaking, one may be changed into another. But there is no reason to believe that either Leucippus or Democritus ever laid claim to any magical powers. They were content to offer what they believed to be a true explanation of the material universe. Democritus said:

"I would rather discover one cause than win the kingdom of Persia."

His writings as a whole have not survived; but many sentences and passages quoted by other writers have come down to us. Some of the most interesting are concerned with family and social life, and politics; but one cannot tell whether any of them have any bearing on life in Abdera. Democritus' outlook is so wide that his political advice contains no hint of provincialism; it might have been written from anywhere. But it has a freshness and originality that may have been due to his freedom from Athenian influence; he easily takes his place with the greatest of the Athenians, though in his lifetime they did not recognize him.

.   .   .   .   .

Abdera continued to be prosperous commercially throughout most of the fifth century. She was on friendly terms with her neighbours, and carried on a busy trade with the interior and with Asia Minor. The deity on whom she chiefly relied for protection was Apollo, whose name, together with his cult-statue, sometimes appears on the reverse of the elegant griffin-coinage. The women's religious festival in honour of Demeter, the Thesmophoria, was also celebrated annually for three days. A story is told of Democritus, that when he was very old and felt death near, he decided to hasten the end by starving himself. The moment came when he was about to die; but the women of his family pointed out that the feast of Demeter was about to begin, and that if he died they would not be able to go; to please them, therefore, he prolonged his life by smelling hot bread, or (as some said) honey. This anecdote doubtless was based on some experiments carried out by Democritus on the nature of odours, which he believed to be atomic in structure.

The passion of the Abderites for scientific philosophy is shown by the issue of a silver four-drachma piece bearing a portrait of Pythagoras—the only surviving named portrait of the fifth century B.C. The die-engraver probably copied the head of a statue preserved at Abdera; Pythagoras himself had been dead for half a century.

One of the names of officials on the coinage of Abdera is that of Nymphodorus. In 431 B.C. at the outbreak of the Peloponnesian War, a man of this name comes forward for a moment into the light of history, as the negotiator of a treaty between Athens and the Thracian king Sitalces. The Athenians wanted the help of Sitalces in the reduction of the Thracian towns and of Perdiccas, King of Macedonia. They now controlled Abdera as one of the member-states of the Athenian Empire. They

therefore sent for the Abderite Nymphodorus to Athens and
made him their representative (Proxenos) in the north. He
achieved for them all that they wanted: a treaty with Sitalces,
and also a reconciliation with Perdiccas.

But by now Abdera, like the other subject-allies of Athens,
was beginning to feel oppressed. In 432 B.C. Athens had issued
a decree forbidding her subjects to mint silver coins on any
standard other than the Attic. Abdera was forced to lower
her standard, a measure which did not at all suit her varied
trade-interests. In the middle of the war, the Athenians passed
a still more drastic decree prohibiting the coining of any silver
by her subjects, and so put an end to the famous coinage of
all four Thracian city-states: Abdera, Thasos, Maroneia and
Aenos. The Athenian "owls" were now the sole legal tender
throughout the Empire. There was bitter discontent; and in
411 B.C. when things were going badly with the Athenians the
Thracian cities all revolted and resumed their own issues, returning to their own types and their own weight-standards.
They also struck some small gold coins.

From now on, Abdera, an Ionian city-state, fought on the
side of Sparta against Athens, until the defeat of Athens in
404 B.C.; but she was too far removed from the scene of activity
to play any important rôle. The city was still prosperous, and
its environs were fertile and productive, especially of corn;
but the climate was not altogether healthy. We possess a star-
tlingly vivid testimony to this in the form of a physician's case-
book dating from the late fifth or early fourth century B.C.
The physician, whose name is unknown, was a follower of the
school of Hippocrates of Cos, whose insistence was on exact
observation, with the use of only rational remedies. Hippocrates himself may have visited Abdera; he writes of fre-
quent illnesses, causing mental disturbance, which occurred
there. This pupil of his evidently established himself on the
island of Thasos, twenty miles south-west of Abdera, and as
was then the custom, travelled about Thrace and Thessaly,
practising for periods in the different towns and recording the

interesting cases. Of the sixteen cases in one of his itineraries, six are from Abdera.

The diseases described, so far as they can now be identified, are mostly some form of malaria, mild or malignant. Malaria was the greatest plague of the Greek and indeed of the whole ancient world. With it was associated "melancholia" (black bile), a term which covered any condition, physical or mental, produced by malaria. To read the doctor's case-book, with its names and addresses of his patients in Abdera, gives a vivid sensation of walking about the town. There was one Pericles, who was seized with acute fever, pain, thirst and vomiting, but who recovered after a violent sweat on the fourth day. Anaxion, who lay ill by the Thracian Gate, developed a fever which quickly led to delirium; warm applications gave no relief. On the eighth day, the doctor records, "I bled him in the arm". He recovered after an illness lasting thirty-four days. Heropythus, who lived near the Upper Road, developed a headache, but refused to go to bed; soon, however, he was compelled to do so, because of deafness, delirium, and pain in the lower limbs. His illness lasted four months. Then there was Nicodemus, who brought his illness on by drinking and sexual indulgence; he recovered after twenty-four days. Another patient was Apollonius, who was ill for a long time without taking to his bed; in spite of pain, flatulence and a swollen abdomen, he dined and drank a large quantity of cow's milk, but became feverish and took to his bed. Still he did not adopt a sensible régime, but drank copiously of milk, both goat's and sheep's, and made himself extremely ill. Insomnia was followed by delirium, at first slight, then raging. On the thirty-fourth day he died. Lastly, there was the unnamed girl who lay ill in a house on the Sacred Way, with fever, nausea, shivering, deafness, delirium; she recovered on the twenty-seventh day.

The methods of Hippocrates and his pupils are often written about as if they emphasized mere diagnosis at the expense of treatment; and it is noted that many of the recorded cases ended in death. It is therefore interesting to see that of the six patients at Abdera, five recovered, and the man who died obviously persisted in disregarding the doctor's orders, which covered diet and rest in bed. The primary object of the case-book is clearly to describe cases that interested the doctor; but treatment is referred to—fomentations and bleeding—and the omission of any mention of drugs does not mean that they were not used. The outstanding quality of the book is the writer's complete honesty, impersonal devotion to his art, and freedom from the common superstitions of his time.

.   .   .   .   .

At the end of the war, and when Athens began gradually to recover, Abdera resumed relations with her, under the influence of the democrat Thrasyboulus. There was no longer anything to be feared from that quarter; the Athenian Empire had gone for ever, together with the Athenian mastery of the Aegean. The blow that was to reduce the prosperity of Abdera came from inland: a sudden incursion of a Thracian tribe named Triballoi who were driven southward from their own territory by famine, and who coveted the corn-harvest. The invaders numbered over thirty thousand; they ravaged Abdera's territory without fear, and were retiring in some disorder when the angry citizens sallied forth in full strength and cut down over two thousand. The barbarians, enraged, turned back into the Abderite cornfields. There was a violent battle, during which those Thracians who had joined the Abderites deserted. The Abderites were surrounded, and almost all who fought in this battle were killed.

While Abdera was reeling under this disaster and expecting to be besieged, suddenly help came. The Athenian admiral Chabrias appeared with his forces and rescued them. He drove the barbarians out of the country, and installed an adequate garrison in the city, which the Abderites in their reduced condition were glad to accept. Thus Abdera became a member of the new Athenian Confederacy, founded on a basis of freedom and equality for the members. One tradition absurdly maintains that Chabrias himself was assassinated at Abdera; it is well known that he lived another twenty years, to fall in battle against the Chians in 357 B.C.

But soon a greater enemy to the freedom of the city-states was to appear. Abdera was easily swallowed up by Philip of Macedon in his Thracian campaign of 340 B.C., and became part of the Macedonian Empire. Her famous coinage now comes to an end for ever, and so does her history as an individual state.

.   .   .   .   .

The scientific tradition of Democritus continued. A vast mass of writing was produced, on the lines of research suggested by Democritus, during the fourth century, and cost later scholars much trouble in their efforts to disentangle from it the genuine works of the master. One philosopher, a native of Abdera, was chosen to accompany Alexander the Great on his campaigns; this was Anaxarchus, who preached the Democritean doctrine of serenity as the key to happiness, and who did not believe in absolute knowledge. His views would not have survived if it had not been for his association with Alexander.

Opinions differed regarding his influence on Alexander. Some said that he checked the King's arrogance, others that he pandered to it. He was accused by some of having taught Alexander that a king is above the law, and of encouraging him to expect servility in his subjects. Others said that he mingled sweet with bitter—blame followed by praise. It was Anaxarchus who instructed Alexander on the Democritean theory that there are innumerable worlds; Alexander wept because he had not yet conquered this one. After Alexander's death, Anaxarchus retired to Cyprus, where it was said that he lived in luxury with a beautiful naked girl as a cup-bearer, and a cook who wore sleeves and a mask to prevent his sweat and breath from contaminating the bread he was kneading.

But Anaxarchus was seized by a native ruler and pounded to
death in a mortar, so the story-tellers said, and died bravely,
with the defiant words: "You can crush—not Anaxarchus but
only his husk."

Another well-known citizen of Abdera during the time of
Alexander was named Hecataeus. He had migrated there from
Teos, and like his namesake of Miletus two centuries earlier,
wrote geographical works. His preference was for the marvell-
lous, based on travellers' tales, and he was a romancer rather
than a scientist. A famous work of his dealt with the mythical
country of the Hyperboreans, an island "not smaller than
Sicily" lying in the northern ocean "off the Celtic land", where
the moon is so near that its mountains can be clearly seen. The
people, he said, worship Apollo, who visits the island every
eighteen years, bringing fine weather, playing the harp and
dancing all night long. In contrast to this legend, Hecataeus'
book on Egyptian theology was erudite and factual, and much
used by later writers; for this work he used Egyptian writers.
But Hecataeus with his passion for the marvellous belongs
much more to the tradition of the Magi than to any genuine
school of research.

Abdera was not a city of poets. Her only writer of verse, so
far as we know, was a *ridiculus mus* named Nicaenetus, and
even he seems to have migrated to Samos. He wrote conventional epigrams, several of which were considered by Meleager
worthy to be included in his Anthology, or "garland" as he
calls it. He likens these poems to myrrh; but to us they seem
poor stuff.

·   ·   ·   ·   ·

By the fourth century B.C. Abdera was considered politically
backward. An Athenian orator of the time of Demosthenes,
sneering at the pro-Macedonian party in Athens, says that
they talk as if they were addressing an audience of Abderites,
not Athenians. We know little of what happened at Abdera
during the struggles that followed Alexander's death; presum-

ably she was too weak to do anything but submit to whoever happened to dominate Thrace from time to time. But her attitude mattered too little to be worthy of separate recording by the historians of those days.

A century or more passes; and then we read how the city was betrayed from within to the army of King Eumenes II of Pergamum, who was besieging it on behalf of Rome. It is an odd little story. A certain influential man named Python was then in virtual control of Abdera, having a bodyguard of two hundred slaves and freedmen. Eumenes' officers, finding it impossible to take Abdera by storm, got into touch with Python and persuaded him to admit them. Having thus won the city, they rewarded Python, as might have been expected, with scant gratitude: he had to look on at the destruction of his native city, and he lived out his remaining days in remorse and despair.

Abdera was now incorporated into the Roman Empire, with the rest of Macedonia and Thrace. But the district was unfortunate in having among its early governors several predatory Roman officials. In 170 B.C., for instance, the consul Licinius and the praetor Lucretius treated the Greeks with cruelty and avarice so great that complaints from Abdera and elsewhere reached Rome. The tribunes were constantly attacking the misdemeanours of Lucretius, who absented himself, pretending to be on active service, whereas in fact he was on his country estate, installing a water-supply with the proceeds of the booty captured in Greece; he also adorned a temple of Asclepius with stolen paintings. The envoys from Abdera, unable to obtain satisfaction from Lucretius, transferred their attacks to his equally voracious successor Hortensius. They appeared before the Roman lawcourt in tears; Hortensius, they said, had demanded a large sum of money from their city. They had asked for time in which to appeal to the consul Hostilius and also to Rome. They had hardly reached the consul when they heard the terrible news that Hortensius had sacked Abdera, beheaded the leading citizens, and sold the rest into slavery.

The Roman Senate, to whom this was reported, were gravely displeased. They despatched two representatives to restore freedom to Abdera, and to carry orders to the consul Hostilius and the praetor Hortensius that they were to seek out all who had been sold into slavery and give them back their liberty.

Abdera remained a free city under the Romans. It is referred to as such in Imperial times; but freedom under Roman rule was not the same thing as the independence of the city-state. The greatness of Abdera was over, though her influence survived in the poems of Lucretius, who expounded to the Romans the atomic theory originated by Leucippus and Democritus nearly four centuries earlier.

The people's reputation for stupidity persisted. Juvenal, speaking of Democritus, who by now was known as the Laughing Philosopher, says:

"In those days, even, he found matter for laughter whenever he met his fellows,
"He whose wisdom shows that it is possible for men of the highest quality, destined to give great examples,
"To be born in a land of blockheads and beneath a heavy clime."

Martial's idea of an insult was to say: "You have the soul of the Abderite populace," meaning: "You belong to a race of half-wits." No doubt the malarial climate had much to do with it; nevertheless, Abdera still appears in Byzantine times, and survives into the Middle Ages.

Today, its ruins on Cape Balastra cover seven small hills, extending from an east to a west harbour, a pleasant and secure position. The site had long been lost when it was rediscovered in the nineteenth century. On the northern side, looking away from the sea, a small village had been built, mostly out of the ancient stones.

9. MASSALIA

(*Massilia, Marseille*)

"*Ville antique sans antiquités.*"—MÉRY.

THE MOST westerly of the Greek city-states was destined to become one of the most important, and to survive as a flourishing port into modern times.

Its founders came from Phocaea in Ionian Asia Minor—a distance of some 1,250 miles in a straight line, and of many hundreds more by sea—in about 600 B.C. Their enterprise was rewarded: they found a harbour, with a semi-circular "theatre-like" site facing southwards on which to build a city; and although possession was for a time disputed by the Carthaginians at sea, the prowess and determination which had brought them so many hundreds of miles served to repel their enemies. The colony flourished, and was reinforced by fresh contingents throughout the century; in particular, in 545 B.C., by a large influx of their fellow-countrymen fleeing from the Persian invasion of Ionia.

The contingent which came at the beginning of the century was not the first to explore the western Mediterranean region. A Greek merchant had already sailed through the Straits of Gibraltar some four or five decades earlier, driven by an easterly wind past Gades (Cadiz) to Tartessus. This was a man

from Samos named Colaeus. He returned home with a cargo
of silver from Spain; and the news of his success must have
stimulated others to similar adventures. The city-state of Phocaea, more enterprising than the rest, organized communal
expeditions of exploration, and provided warships as escorts.
These expeditions resulted in the founding of a chain of trade-
ports on the Mediterranean coast: in Italy near Naples, in Sardinia, the Balearic Isles, and Spain. The explorers also sailed
along the south coast of Gaul, and a small group, going ashore
near the mouths of the Rhone, was so much taken with the
charms of the place that they returned home and asked for
reinforcements. The leaders of the second expedition were
called Simus and Prôtis.

When this contingent arrived, the two leaders went inland
to try to obtain the friendship of the native king, whose name
was Nanus. It so happened that Nanus was about to arrange
for the marriage of his daughter Gyptis. It was the custom in
his tribe for the king to hold a banquet for the suitors and
allow his daughter to choose her own husband there and then.
As the Greek visitors happened to come at this time, they too
were invited. In due course, the princess was called in and
presented to the company; and according to custom, she was
told to indicate her choice by serving the favoured suitor with
water. Gyptis passed over all her fellow-countrymen and
handed the water to Protis. Thus the Greek colony started on
good terms with the natives, and was not obliged to waste its
energy in fighting them, but could devote itself to establishing
a firm position on the "Gallic Gulf" (the Gulf of Lions).

The Phocaeans attributed their happy choice of a site to the
guidance of Artemis of Ephesus, whose priestess, a Phocaean
noblewoman, had had divine direction in a dream. On the highest point, the acropolis, of the site, therefore, they built a
temple to the Ephesian Artemis, and another to the Delphinian
Apollo, whose worship was common to all Ionians. They had
brought with them cuttings of olive and vine, which they now
planted, thus introducing the cultivation of these to Gaul. The

soil was too dry and stony for the cultivation of grain in any great quantity, and was very difficult to work; the Greeks therefore employed the tougher native Ligurians, women as well as men, for the hardest toil. In time, Massalian wine came to be valued by those who liked its thickness and rough taste. It was drunk by well-to-do Greeks, but was disliked by those with more refined palates, such as the Romans.

Throughout the sixth century B.C. Massalia continued to expand from a small outpost to a city, and to send out colonists to the east and west along the coasts of Gaul and Spain. Eastwards, she planted Monaco, Nice, Antibes, Hyères (then called Olbia, "Prosperity"); westwards, a number of smaller settlements. She also occupied the Stoichades Islands, off Hyères. Inland, she founded Avignon and Cavaillon. All these posts were fortified, and Massalia itself was surrounded on the landward side by a high wall with turrets. The harbour, then called Lacydon (today Vieuxport), was the best in southern Gaul, completely sheltered from the wind by the surrounding heights, and having an entrance only a hundred yards wide; it was far enough from the Rhone delta to avoid the danger of silting, which was a constant menace to cities built near large rivers, and might mean eventual extinction. The town was built in terraces, on the peninsula north of the harbour; the hill nearest the sea, only about eighty feet high, was chosen as the acropolis and the site of the two temples. The circumference of the old town was probably about a mile and a half, and the population, including the outposts, is reckoned at about 5,000—very small, as Greek city-states go. But the hard work was done, whenever possible, by employing native labour. Massalia was a city of merchant-aristocrats, and remained so throughout its history.

After the influx of colonists in 545 B.C. Massalia became the principal power in the western Mediterranean. Her occupation of the coasts to east and west alarmed the Carthaginians into hostile action, but the energetic Massaliots defeated them at sea in 540, and repelled another attack shortly afterwards.

For these successes they sent a statue of Apollo to Delphi as a thank-offering. It was probably taken to Delphi by one Apelles, who died there: his tomb with its inscription was found at Delphi in 1894.

The Massaliots were great travellers: it was at about the same time that a certain Euthymenes attempted to explore the coast of West Africa, and reached the mouth of the river Senegal, where he saw crocodiles and so thought that this river must be connected with the Nile. He wrote a book on his travels; this is now lost, but it survived for nearly a thousand years, and was translated into verse by a late Roman poet, Rufus Festus Avienus.

Throughout the great period of Greek history, the fifth and fourth centuries B.C., Massalia stands outside the main stream, developing her trade by land and sea. Already in the sixth century B.C. she had begun minting her own coinage. The coins were like those of the Ionian land her people had left, but were of silver instead of electrum. As a regular device Massalia adopted the lion, with the letters MASSA above; on the obverse of the coin, the head of Artemis wreathed with olive, or of Apollo, became the most popular types. These coins spread far and wide throughout Gaul and beyond it, influencing the native tribes to produce coins of their own. Commerce oversea was carried on all over the Mediterranean, and Massaliots are mentioned as captains of cargo-vessels hired to carry grain from one Greek city to another—for example, from Syracuse to Athens. Shipbuilding was therefore an important industry. Gradually the arsenals and warehouses at the docks were filled with every device necessary for war- and merchant-vessels, until the Massaliot fleet became one of the best-equipped and best-handled in the known world. The land-trade with the Gauls took the traders up the Rhone valley, along which discoveries of coins point the way.

The Gulf and the many lagoons near the town were rich in fish. The Massaliots had an important fishing-fleet, and they also practised a special sort of fishing by means of pits in the shallower waters. Red mullet were plentiful, and oysters. Coral was found on the Stoichades (Îles d'Hyères) and sent inland for the use of the Gallic natives, especially to the Marne district. The only products of the land which could be exported were olives and wine.

In the neighbourhood were stone quarries, including granite for building; but hardly any trace of Massaliot architecture has survived. The Temples of Artemis and Apollo, as well as one of Athene, have perished. The walls were remarked upon in antiquity, and it was said that the Gauls learnt from the Massaliots the art of surrounding their towns with walls. Vitruvius, the Roman architect, writes that the private houses of the Massaliots were not roofed with tiles but with a mixture of clay and chaff. The remains of their pottery are meagre and second-rate; but their coinage developed a style of considerable beauty.

The Massaliots were Ionians, and for a long time kept up their connection with their mother-city in Asia Minor, as well as many of her customs. They worshipped Ionian gods, and celebrated the Ionian festivals of Anthestêria and Thargêlia. The Anthesteria was an ancient festival of Dionysus, which fell in early March, when the previous year's wine was opened. The Thargelia, perhaps even more ancient, was held in honour of Apollo and Artemis, and, originally at any rate, was accompanied by the sacrifice of a human scapegoat (probably a condemned criminal kept for the purpose) who was flung into the sea. The Massaliots, early in their history, created a Treasury at Delphi to house their offerings to Apollo there, especially on the occasion of victories; and Massalia itself was adorned with many trophies and statues.

The Massaliots, living thus far from their place of origin, and planted among the barbarian peoples of the West, were from the first driven to an extreme conservatism in manners and politics which contrasted strikingly with their adventurousness as explorers. They wore the long Ionian dress on formal occasions, and retained an Ionian fondness for bright colours;

but they did not bring any oriental love of luxury with them, and they preserved a simplicity, moderation and dignity of behaviour which endeared them to the Romans, from whose friendship they greatly benefited. In later times, many Romans remarked on their conservatism, their discipline and grave bearing, and above all, on the admirable strength of character which had enabled them to maintain the Greek way of life pure and unadulterated. Others declared that Massalia was influenced by her Gallic neighbours; but although some influence must have been unavoidable, the consensus of opinion was that for a thousand years, throughout her independence and under Roman rule, Massalia remained distinctively Greek, and became a centre of advanced education to which Roman aristocrats sent their sons to study instead of to Athens. And the city was always a source of culture and civilization for the Gauls, especially after the Roman conquest of southern Gaul in the late second century B.C.

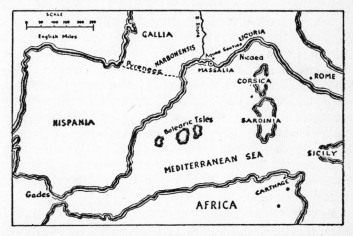

Massalia produced no outstanding writers; the most famous books by Massaliots were both by explorers: Euthymenes in the sixth century B.C., Pytheas in about 300 B.C. In later times a number of scholars and physicians are mentioned, and one poet, named Charmis, who wrote on the song of the nightingale. There was also an early epic poem, after the model of Homer, which told the story of Massalia and its founding, and was often quoted.

.   .   .   .   .

Owing to its remote position, Massalia was spared the bitter struggle with Carthage that engaged the Sicilian Greeks during the fifth and fourth centuries, and brought ruin on some of the most prosperous of them. Massalia stood aside, and probably benefited. In the beginning of the fourth century the signs of a growing friendship with Rome begin to appear. In 396 B.C. the Romans sent a golden mixing-bowl to Delphi as a thank-offering for a victory in Italy; this was housed in the Treasury of Massalia there. Throughout the century it must be supposed that this friendship grew, as the Massaliots realized the importance of Rome for the preservation of civilization in the western Mediterranean.

Nevertheless, when Rome came to grips with Carthage in the First Punic War (264 to 241 B.C.) Massalia remained neutral. But before the Second Punic War (218 to 201 B.C.) the friendship had become an alliance, and a Roman embassy was sent to Massalia to obtain information concerning Carthaginian activities in that region. During the war Massalia rendered valuable help to Rome, especially with her navy, which was now of excellent quality, and by sending to Rome information about the movements of Hannibal. Massaliot reconnoitring-vessels brought news of the manœuvres of the Carthaginian fleet. Massaliot mercenaries acted as guides to the Roman cavalry moving inland to keep watch on Hannibal's army. Massaliot war-galleys played a notable part in a victory over the enemy; their captains and sailors by their inspiring example and skilled tactics helped the Romans to win the day. Any movements of the Carthaginian generals in Gaul were at once reported by the Massaliots to Rome. The Romans were extremely grateful for all this help. The destruction of Carthage in 146 B.C. removed Massalia's most dangerous trade-rival, and her position was improved by the conquest of Sicily by Rome. From now onward Massalia, still a Greek city-state, was nevertheless completely bound up with the fortune of Rome.

. . . .

For two centuries, between 500 and 300 B.C., the Massaliots had been prevented by the Carthaginians from continuing their explorations to the west. Carthage had closed the Straits of Gibraltar against further expansion by strengthening the old Phoenician tradepost of Gades. The Carthaginians had control of the valuable tin-trade of Cornwall and the Scillies. But somewhere about 300 B.C. a Massaliot sea-captain slipped through the Straits while the Carthaginians were busy defending themselves against the Syracusans. Pytheas was not only a trader: he was a skilled astronomer and geographer, and during his voyage he took observations which were of the greatest help to later scientists. He coasted northwards to Brittany, and crossed to Land's End, where he went ashore and inspected the tin workings. He found the natives hospitable and friendly, owing to their intercourse with foreign traders; and he describes their skilful method of extracting tin. From Land's End he circumnavigated the coast of Britain, describing it as a triangle and giving measurements. Sometimes he went ashore, and in fact claimed to have "walked all over Britain", though his tale was on the whole not believed. He wrote a detailed account of the inhabitants and their way of life: they were simple in their ways, he said, and far removed from the knavishness of modern man. Their diet was cheap and primitive, unlike the luxury bred of wealth, and their many chieftains lived on the whole at peace with one another. When they fought, they used chariots of which the wheels were armed with knives. Britain, he said, was thickly populated and had a very chilly climate.

While in Scotland, Pytheas heard stories of an island further north, called Thule, the identification of which is still a matter of controversy. He extended his travels, apparently, as far as the mouth of the Elbe. Great doubt was cast on his veracity by ancient writers; but modern opinion holds that it was the very magnitude of Pytheas' discoveries which prevented their appreciation, and that his record, though sometimes mistaken in detail, is essentially true. After him, no Greek followed for a hundred and fifty years, as the Straits were soon afterwards closed to traffic by the Carthaginians, until the destruction of Carthage in 146 B.C.

    ·   ·   ·   ·   ·

Massalia had the reputation of being one of the best-governed states of ancient times. Its constitution attracted the attention of Aristotle, who selected it as one of his examples in his book of Constitutions. It was at first completely oligarchic, governed by the descendants of the original chief settlers; its founders did not, as at Cyrene and elsewhere, become kings. This, however, had been somewhat modified before Aristotle was writing, in the latter half of the fourth century B.C. At some time, a selection had been made from those hitherto considered unfit to rule, and these were given a share in the government. But in spite of this addition to the small class that originally held all the power, the régime remained oligarchic. The masses were almost without privilege, and Roman observers like Cicero, writing in the first century B.C., thought that their condition was practically slavery.

The government consisted of a Council of six hundred men called Timouchoi ("Holders of Office"). These were appointed for life, and, in the first century A.D. at any rate, had to come from a family who had held citizen rights for not less than three generations. Doubtless in earlier times the field was even more limited. Only men who had sons were eligible as counsellors. Since their office was vacated only on death, they were on the whole elderly. Any citizen who proposed an illegal motion was punished with loss of citizen rights.

From the Council of Six Hundred, fifteen members served

as a committee to manage current affairs. These held almost dictatorial power: Cicero compared them to the Thirty Tyrants at Athens. Of these fifteen, three were selected as presidents; and of the three presidents, one was the chief. This constitution, like the coinage of Massalia, was sometimes imitated by admiring Gauls.

The laws of Massalia, although aristocratic, were published for all to know, unlike those of early Greek oligarchies. A few of the most curious have been preserved by Roman writers, and show that the State supervised the citizen, even in their private lives, in a patriarchal manner. For instance, women were carefully controlled: they were not allowed to drink wine, and their dowries were limited to a hundred gold pieces in cash, together with five for the wedding-dress and five for gold jewellery. Law and order were rigidly maintained. Every foreigner on entry had to surrender his weapons; mendicant priests were debarred from entry. Indecent theatrical performances were prohibited: this is all we know of the drama at Massalia. The death penalty was carried out by decapitation; a sword was used—the original sword, so it was said—which had become so badly rusted as to be scarcely adequate. Any citizen who wished was allowed to apply to the Council of Six Hundred for a permit to commit suicide; if the Council, on examining the case, agreed, a portion of State hemlock kept for the purpose was served out to the applicant. If a master had granted freedom to a slave and was later swindled by him, he could withdraw the freedom; this was allowed three times. On the fourth occasion the master could no longer do so, as it was thought that he had only himself to blame for any damage he then suffered.

Massalia never became a democracy. It preserved its aristocratic constitution until the second century A.D., when Roman colonial officials took the place of the original counsellors. No doubt its long preservation was due to Roman admiration: Cicero says that its virtues were more easily praised than imitated. Its rulers were picked, outstanding citizens of the greatest integrity; and the efficient management of the city-state was shown in its freedom from political strife, its superb military and naval equipment, and its widespread commercial connections by land and sea.

.   .   .   .   .   .

During the second century B.C. the influence of Massalia with Rome was powerful. In 196 B.C. the Council of Six Hundred was able to help the Greek city-state of Lampsacus (also a colony of Phocaea) on the Hellespont to succeed in a plea before the Roman Senate. In 130 B.C. Massalia was able to intervene on behalf of her own mother-city Phocaea and save it from Roman vengeance. But the protection and friendship of Rome, here as elsewhere, brought a gradual neglect of military duties. In 181 B.C. Massalia, formerly the breeder of daring sailors, had to ask Rome for help against Gallic pirates. This happened a second time in 154 B.C., when the pirates turned their attention to Massalia's colonies, Antipolis (Antibes) and Nicaea (Nice). Rome again granted help, and the sea-robbers were severely defeated. In 125 B.C. Rome for the third time came to the rescue against an inland tribe (the Salluvioi); a Roman army cleared the coastal strip of the Gallic enemy, and its commander, the consul L. Calvinus Sextius, established a fort at some hot springs called after him Aquae Sextiae (Aix), eighteen miles north of Massalia. The Roman operations against the Gallic tribes resulted in the incorporation of southern Gaul in the province Gallia Narbonensis; and the territory of Massalia, which alone remained at least nominally independent, was enlarged. She was given charge of the road which the Romans began to build along the coast, connecting Italy and Spain, and was granted the coastal strip from the Italian frontier to the Rhone.

Then came the wars of Marius against the Cimbri and Teutones at the end of the second century B.C. Massalia rendered him active help, and as a reward she was given control of the canal constructed by Marius from Arles to the sea, and called after him. Massalia drew a large income from the customs dues of this canal. After Marius' final victory at Aquae Sextiae, it is said, the Massaliots used the bones of the enemy dead to make fences for their vineyards, which were so heavily fertilized by the rotting corpses of this massive slaughter that they gave an unprecedented harvest in the following season.

During the years 76 to 74 B.C. the governor of the province of Gallia Narbonensis was M. Fonteius, who on the expiration of his office was accused by the Gauls of oppression. His defence was undertaken by Cicero, and among the witnesses on his side were delegates from Massalia, who praised him highly, as was natural, since no doubt his treatment of the Massaliots had been very different from his treatment of the natives. Massalia was regarded as Rome's faithful ally and supporter against Gallic unrest. But an unexpected blow of fate was soon to fall.

Massalia would never have taken sides against Rome herself; but when two great Romans quarrelled, how could she know which would be the winner? In the war between Pompey and Caesar, Massalia, which had received accretions of territory from both men, decided to support the cause of Pompey, and so found herself besieged by the greatest soldier of the age.

.   .   .   .   .

The siege of Massalia by Caesar's forces in 49 B.C. is described by Caesar himself, though he was not present except at the outset. The possession of the city, with its excellent harbour and its position on the coastal route from Italy to Spain, was essential to success. But the Massaliots had already decided to help Pompey. They had enrolled native troops and brought in corn from their furthest confines; they had set up arsenals in the city and repaired their walls, gates and ships. When Caesar arrived, they closed their gates against him.

At his summons, the Committee of Fifteen came out to meet him, and reported, on the authority of their Council, that

Massalia could not take sides in a quarrel which divided the Roman people: it was not their place to decide between the two men and the two causes. Both, they said, had benefited them, and they must therefore treat both alike—help neither and admit neither.

This sounded reasonable. But during the conference, an officer of Pompey's, Domitius, arrived by sea, and was not only admitted but given full command of the city and the fleet. Preparations for war proceeded rapidly; stores and war-material were accumulated within the walls, and the spirit of resistance to Caesar rose high.

Caesar, unable to stay at Massalia himself, brought up three legions and siege-engines under the command of Decius Brutus and Caius Trebonius to invest the city. He also put in hand the building of twelve warships at Arles; this was completed in thirty days. The Massaliots had fitted out seventeen ships, as well as many smaller vessels; large crews of archers and Albicians (a Gallic tribe with a long tradition of loyalty to Massalia) were put on board. Caesar's fleet, when ready, took up station off the harbour.

In the sea battle that followed, the Massaliots and their native allies fought with the greatest courage and skill, as Caesar generously allows. His own crews were less skilled, and the newly-built ships, being of unseasoned timber, were slower as well as fewer. Nevertheless, with the help of grappling-irons they managed to tackle two Massaliot ships at a time, and won a victory which cost Massalia nine vessels taken or destroyed.

Trebonius, the lieutenant, was now in charge of the siege-operations. Massalia was a promontory, washed by the sea on three sides; the fourth side presented great difficulty because of its natural steepness and the lofty fortifications. Trebonius, calling in men and transport animals from the whole province, began by building a huge rampart eighty feet high. But Massalia possessed such numbers of war-weapons, stored for a long time past, and in particular of ballistic machines, that no protection was proof against them; and the trusty Albicians

were always ready to sally forth against the Roman engineers.
The attacks were beaten off, but the operation was delayed.

Meanwhile, the Massaliots were preparing for another naval
battle. They brought out their old ships from the dockyards
and refitted and rearmed them, working with the greatest
energy; they manned them with numbers of rowers and helms-
men, and added fishing-vessels which they armoured against
missiles and manned with crews of archers and slingers. When
this new fleet was ready, the men, urged on by the tears and
prayers of all the non-combatants—old men, mothers and girls
who begged them to save their country in its extreme danger
—went on board with a confidence unimpaired by the earlier
defeat. Confidence in the unknown, as also the fear of it,
Caesar remarks drily, is a common weakness of human nature
—as it then proved to be. The arrival of Pompey's lieutenant
Nasidius with reinforcements to the fleet confirmed the hope
and enthusiasm of the Massaliots. When a suitable wind arose,
their fleet sailed out of the harbour in formation to give battle
to Caesar's fleet led by Decius Brutus, who had the twelve
ships built at Arles as well as six captured from the Massaliots
in the earlier battle and repaired by the Romans.

From the Roman rampart inland, and from all higher ground,
it was easy to see across into the city. All the young were
left behind, all the older men, with the women and children,
and the state officials, were holding up their hands to heaven
in prayer, or visiting the temples of the immortal gods and
throwing themselves before their statues imploring them to
grant victory. Every Massaliot knew that his fortunes depended
on the issue of that day; among those who had gone out to
fight, the noblest had been appealed to by name and besought
to realize that defeat would mean the end of everything. Those
who were now left behind could do nothing but flock to the
Acropolis and pray to their patron gods Apollo and Artemis
to protect them.

The battle was joined. The Massaliot crews fought with
desperate courage. But the issue went against them, this time

as before. Five ships were sunk, four captured, and one fled. Another sped to the city with the bad news. As it approached, the whole population poured down to the harbour; and when they heard the truth, such lamentation overwhelmed them that the city was like one already captured by the enemy. Still, with dauntless courage they set about preparing for their defence.

Trebonius' investing works now proceeded rapidly. A six-storey tower was built at a new point against the wall. The Massaliots tried to destroy the new works with rocks and fire, but in vain. The wall was breached; and the citizens, terrified, surrendered.

The most distinguished citizens approached the Roman commander, and pleaded eloquently for restraint until Caesar should come and make terms. They feared that the army would sack the town. The Roman officers listened to their pleas, and were moved to pity. An unofficial truce was observed during the time of waiting for Caesar's arrival; the soldiers were restrained from plunder, and guards were posted. Not a single dart was thrown; all military vigilance was relaxed, as if the operation were concluded. Caesar himself sent letters to Trebonius prohibiting any pillaging or slaughter.

It was therefore a shock to the Romans when the Massaliots, after a few days, when the army was relaxing at noon and all arms were piled, chose this moment to break the truce and launch a sudden attack. They set fire to the Roman siege-works, and hurled missiles from the walls at the Roman soldiers as these rushed to arms. In a moment the work of months was destroyed, "by enemy guile and the weather," says Caesar— for a strong wind was blowing at the time. Next day a similar attempt was made; but this time the Romans were ready, and the attack was repulsed with great loss. Against all expectation, the Romans repaired the damage quickly, and the Massaliots, realizing that their effort was hopeless, surrendered for the second time.

Caesar now arrived.

The Massaliots were worn out with misfortunes: the greatest

dearth of provisions; two naval defeats; attacks; severe illness due to the long blockade and change of diet—for they were all living on old millet and rotten barley which had been collected a long while before and stored in the public granary; much of their fortifying wall in ruins. No help was to be expected from any quarter now that Caesar had all in his power. They had no choice but to accept any terms imposed by the victor. But Caesar, in spite of provocation, was lenient—rather, he says, because of their name and ancient fame than because of their deserts towards himself. The city was not sacked, and there was no massacre.

The Massaliots were ordered to surrender their weapons and sling-engines in the city, and their ships from the docks; but this was all. Their independence as a city-state was not taken from them, though they had to submit to a Roman garrison of two legions; and a few years later they lost all the territory formerly granted to them by Rome, retaining only a narrow strip of coast and the Stoichades Islands. Nevertheless, Rome remembered that without the help of Massalia her conquests over Carthage and over the Gauls would have been rendered more difficult; and those who saw Massalia represented in Caesar's triumphal procession in Rome reflected that this was the city that had once shared in Rome's triumphs over the transalpine tribes.

·　　·　　·　　·

Throughout Roman imperial times, Massalia still kept a certain independence, moral rather than political. She kept the right of asylum, and was sometimes rewarded with a bequest from a grateful refugee. Her citizens made money: in Nero's reign (A.D. 54 to 68) the Massaliot physician Crinas was able to repair the walls at his own expense. Massalia was no longer a political force; but the city remained a centre of culture, for Gauls and even for Romans, as well as an interpreter between the two. The educated citizens had long been trilingual, speaking Greek, Latin and Gallic; and they were also skilled in all the devices of oratory. In time, the education they had passed on recoiled upon them; a Gallic rhetorician in the fourth century A.D. calls them "Greeklings". But they retained their Greek character until the Frankish domination of Provence in the sixth century A.D. Then at last a Byzantine historian (Agathias) could write:

"Now the city that was Greek has become barbarian."

10. BYZANTIUM

BYZANTIUM, on the European side of the Bosphorus, was destined to reach its highest importance long after Athens and even Rome had declined. In A.D. 323 Constantine the Great defeated his rival Licinius in a battle; Licinius fled to Byzantium and was besieged. Constantine entered, was captivated by the place, and decided to remove his residence there. Thus the Greek city, already a thousand years old, began another millennium of a quite different kind of prosperity, in which a new civilization, in many ways opposed to the past, was created. But what of its preceding history? Much is known of Constantinople, the new capital of the Roman Empire; what of the Greek city-state on which the new structure was based?

Byzantium was built on the most easterly of the seven hills of Istambul. Near by is a curved inlet known as the Golden Horn because of its fisheries. The city, which like Massalia was surrounded on three sides by the sea, in time extended westwards to cover two other hills (the modern Serail and Hippodrom), and the whole was enclosed within a wall.

The walls of Byzantium, added to throughout its history, were famous: they were said, with those of Rhodes, to be the strongest known, with the exception of Messina's. They were made of square blocks so well put together that they looked as if built of one unjointed stone. The ruins still show the skill of the builders and the efforts of the destroyer. Byzantium was destined to endure one of the most determined siege attempts ever made on a Greek city, and unlike almost all the others, to resist triumphantly. A detailed description of the walls by a historian of the second century A.D. tells of the very high wall on the landward side, and the strong though less high walls encircling the city on the seaward sides. There were twenty-seven towers in all; of these, a wonder of the age were the seven towers which ran from the Thracian Gate to the Horn; they were built on an acoustic plan so skilled that any sound was echoed successively from one to the other. There were two harbours on the Horn; both could be closed by a chain, and were protected by moles and towers.

The first settlers came in the middle of the seventh century B.C. They had been led to the spot by the enterprise of an earlier band, who, seeing the advantages of a position on the Strait, but fearing the attacks of the wild Thracian tribes on the European side, had founded the city-state of Calchêdon opposite. Calchedon was later called "the City of the Blind", in derision at the stupidity of its founders, who had failed to see the advantages of the site chosen by the founders of Byzantium. Henceforward, the fortunes of Byzantium and Calchedon were linked; but Byzantium far outgrew its *vis-à-vis* in importance, because of its splendid position on the promontory that dominated the Strait.

The founders of Calchedon came from Megara; but the mother-city of Byzantium, strangely enough, is not certainly known. It was not Miletus, which sent most of the colonies to the Black Sea, nor was it Athens. The dialect of Greek spoken

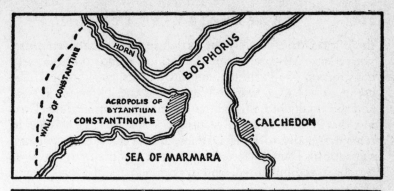

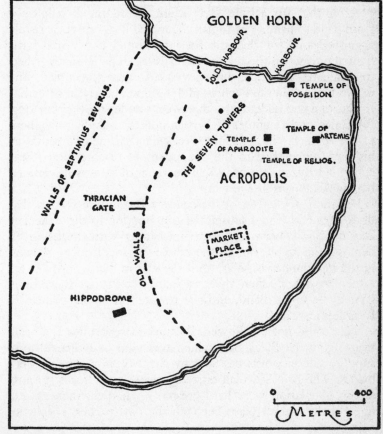

there was Doric. Possibly the settlement was a joint enterprise, with a large Megarian element. Nothing is known of the early constitution of Byzantium, and little of its early history. The community had to ward off attacks of the Thracians at first, and this no doubt hastened the building of fortifications. During the Persian Wars, Byzantium seems to have wished to remain friendly to King Dareius, and even to have lent him ships for his Danube fleet; but later the city incurred his anger by some act unknown, and was conquered by his general Otanes.

After this, for a time, Byzantium passed rather helplessly from hand to hand. The Ionians occupied it during their revolt against Persia; for this, the Persians visited Byzantium with their wrath when the revolt was crushed. The Byzantines had to evacuate their city, which was sacked and occupied. But in 478 B.C., when the Persians under Xerxes had been defeated, Byzantium was liberated by the Greeks under the Spartan king Pausanias, and a number of Persian nobles, including members of the royal family, fell into Greek hands. Then Pausanias in his turn succumbed to the allurement of oriental despotism, and ruled Byzantium for seven years, until he was driven out by the Athenians in 470 B.C.

For most of the rest of the century Byzantium was an ally of Athens and paid a substantial contribution to the Athenian League. She wavered at one point, siding with the island of Samos in its revolt; but on the whole she was loyal to Athens in the Peloponnesian War, until the war in Sicily ended in an Athenian defeat; then the pro-Spartan party in Byzantium gained the upper hand, and she revolted from the Athenian League in 411 B.C.

This could not be allowed. Byzantium controlled the corn route from the Black Sea, which was vital to Athens' food-supply. The city was besieged by the Athenians under Alcibiades. The pro-Athenian citizens opened their gates to him, as the population were hard-pressed by famine; there was a fight in the market-place between the two parties, a fight in which the Spartan garrison also engaged, and a number of Byzantines were killed. The fighting ended when Alcibiades proclaimed a pardon to all Byzantines who surrendered. The city was in Athenian hands again.

This was in 409 B.C. Four years later Athens was finally defeated at Aegospotami on the Hellespont, and surrendered to Lysander. The Athenian garrison left behind at Byzantium by Alcibiades were released by agreement, and managed to get back to Athens by a roundabout route, so that when Lysander came Byzantium again fell under the domination of Sparta.

.   .   .   .   .

Thus throughout the two hundred and fifty years after its foundation, Byzantium, though never taking a leading part in Greek politics, yet was constantly subjected to the pressure of warring claims. The possession of the place was contested; the friendship of the community was eagerly sought; the city-state, while remaining nominally free, was always under the control of some foreign power, Persian or Greek, Athenian or Spartan. Nevertheless, unlike so many of the other Greek city-states during these troubled times, Byzantium emerged from these ordeals even more prosperous than before. Nothing could finally get the better of her incomparable resources.

The excellent harbours were by now a centre for trade, which included an immense traffic in grain from the Black Sea, especially to Athens; and from the same quarter, slaves, fish salted or smoked, hides, honey, wax. The Black Sea cities imported oil, wine and clothes. All passed through Byzantium, bringing her a huge income in customs dues. She also controlled not only the passage through the Strait but the landward route at this point to Asia, for military movements as well as for commerce. Then too she had her own products.

The site itself was dry and rocky, and cisterns had to be built to conserve drinking-water; but the surrounding territory was of a remarkable fertility. Ears of corn and bunches of grapes figure on the Byzantine coinage, with the heads of Demeter and Bacchus; and the abundance of figs is praised. Further, the peculiarity of the current brought to Byzantium every year shoals of tunny-fish on their journey from the Black Sea, and provided an easy prey; Byzantium was called by the poets "the tunny's metropolis", and "mother of tunnies in their youthful prime". Oysters too were plentiful, as well as other fish. The sale of salt was also a profitable industry, and may at one time have been a state monopoly; in later years, when new sources of revenue were sought, the Byzantine government imposed taxes on fishermen, salt-merchants, apothecaries, magicians and seers, as well as a purchase-tax and a bank-monopoly. They also took to selling the citizenship and other rights such as the inheritance of land. Formerly, citizen rights had depended on birth from citizen parents, but the franchise was extended to include certain immigrants as the city's population grew.

.   .   .   .   .

In 400 B.C., while the city was still in Spartan hands, an event occurred which led to fighting and bloodshed. Xenophon, returning with the remains of the Greek mercenary army which had struggled back to the Black Sea from the heart of Mesopotamia, reached Byzantium. They came there by invitation of the Spartan admiral Anaxibius, who offered to enrol the men for a further term of mercenary service. But instead of giving them the promised pay, he treacherously induced them to leave the town without provisions; and the gates were closed against them.

At this, the soldiers were enraged, and began a violent assault on the gates, while others ran down to the sea and climbed up on to the wall on that side, by way of the mole. Others who had been left inside the city, seeing their comrades attacking the gates, broke down the bolts from the inside. The gates flew open, the inhabitants fled to their houses or away, some took to the boats in the harbour, others began to go on board the war-ships. All thought that the city was captured and that they were lost.

Anaxibius, the cause of the trouble, managed to sail round in a fishing-boat and reach the city's acropolis, from where he despatched urgent messages for help to Calchedon across the Strait. But Xenophon, fearing that his soldiers would sack the town, managed to make his way in and prevail on them to listen to him, saying:

> "What will our fellow-countrymen at home think of us if we sack the first Greek city we enter? I pray that before I live to see such a sight I may be a myriad fathoms below ground. You are Greeks. Follow my advice and try to obtain your rights under the guidance of your Greek commanders!"

The soldiers listened and were calmed. Byzantium was saved. But this did not prevent Anaxibius from arranging later for the sale of four hundred of those left behind into slavery.

Ten years afterwards, Spartan rule in Byzantium was ended by the Athenian general Thrasyboulus, and the city was given back her old control of the Strait. Byzantines who had helped were awarded Athenian honours for their share in this result.

.   .   .   .   .

For the next half-century Byzantium alternated between friendship with Athens and flirtation with other powers. The Athenians still depended on Black Sea corn for their existence; but their control of this life-line depended on their strength at sea. At one time, when the anti-Athenian party was uppermost in Byzantium, the government compelled Athenian ships to put into the harbour and unload their cargo, so that Athens was compelled to send an expedition to protect the grain fleet, and eventually to blockade Byzantium itself. The quarrel was ended by a treaty somewhat in favour of the Byzantines.

When Philip of Macedon began his career of conquest Byzantium was at first friendly towards him, though she took no part in his war against Athens. At last, her refusal to join him against Athens led to a breach. Philip recognized the importance of the Strait, and decided to make an attempt to seize Byzantium by force; and though he was deflected for a time, he returned to this project in 340 B.C. and set to work to besiege the city.

The siege of Byzantium by Philip was memorable. In later times it gave rise to many legends, and its story was often told. The Byzantine leader was Leon, a pupil of Plato. The Greek city-states which had to fear the aggression of Philip recognized the importance of the siege; Athens especially declared war on Philip, and sent help under able commanders. Demosthenes used all his influence to stimulate Athenian enthusiasm, and equipped a war-ship at his own expense. The Byzantines submitted to a discipline which was new to them. Philip on his side brought every art to bear against the city, including a siege-machine which marked a fresh epoch in military invention. He also built a bridge across the Golden Horn against the wall on that side, and destroyed a Temple of Pluto outside the city for material.

How long the siege lasted is not known; but the stubborn defence, assisted by Athenian skill, held out, and Philip was obliged to withdraw. Byzantine gratitude to Athens was recorded in a decree granting Athenians special rights and honours, including the erection of three statues on the Bosphorus showing the People of Athens being crowned by the People of Byzantium and their allies, and the proclamation of the decree at the great national festivals of Olympia, Delphi, Nemea and the Isthmus, "so that all Greece shall recognize Athenian merit and Byzantine gratitude".

.   .   .   .   .

The conquest of the Greek city-states by Philip and then by Alexander affected Byzantium hardly at all. She retained her independence, and went on minting her own coinage and pursuing her commercial aims. She took little part in the struggles between Alexander's generals, though she was sometimes

wooed and sometimes threatened. Her greatest difficulties during the third century B.C. were caused by an invasion of Celtic
tribes in 278 B.C., who for a time dominated the surrounding
country and even levied tribute. The Byzantines appealed for
help to the other Greek states, but obtained very little; and
after a while the Celts, having exhausted the countryside,
moved on into Asia, leaving behind them a bitter memory. At
the end of the century a brief war with the island of Rhodes
over the levying of the Bosphorus tolls led to a renunciation of
the toll by Byzantium as well as to a loss of territory.

During the following century, the second before Christ,
Byzantium came into contact with Rome, and had the wisdom to take the side of the Romans in their wars in Greece.
For this, Byzantium was rewarded with a formal treaty of
alliance. Throughout the first century B.C. likewise, Byzantium
in spite of some sufferings remained faithful to Rome, and in
imperial times was often used by the Roman army as a crossing-
place to Asia. At the end of the second century A.D. the city's
prosperity stood as high as ever, thanks to the fisheries, the
customs dues and the fertility of the land. The fortifications
were in good repair, and engines of war stood ready in great
numbers on the walls. Then came a terrible disaster: Byzantium
incurred the displeasure of the Emperor Septimius Severus by
befriending his rival Pescennius Niger; and a siege was begun,
in the winter of A.D. 193.

This siege lasted two years, until in the end, it was said,
hunger led even to cannibalism in the city. Resistance continued after Severus had captured Pescennius, beheaded him
and sent his head to Byzantium as a proof of victory and an invitation to surrender. In the summer of A.D. 196, however, the
city gave way; and the harshness of its treatment shocked the
Greek world.

Soldiers and magistrates were put to death. The city lost its
freedom and civic rights, and was placed under tribute. As a
further humiliation, it was handed over to the Thracian city
Perinthus, a former ally, as a "village", and was treated by the

Perinthians with merciless arrogance. The walls were partly pulled down, and considerable damage inside the city was perpetrated. Later, Severus repented of his cruelty. He restored Byzantine civil rights, and instituted a new building-plan, which included a colonnade with hot baths, a theatre for gladiatorial displays, and the restoration of the Temple of Apollo on the Acropolis.

The third century A.D. saw a fresh irruption of Goths, which the Romans were not able entirely to repel; in fact, Byzantium suffered severely from a mutiny of Roman soldiers, during the disastrous reign of Gallienus (A.D. 260 to 268). In the year after Gallienus' death, the Goths appeared before the very walls of Byzantium, but were not able to break in. All these ravages, however, had so much weakened the once prosperous city that when Diocletian redivided the Roman Empire, Perinthus and not Byzantium was declared the capital of the Province of Europe.

But this was soon to be ended. In the struggle for empire between Maximinus and Licinius, Byzantium fell first to one, then to the other. Then, as the adversary of Licinius, came Constantine, with the result that in A.D. 323, almost by chance, the ancient city found itself chosen as the capital of the Roman world, and the birthplace of a new culture.

.   .   .

In pre-Constantinian times Byzantium was not a centre of learning or the arts. We hear of an occasional painter, musician, actor or historian; there is even a poetess named Myro, and a poet named Alcibiades described on an inscription as "the most tuneful songster of all Hellas", but none of his work survives. Byzantium produced one great critic named Aristophanes, who specialized in Homer; but he spent most of his life in Alexandria under Ptolemy II and III. The names of a few scientists, orators and engineers also are known; but none achieved universal fame. Nor were the Byzantines distinguished in athletics; they had a Treasury at Olympia, but are not known to have ever won an Olympic victory.

Nothing is known against or for their manner of life; there are a few unauthenticated stories which contradict one another. One writer (Theopompus) much given to censure says that trade and democracy had caused deterioration, and that the bad example of Byzantium had corrupted Calchedon across the Strait; but Byzantine history shows that the citizens could defend themselves with courage and determination if necessary, though they kept as much as possible out of the quarrels of Greece and Rome. They worshipped the orthodox gods of Greece: Apollo and Artemis, who had temples on the Acropolis; Aphrodite, who had a temple on the seashore; Demeter and Persephone, whose temple was on the Horn; Hera and Poseidon and the rest. There is no proof that the citizens' traditional Dorian sobriety was corrupted by contact with the East, though the names of oriental deities such as Cybele and Serapis are mentioned in later times.

Their constitution, after early attempts at tyranny, alternated between oligarchy and democracy, as elsewhere. They had the usual Council and People's Assembly, with officials called Generals, and a division of the population into "hundreds" for administrative purposes. They had a priesthood going back to ancient times.

No great thinker or philosopher was born here. Byzantines went to Athens or elsewhere to study. The lack of a high standard of culture opened the door to charlatans: Apollonius of Tyana, the celebrated Pythagorean miracle-worker of the early Christian era, carried on his activities in Byzantium, and, as has been already said, the state was able to treat magicians and seers as a group for purposes of taxation as early as the third century B.C.

We know nothing particular about the daily life of the inhabitants, except for a few incongruous details such as that they liked well-salted food; that the men could not be prevented even by law from shaving off their beards; and that a favourite annual event, as at Athens and elsewhere, was the torch-race down to the harbour, here called the Bosporia. Even the exact date of the advent of Christianity is not known, though Byzantium was destined to become the head of the Eastern Church; all that can be said is that up to the time of Constantine a line of twenty-two bishops can be traced.

Such was the city on the Strait, chosen to be the capital of two successive empires, and to survive into modern times. Nothing in its first thousand years of existence presaged its future greatness. A complete lack of aggressiveness combined with an unsurpassed obstinacy in defence enabled it to survive; but its singular good fortune in being selected as Constantine's capital was really due to the perspicacity and courage of the unknown founders, who planted their settlement on a site so superb.

11. CONCLUSION

WHAT caused the failure of the Greek city-state system? It is usual to speak of the "particularism" that was the bane of Greece, since it is obvious that the collapse of the Greek world was due to the failure of its many small units to combine against outside attack. It is often added that there was something in the Greek character that precluded unity: and the same characteristic is thought to be displayed by the Greek nation today: the irreconcilable cleavage between Left and Right which ran through every Greek *polis*, and which in its modern form is again threatening the peace of Europe.

Is this true? Does "lack of unity" provide a complete answer to the problem?

First, in considering this question, let us remember that unity does not necessarily mean survival. The ancient kingdom of Egypt came to be "united" in the sense that its citizens were not allowed to form parties, to argue and discuss, to take any share in government except that allotted to a chosen few. Egypt was united under the sacrosanct rule of king and hierarchy and their appointed ministers; but Egypt fell before the attacks of the Persians, whereas the Greeks repelled the invader. Two centuries later Egypt, no less than Greece, proved unable to resist Alexander. The Persians, under Xerxes, were united, in that the will of the king, however capricious, cruel or foolish, was law; yet they failed before the determined resistance of the Greek fleet, whose commanders were so far from being united in counsel that to this day it is uncertain whether the Athenian Themistocles was a patriot or was playing a double game which would safeguard him no matter which side won the battle. The unity of the Egyptians and the Persians was not a unity of conscious choice; it was imposed on them from above, and its acceptance was a proof of moral and intellectual inferiority. When the modern world sighs for unity within nations or between nations, let it remember that the only unity which gives strength is that of genuine agreement and consent; that of compulsion from above, and of ignorance or servility below, is of little use in time of danger. The Greek city-states were united in one thing: each desired to keep its independence and its own way of life; and that proved sufficient.

Secondly: is the inclusion of the smaller unit in the larger necessarily a gain, from the point of view of human progress? In ancient Greece it does not seem to have been so. The existence of these hundreds of small units with separate administrative systems seems uneconomic nowadays, when economy of effort is accorded a growing place in the theory of government. But certain of these small units created the beginnings of movements which transformed the world, and ultimately gave Man his present control over Nature. The first known electrical experiment was observed in Miletus; the first atomic theory in the town of Abdera in Thrace; the first statement of the transcending importance of numerical formulae for the understanding of matter came from Pythagoras, an islander from Samos, who migrated to Italy. The first geometrical proofs demanding an assumption of moving lines and planes were evolved at Tarentum, Sparta's only colony, by its admirable chief magistrate Archytas. It was the small unit, the independent city-state, where everybody knew all that was going on, that produced such intellectual giants as Thucydides and Aristophanes, Heracleitus and Parmenides. If these conditions were not in part responsible, how is it that philosophy, science, political thought, and the best of the literary arts, all perish with the downfall of the city-state system in 322 B.C., leaving us with the interesting but less profound and original work of men such as Epicurus and Menander? There is only one major poet after 322: Theocritus of Cos, a lyric genius of the first rank, who nevertheless (unlike Sappho) wrote much that was second-rate also, when he was pandering to possible patrons like the rulers of Alexandria and Syracuse. The modern nation that has replaced the *polis* as the unit of government is a thousand times less intellectually creative in proportion to its size and resources; even in building and the arts and crafts it lags behind in taste, and relatively in productivity.

Thirdly, it must also be remembered that racial unity does not necessarily make for peace. The larger the conglomeration, and the less room for discussion and difference of opinion within it, the greater the potential menace to the rest of the world. A united Germany was a greater menace to peace than the many separate kingdoms, dukedoms and the rest that it superseded. Suppose the Hellenes had united: would the world have been better off? Might they not have felt themselves strong enough to attack their neighbours, and have wasted their energies in overrunning North Africa, Asia, and the rest of Europe, in the name of security: pushing their frontiers outwards further and further as the Romans were later to do? The spread of Greek culture, even in the diluted form brought by conquerors, would have been an advantage, but the essential quality of the Greek genius would have been dissipated, as it was in the territories ruled by the successors of Alexander, and in the Byzantine Empire. If, as at present seems likely, the world is about to abandon the national principle for that of larger units composed of a number of nations; if we are to have groups such as the U.S.S.R. and its satellites in Europe and Asia, the Western European Union, the United States becoming perhaps the Union of the Americas, and so on: will the material advantage and the increase in certain kinds of efficiency be offset by a loss in the quality of the contribution made by the separate nations, for instance, that of an intensely individualistic nation like France? Moreover, will not the inevitable clash of interests between such powerful blocs lead to wars so terrible that one half of the human race will in the end destroy the other, as little Croton once obliterated little Sybaris?

Further, suppose the whole of human kind, white, yellow, brown and black, at length united under a World Government: will the result be like running cold water into hot, a tepid mixture from which nothing can be expected except usefulness, orderliness, a humdrum industry, and a general indifference to all wider interests; material prosperity and peace, but intellectual and cultural stagnation? The human race might then perish from another cause: inanition, the despair that already seems to be afflicting many advanced modern minds, the confused pessimism of the Teutonic death-worshippers and the Existentialists. Nothing could be further removed from the temper of the Greek of the city-state even in the midst of his greatest trials. Human progress is achieved not by groups but by individuals, and the soil in which personality can best flourish without damage to its fellows is that which best nurtures progress.

What, then, do we wish that the city-states of Greece had done and not done?

First, we wish that they had learnt to settle their internal differences by constitutional machinery and not by force: most of them had such legal machinery, but it did not always work. Still more, we wish that they had learnt a way of avoiding inter-state wars. Why could they not do so? Because their governments were, on the whole, actuated by immediate self-interest as they saw it, and nothing in their thought or their education taught them to see that immediate self-interest means ultimate disaster.

What would have been the remedy? Education: an education that while encouraging individuality to the highest degree, yet discouraged immediate self-interest. Today, the emphasis is reversed. We need a universal propaganda showing two things: that immediate self-interest must be given up in favour of the longer view, but that this does not mean the abandonment of the individual way of life of smaller units, nations great and small. The passionate fervour aroused by the new, self-conscious nationalism especially of small countries has in it a considerable admixture of self-interest on the part of those who preach it; but those who respond are actuated by a deep love of a particular way of life, a love which calls out their greatest energies and makes them produce of their best. If their response to the ideal of a World State is lukewarm, this is because they fear that the blending of their group in a larger union, however excellent the purpose of such blending, is going to mean the loss of that loved way of life and that precious emotion. For the next century or so let education encourage nationalism and even regionalism. But let every individual, every village, every group, every nation, learn to accept the basic truth that the passion for immediate self-interest must be —to quote Heracleitus—"quenched as if it were a conflagration", not necessarily because it is wrong, but because it is always dangerous and frequently suicidal.

The way to inculcate this doctrine? There is only one way, which so far has never been seriously and systematically tried: through the cultivation of that least developed and most neglected faculty of the human mind—imagination.

BIBLIOGRAPHY

References to ancient writers have not been given in detail, in order not to overload the text with numbers and notes. They can be found in:

Pauly-Wissowa, *Realencyclopädie der Altertumswissenschaft*, under the names of the particular city-states.

Out of many modern works consulted, the following have been of special help:

The Journal of Hellenic Studies.
The Proceedings of the British School of Archaeology.
The American Journal of Archaeology.
The American Journal of Philology.
Archivio Storico per la Calabria e la Lucania.
Milet: Ergebnisse der Ausgrabungen und Untersuchungen seit der Jahre 1899, ed. Th. Wiegand (1906–8).
Pape, W., *Wörterbuch der griechischen Eigennamen* (1911).
Cary, M., and Warmington, E. H., *The Ancient Explorers* (1929).
Cary, M., *The Geographic Background of Greek and Roman History* (1948).
MacIver, Randall, *Greek Cities in Italy and Sicily* (1931).
Dunbabin, T. J., *The Western Greeks* (1948).
Hicks, E. L., *Manual of Greek Historical Inscriptions* (1882).
Tod, M. N., *A Selection of Greek Historical Inscriptions* (1946, 1948).
Farnell, L. R., *Cults of the Greek States* (1896–1909).
Hill, G. F., *Historical Greek Coins* (1906).
Seltman, C. T., *Greek Coins* (1933).